Britain's Soldiers

Rethinking War and Society, 1715–1815

EIGHTEENTH-CENTURY WORLDS

SERIES EDITORS:
Professor Eve Rosenhaft (Liverpool) and Dr Mark Towsey (Liverpool)

Eighteenth-Century Worlds promotes innovative new research in the political, social, economic, intellectual and cultural life of the 'long' eighteenth century (c. 1650–c. 1850), from a variety of historical, theoretical and critical perspectives. Monographs published in the series adopt international, comparative and/or interdisciplinary approaches to the global eighteenth century, in volumes that make the results of specialist research accessible to an informed, but not discipline-specific, audience.

Britain's Soldiers

Rethinking War and Society,
1715–1815

Edited by
Kevin Linch and Matthew McCormack

Liverpool University Press

First published 2014 by
Liverpool University Press
4 Cambridge Street
Liverpool
L69 7ZU

British Library Cataloguing-in-Publication data
A British Library CIP record is available

ISBN 978-1-84631-955-6 *cased*

Typeset in Caslon by Carnegie Book Production, Lancaster
Printed and bound by Booksfactory.co.uk

Contents

Part 3: Discipline

Part 4: Gender

Part 5: Soldiers in Society

List of tables and figures

TABLES

FIGURES

Acknowledgements

THE CHAPTERS of this volume are versions of papers presented at the 'Britain's Soldiers, c. 1750–1815' conference held at the University of Leeds in July 2011. We would like to thank all of those involved in the conference for a stimulating two days, the only downside of this event being that we were not able to incorporate more of the presentations into this edited collection. The conference was part of a wider research project – 'Soldiers and soldiering in Britain, c. 1750–1815' – funded by the Arts and Humanities Research Council. Without this generous assistance, funding research leave for both of the editors and contributing to the costs of the conference and related workshops, the creation of this edited collection would have been much harder, and no doubt would have taken longer to reach fruition. Likewise, the edited collection and the research that underpins the chapters that follow are indebted to a range of colleagues and professionals: we would like to offer our particular thanks to the staff at archives, libraries and museums who have helped with our enquiries and shared our enthusiasm for the subject; to the readers at Liverpool University Press for their comments and support in the drafting of this book; and to Alison Welsby at LUP for her work in helping to produce this volume.

The editors gratefully acknowledge the Metropolitan Museum of Art, New York for permission to reproduce John Trumbull (1756–1843), *The Sortie Made by the Garrison of Gibraltar* (1789, New York, Metropolitan Museum of Art. Oil on canvas, 180.3 × 271.8 cm, Purchase, Pauline V. Fullerton Bequest; Mr and Mrs James Walter Carter and Mr and Mrs Raymond J. Horowitz Gifts; Erving Wolf Foundation and Vain and Harry Fish Foundation Inc.

Gifts; Gift of Hanson K. Corning, by exchange; and Maria DeWitt Jesup and M; Acc.n.: 1976.332. Photo: Geoffrey Clements. © 2012. Image copyright The Metropolitan Museum of Art/Art Resource/Scala Florence, © Photo SCALA, Florence) and John Singleton Copley (1738–1815), *Study for 'The Siege of Gibraltar': Figure Reaching; Sprawling Figures; Cheering Group; Dying Sailors* (1785–6, New York, Metropolitan Museum of Art. Black chalk and white chalk heightening on light blue laid paper. 14⅝ × 23 in. (37.1 × 58.4 cm). The Metropolitan Museum of Art, Harris Brisbane Dick Fund, 1960 (60.44.15). © 2012. Image copyright The Metropolitan Museum of Art/Art Resource/ Scala, Florence © Photo SCALA, Florence). The Guildhall Art Gallery, City of London for permission to reproduce John Singleton Copley, *The Defeat of the Spanish Batteries at Gibraltar, 13th–14th September 1782* (painted 1783–91, oil on canvas, 302 × 762 cm) and Birmingham Museums and Art Gallery for Thomas Rowlandson, *The Wonderfull Charms of a Red Coat and Cockade* (c. 1785–90). Also to the Trustees of the British Museum, London for permission to reproduce: *Longings after a Red Coat* (1797); *Heros in Council – or a Military Squabble about Dress* (1798); Francesco Bartolozzi, *Mr Copley's Picture of the Siege of Gibraltar as Exhibited in the Green Park near St James's Palace (1791) Admission Ticket* (c. 1850s–60s); J.S. Copley, *Study of General Elliot on Horseback, Mounted on Hearing horse to Left, Preliminary Drawing for the 'Defeat of the Spanish Batteries* (c. 1780s), *Proposal for Publishing by Subscription, An Engraving from the Historical Picture of the Siege and Relief of Gibraltar* (1791) and *The Siege and Relief of Gibraltar, while exhibiting in a pavilion in Green Park, including a key to the principal figures in the centre pages; with the plans for a building sketched in ink on the back page* (c. 1791); Isaac Cruikshank, *Female Opinions on Military Tactics* (1798); Thomas Rowlandson, *The Light Horse Volunteers of London & Westminster, commanded by Col. Herries, reviewed by His Majesty on Wimbledon Common 5th July, 1798* (1798), *None but the Brave Deserve the Fair* (1813) and *The Reconciliation or the Return from Scotland* (1785); after John Trumbull, *References to the Print of The Sortie made by the Garrison of Gibraltar* (1810); and Charles Williams, *The Consequences of Invasion or the Hero's Reward* (1803).

Kevin Linch
Matthew McCormack

Notes on the contributors

Kevin Linch is a Principal Teaching Fellow in History at the University of Leeds and works on the military in Georgian Britain. His monograph, *Britain and Wellington's Army: Recruitment, Society, and Tradition 1807–15*, was published in 2011 and other recent publications include chapters in *Soldiers, Citizens and Civilians: Experiences and Perceptions of the Revolutionary and Napoleonic Wars, 1790–1820*, *Soldiering in Britain and Ireland, 1750–1850: Men of Arms* and *Transnational Soldiers: Foreign Military Enlistment in the Modern Era*.

Matthew McCormack is Associate Professor of History at the University of Northampton. He works on Georgian Britain and has published widely on the role of masculinity in politics and warfare. He has published articles in *The Historical Journal*, *War in History*, *Gender & History* and *Cultural & Social History*. His monograph *The Independent Man: Citizenship and Gender Politics in Georgian England* was reissued in paperback in 2012, and he edited the collections *Public Men: Masculinity and Politics in Modern Britain* and (with Catriona Kennedy) *Soldiering in Britain and Ireland, 1750–1850: Men of Arms* for Palgrave.

Ilya Berkovich completed his PhD thesis 'Motivation in Armies of Old Regime Europe' in Peterhouse, Cambridge, where he was a recipient of a research studentship. He currently serves as Golda Meir Postdoctoral Fellow at the Hebrew University of Jerusalem.

Louise Carter is Lecturer in History at University Campus Suffolk. She gained her PhD from the University of Cambridge and her research interests are in war, gender and empire in the eighteenth and nineteenth centuries. She has published in *Gender & History* and is currently working on a monograph.

Bruce Collins is Professor of Modern History at Sheffield Hallam University. His recent publications include *War and Empire: the Expansion of Britain 1790–1830* (2010); 'Defining Victory in Victorian Warfare, 1860–1882', *Journal of Military History* 77:3 (2013); and, edited with Nir Arielli, *Transnational Soldiers: Foreign Military Enlistment in the Modern Era* (2013).

Stephen Conway is a professor of history at University College London. His publications include *The War of American Independence, 1775–1783* (1995); *The British Isles and the War of American Independence* (2000); *War, State, and Society in Mid-Eighteenth-Century Britain and Ireland* (2006); and *Britain, Ireland, and Continental Europe in the Eighteenth Century: Similarities, Connections, Identities* (2011).

Graciela Iglesias Rogers is Tutor and Lecturer in Modern History at St Peter's College, University of Oxford, where she read history for a degree followed by a doctorate, after life as a Reuters fellow with a long career in journalism. Her broad fields of interest are the political, cultural and social history of the Atlantic world, including Britain, with particular attention to developments in Spanish-speaking countries from the eighteenth to the twentieth centuries. Her publications include *British Liberators in the Age of Napoleon: Volunteering under the Spanish Flag in the Peninsular War* (2013).

Caroline Louise Nielsen is currently working on a PhD in Historical Studies at the University of Newcastle, where she also teaches. Her AHRC-funded PhD project is entitled 'The Chelsea Out-Pensioners: Image and Reality in Eighteenth-Century and Early Nineteenth-Century Social Care', which examines the pension experiences of the thousands of elderly and disabled men who left the army between 1715 and 1827.

Cicely Robinson completed a BA and MA in History of Art at the University of Bristol. She is now working towards the completion of an AHRC-funded collaborative PhD in History of Art with the University of York and the National Maritime Museum. Her thesis, entitled 'The Foundation of the National Gallery of Naval Art (1795–1845)', investigates the display and reception of naval painting, sculpture and maritime curiosities within Britain's first 'national' gallery, which was situated in the Painted Hall at Greenwich Hospital from 1823 until 1936.

William P. Tatum III is the official government historian for Dutchess County, New York, USA. He completed his BA in History and Anthropology at the College of William and Mary in 2003 and his MA in History at Brown University in 2004. He is presently finishing his doctoral work at Brown University, focusing on the role of the eighteenth-century British military justice system in civil-military relations.

Introduction

Kevin Linch and Matthew McCormack

B RITAIN had a complex relationship with its soldiers in the eighteenth century. On the one hand, Georgians celebrated their victories, championed military heroes and sympathised with the plight of the injured soldier or the bereaved family. This response is comprehensible today. The wars in which Britain has been engaged since 2001 have been far less popular than those of the eighteenth century were at the time, but the soldiers who have been fighting in Afghanistan and Iraq have enjoyed almost universal public esteem. For example, the charity 'Help for Heroes' has achieved a high media profile and has raised millions of pounds for service personnel injured in these conflicts: if its attitude towards the wars themselves is avowedly apolitical, its language of heroism, sacrifice and national pride has served to celebrate the figure of the soldier.[1]

By contrast, any celebration of the soldier in the Georgian period was more than counterbalanced by some very negative prejudices. These could themselves be contradictory. Soldiers could simultaneously be accused of being both a tool and a victim of oppression; of being the strong arm of the law whilst being lawless themselves; of being both brutishly hypermasculine and attached to foppish uniforms; of being addicted both to violence and to the excesses of politeness. All ranks of the army came in for criticism. Officers could be condemned both as social climbers and as unqualified men

---

1 Help for Heroes states 'We fund projects and initiatives that make a real difference to the lives of our wounded heroes. We do not seek to criticise or be political.' <http://www.helpforheroes.org.uk> [accessed 17 January 2012].

of privilege, while the common men were apparently drawn from the very dregs of society.

The Duke of Wellington famously – and repeatedly – referred to the latter as the 'scum of the earth'. As Philip Haythornthwaite reminds us, however, this was not simply an aristocrat disdaining his social inferiors. On one occasion, he employed the phrase to distinguish the British system of voluntary enlistment with continental forms of conscription:

> The conscription calls out a share of every class – no matter whether your son or my son – all must march; but our friends [British soldiers] are the very scum of the earth. People talk of their enlisting from their fine military feeling – all stuff – no such thing. Some of our men enlist from having got bastard children – some for minor offences – many more for drink; but you can hardly conceive such a set brought together, and it is really wonderful that we should have made them the fine fellows they are.[2]

While conscripts were necessarily a cross-section of society, Wellington argued, an army such as Britain's would inevitably be the recourse of the poor and the desperate. In describing them in these terms, however, he paid a compliment both to the men for becoming 'fine fellows' and to the army that 'made them' that way. The reputation of the soldier was therefore a complex one: among other things, Wellington reminds us that we have to bear in mind the soldier's relationship with the society of his day, and the transformative experience involved in being a member of an institution like the army.

Britain's Soldiers seeks to explore the figure of the soldier in the century from the Hanoverian accession to the Battle of Waterloo. This was a century of almost continuous conflict – especially from the 1740s onwards – in which Britain established itself as the world's leading military and imperial power. This unprecedented effort involved an unheard-of mobilisation of manpower, from within Britain itself and from without (including from its allies, and from among its colonists and colonised). Strikingly, and in pointed contrast to the continental militaries described by Wellington, this mass mobilisation largely occurred outside of the regular army. Britain had long had an 'amateur military tradition' – with ancient institutions such as the militia, the *posse comitatus* and the trained bands that could put men in arms in case of invasion or internal disturbance – but the period from the Forty Five onwards saw a proliferation of novel forms of military service.[3] The chapters below will

---

2 Quoted in Philip Haythornthwaite, *Wellington: The Iron Duke* (Washington DC: Potomac, 2007), p. 52.
3 Ian Beckett, *The Amateur Military Tradition 1558–1945* (Manchester: Manchester University Press, 1991).

explore new institutions such as the reformed militia, the volunteers and the yeomanry, to name but a few. The existence of these part-time and auxiliary forces complicates our definition of what constitutes a 'soldier' and how we conceptualise his relationship with civil society.

This collection of essays therefore seeks to explore Britain's military by focusing in detail upon its combatants. In particular, it wants to rethink historical approaches to soldiers' relationship with the society and culture of their day. As we argue below, there have been many valuable studies of 'war and society' in this period, but these have often concentrated on wartime civil society rather than on war itself. By contrast, *Britain's Soldiers* argues that 'war and society' should refocus on war by using techniques from social and cultural history in order to study the lives of its combatants, and to think about their place *within* society and culture. This was a period when as many as one in four men had some experience of military service,[4] but when it was usually part-time or a phase of their lives. The sheer pervasiveness of this experience suggests that 'war' cannot be separated from 'society'. Rather, we argue that historians should study the soldier holistically if they are to understand him as a combatant.

This introductory essay will proceed by thinking about the terms in the book's title, in order to demonstrate how its ten chapters will engage with five key themes: the 'Britishness' of the British soldier; the nature of the military institution, as a hierarchy and a profession; the soldier's relationship with military discipline; how soldiering was represented and lived in terms of gender; and the place of soldiers within society, both during and after their period of military service.

BRITAIN'S SOLDIERS

OF ALL THE TERMS in the title, 'Britain' might appear to be the most descriptive and uncontentious. When George I succeeded to the throne, however, Great Britain was of relatively recent creation, and a fairly pragmatic one at that. Military motivations for the 1707 Act of Union with Scotland were paramount, seeking to take the sting out of Jacobitism and to remove England's land border with a country that had historically allied with France: tellingly, an English army stationed over the border urged its passage. Jacobitism was thereafter committed to the dissolution of Britain as a state, and remained a key security threat for four decades.

---

4 Stephen Conway, *The British Isles and the War of American Independence* (Oxford: Oxford University Press, 2000), p. 28.

Britain was indeed a state at the beginning of this period, a political and administrative entity rather than a nation with which people could identify and to which they could have a sense of belonging. War was central to the creation of Britain in this latter sense too. Linda Colley has argued that it was the prolonged experience of conflict with France in the eighteenth century that encouraged the English, Scots and Welsh to see themselves as 'British'. France became the 'other' that encouraged Britons to emphasise what they had in common, and wartime fostered a culture of patriotism and active citizenship. In particular, Colley tests her thesis at the end of the period by examining how many men pledged to fight for this new nation in the volunteering movement of the Napoleonic Wars: soldiers were therefore the engine and the product of 'forging the nation'.[5] Colley's *Britons* has helped to open up the cultural history of war in eighteenth-century studies, although it largely views the armed forces themselves through the lens of contemporary representation. Military scholars such as Stephen Conway, Austin Gee and John Cookson have subsequently explored how far her thesis can be applied in practice to particular regions and branches of the service,[6] and there is potential for further study of the national identity of soldiers as a group and the army as an institution.

'Britishness' is an important consideration in a further sense. We are accustomed today to think about armies as national entities, in both an organisational and a cultural sense. In the eighteenth century, however, Britain routinely hired regiments wholesale from its allies and even deployed them within Britain to guard against invasion: this in itself hints at a very different attitude towards 'national' armed forces. In this volume, Conway further considers the Britishness of the British soldier, by emphasising how armies of the *ancien régime* could in fact be cosmopolitan in their composition, attitudes and practices. For Conway, it is rather the *Europeanness* of the British military that is striking: this serves as a counter to the usual assumptions about the exceptionalism of the British (or Anglo-American) military tradition, which the 'Britons' cultural thesis had arguably helped to shore up.[7] This theme is returned to in chapter 10, where Kevin Linch examines the creation of new military identities in Britain, which

5 Linda Colley, *Britons: Forging the Nation, 1707–1837* (New Haven: Yale University Press, 1993), ch. 7.

6 Conway, *British Isles*, ch. 5; John Cookson, *The British Armed Nation, 1793–1815* (Oxford: Oxford University Press, 1997); Austin Gee, *The British Volunteer Movement, 1794–1814* (Oxford: Oxford University Press, 2003).

7 For a recent example of British history that looks across the Atlantic rather than the Channel, see Paul Kleber Monod, *Imperial Island: A History of Britain and its Empire 1660–1837* (Oxford: Wiley Blackwell, 2009).

partly drew upon wider European ideas of soldiering. The trans-national nature of armies is underlined by the phenomenon of officers serving in foreign militaries, with whom they shared a common sense of professionalism. Endorsing the critique of 'methodological nationalism',[8] in chapter 2 Graciela Iglesias Rogers takes up the story from the 1790s, by thinking about British and Irish soldiers who served in the armies of France and Spain. In the era of democratic revolutions, we might assume that armies were more closely identified with their nation and their citizenry, but Iglesias Rogers considers the extent of cross-cultural contact in a context where soldiers signed up to fight in another nation's cause.

A definition of Britain necessarily requires an exploration of England's relationship to the other parts of the British Isles, most notably Ireland. Despite being titled *Britain's Soldiers*, this volume does not overtly exclude Ireland and the Irish military experience. Although Ireland had a separate military establishment through this period, and even the Union in 1801 left many aspects of the military relationship between the two islands unresolved,[9] Irishmen were a consistently large portion of the British Army, and its auxiliary forces were an important part of military power at the disposal of the governments in London and Dublin.[10] Indeed, regiments of the British Army were regularly shipped to Ireland, often before being sent further overseas, and so it was usual for a regiment in the British Army to have a contingent of Irishmen (notable exceptions were the Scottish Highland regiments).[11] Equally, the titled Irish regiments were not necessarily wholly Irish.[12] Therefore, in chapters that focus on the British Army, Irish soldiers are inherently present within the parameters of the analysis. Where there

---

8 Andreas Wimmer and Nina Glick Schiller, 'Methodological Nationalism and Beyond: Nation-State Building, Migration and the Social Sciences', *Global Networks*, 2.4 (2002), pp. 301–34.

9 Alan J. Guy, 'The Irish Military Establishment, 1660–1776', in *A Military History of Ireland*, ed. by Thomas Bartlett and Keith Jeffery (Cambridge: Cambridge University Press, 1996), pp. 211–30; Alan Blackstock, 'The Union and the Military, 1801–c.1830', *Transactions of the Royal Historical Society*, 10 (2000), pp. 329–51.

10 Alan Blackstock, 'A Forgotten Army: The Irish Yeomanry', *History Ireland*, 4.4 (1996), pp. 28–33; Stephen Conway, *War, State, and Society in Mid-Eighteenth-Century Britain and Ireland* (Oxford: Oxford University Press, 2006), pp. 60–2; Ivan F. Nelson, *The Irish Militia, 1793–1802: Ireland's Forgotten Army* (Dublin: Four Courts Press, 2007).

11 For a visual representation of this movement of regiments, see Appendix B of J. A. Houlding, *Fit for Service: The Training of the British Army, 1715–1795* (Oxford: Clarendon, 1981), pp. 409–14.

12 For the national proportions in British Army in the Napoleonic Wars, see Kevin Linch, *Britain and Wellington's Army: Recruitment, Society and Tradition, 1807–1815* (Basingstoke: Palgrave Macmillan, 2011), pp. 60–3.

was a separation between the British and Irish military institutions, this is reflected in the limits of particular chapters: Caroline Nielsen's chapter explores Chelsea Pensioners, but necessarily excludes a detailed analysis of Chelsea Hospital's sister institution at Kilmainham. For the chapters that investigate wider relationships between soldiers, society and culture, our geographical scope is somewhat harder to define – but their arguments and conclusions are not exclusively limited to the eastern side of the Irish Sea.

Much like the definition of 'Britain', identifying 'soldiers' can appear equally straightforward at first glance; a simple answer would be the members of the established armed forces. As mentioned above, however, a large portion of the growth of Britain's armed forces in the period covered by this volume was outside of the British Army. These men, who can be broadly termed auxiliary soldiers, were an important component in the numerical strength of Britain's military forces. This was particularly the case in the French Revolutionary and Napoleonic Wars, when the British Army expanded from 40,000 in 1792 to a peak of 250,000 in 1813, whilst the part-time volunteers totalled some 400,000 at their peak in 1805. The scale of mobilisation may have been exceptional, but it was not without precedent for both the Seven Years War and American War of Independence had witnessed the establishment of large numbers of auxiliary soldiers.[13] As a result of this expansion, a unitary military institution did not exist in Britain, and there were multiple lines of authority for its armed forces. This sometimes bewilderingly complex arrangement meant that separate government branches held responsibilities for different aspects of military administration and the lifecycle of soldiering.[14] Militiamen, for example, were raised by county authorities, who in turn were responsible to a civilian Secretary of State, though once mobilised ('embodied' as it was termed), the men came under the jurisdiction of the Secretary at War and general officers appointed by the Commander-in-Chief or the King. At the same time, the Lord Lieutenant of the county and the colonel of militia still retained control of the county militia regiment and often had to navigate these various bureaucratic channels in order to manage it.[15]

These auxiliary soldiers were largely untested in a military sense, as they were involved in combat on only a few occasions, most notably in the

---

13 Conway, *War, State, and Society*; Conway, *British Isles*.

14 The standard reference work on this remains Charles Mathew Clode, *The Military Forces of the Crown: Their Administration and Government*, 2 vols (London: J. Murray, 1869).

15 As an example of the advice given to those in charge of militia regiments, see *Advice to the Lord Lieutenants of counties, Commanding Regiments of Militia. Dedicated to the author of advice to the officers of the British Army* (London: J. Walker, 1786).

Irish rebellion of 1798. If they used their weapons in anger at all, it would probably have been against civilians in support of the civil power, which is an unpromising basis for a positive martial identity. In the absence of an identity predicated on armed combat, these men created themselves as soldiers and reinforced this persona in other ways. Although the training of armed forces was in fact fairly standardised (a phenomenon explored in the last chapter), these new soldiers had some say in the identity that they created, whether it was through their outward appearance or their behaviour. To borrow a phrase from E. P. Thompson, these soldiers were present at their own making, and were an active agent in the process through which they became soldiers. This is significant because, through the waves of mobilisation that occurred in the latter half of the eighteenth century, successive cohorts of men engaged in some way with a new identity as a soldier. In some cases, men and officers could experience different forms of soldiering in their lifetime. At the end of conflicts most of these soldiers were disbanded and they then returned to their civilian lives; some later returned to the profession of soldiering, but in a different force. Although a direct transfer from one service to another was unusual, and indeed specifically outlawed until 1799 in the case of men moving from the militia to the regulars, militia and volunteer units actively sought out former soldiers to act as non-commissioned officers. Letter books to the Secretaries at War and Commanders-in-Chief of the period are saturated with offers from half-pay officers wanting to serve in some capacity.[16]

This close relationship with civil society meant that soldiers often brought into the forces pre-conceived patterns of behaviour, ideals and expectations. At an individual level, soldiering could have different meanings at different times; to address this, the volume considers the full lifecycle of the soldier's service, which stretches to cover the periods after these men had served. The complex identity of the 'old soldier' and attitudes towards them are explored in Nielsen's chapter on Chelsea pensioners. In this study, wider social debates over the deserving poor and fraud were echoed in the discourse around the substantial numbers of men who held a pension because of their service in the armed forces. The sheer number of former soldiers in Georgian society means that this group has to loom large in any account of civil-military relations.

---

16 For examples see: The National Archives, London, Secretaries of State: State Papers Military, SP41/30 (sergeants for the militia in 1759); CO 5/171, Charles Jenkinson to Duke of Northumberland, 22 July 1779 (sergeants from the Guards for the Westminster Association); WO34/153, In letters to Lord Amherst, Commander in Chief, 1779.

By taking a broader view of soldiers and the practice of being a soldier, this volume consciously analyses soldiers across the military and institutional boundaries of the time. This bucks the tendency of historical analysis (and often the cataloguing of primary sources) to adopt contemporary military divisions and to study the British Army, the militia, and part-time soldiers separately from each other.[17] John Cookson's exploration of a military 'service' ethic across all of Britain's auxiliary forces, part of a wider political culture, has demonstrated the value of research that transcends the boundaries of the military administration of the time.[18] With a similar focus, Bruce Collins shows in chapter 3 how a broader perspective can shed new light on the conflicting opinions about British officers in the period, and identifies three categories of officers, each of which had various roles to play, assorted reasons for holding a commission from the King, and different relationships to civilian politics and society. With similarly broad parameters, in chapter 10 Kevin Linch explores how the new military identities of the auxiliary soldiers were created, covering both full-time and part-time soldiers, and reveals how a fairly consistent military culture emerged in Britain as these men sought to legitimise their position in society. The focus on all ranks in this volume enables us to examine how soldiers were defined in the period 1715–1815, both by themselves and by society.

RETHINKING WAR AND SOCIETY

THE STUDY of 'war and society' in Britain is almost as old as social history itself. Over the last four decades, a rich body of work has emerged, which has shed much light on Britain's armed forces and their relationship to society and politics. In the process, this has served to broaden the remit of military and social history alike. Breaking free from a tradition of studies of military operations and the history of the 'regiment', new

---

17 J. E. Cookson, 'The English Volunteer Movement of the French Wars, 1793–1815: Some Contexts', *The Historical Journal*, 32.4 (1989), pp. 867–91; Gee, *British Volunteer Movement*; Kevin Linch, '"A Citizen and Not a Soldier": The British Volunteer Movement and the War against Napoleon', in *Soldiers, Citizens and Civilians: Experiences and Perceptions of the French Wars, 1790–1820* ed. by A. Forrest, K. Hagemann and J. Rendall (Basingstoke: Palgrave Macmillan, 2009), pp. 205–21; John R. Western, *The English Militia in the Eighteenth Century: The Story of a Political Issue, 1660–1802* (London: Routledge & Kegan Paul, 1965).

18 J. E. Cookson, 'Service without Politics? Army, Militia and Volunteers in Britain during the American and French Revolutionary Wars', *War In History*, 10.4 (2003), pp. 381–97.

analyses of British military power and the impact of war have emerged, and the methodological framework has extended to include economic, social and cultural approaches.[19]

These have often involved the study of institutions rather than events. Titles such as John Brewer's *Sinews of Power* have redefined the parameters for studying Britain's armed forces, in this case through an examination of the financial muscle of the British state that created a 'fiscal-military juggernaut' which proved more capable of sustaining war than its rivals.[20] Jeremy Black has criticised such a structural and deterministic argument about the relationship between military success and political and social factors. Taking up this challenge, further work has investigated the military-society relationship,[21] and new work on military medicine and the supply chain has fleshed out Brewer's thesis about Britain's military infrastructure.[22] Additionally, research has highlighted the impact of war on British society and the close relationship between the two, such as the crippling economic and social effects of war on domestic food supplies uncovered by Roger Wells.[23] These works contest the long-held view that war was remote and offshore for most people in the British Isles.

Nevertheless, a fundamental separation remains between 'war' and 'society' in much of the historiography about the subject. Works explore how men were mobilised for war, how women were involved in auxiliary capacities, or how war affected the economy, society or culture.[24] They often have little to say about soldiers as a social group, or as combatants. Inherent in many of these is a natural focus on periods of actual or impending conflict. These

---

19 For an overview of this large literature, see M. Neiberg, 'War and Society' in M. Hughes and W. Philpot (eds), *Palgrave Advances in Modern Military History* (Basingstoke: Palgrave, 2006).

20 John Brewer, *The Sinews of Power: War, Money and the English State, 1688–1783* (London: Unwin Hyman, 1989). Other examples include Gordon Bannerman, *Merchants and the Military in Eighteenth-Century Britain: British Army Contracts and Domestic Supply, 1739–1763* (London: Pickering & Chatto, 2008); Javier Cuenca Esteban, 'The British Balance of Payments, 1772–1820: India Transfers and War Finance', *The Economic History Review*, 54.1 (2001), pp. 58–86; H. M. Scott, 'Britain's Emergence as a European Power, 1688–1815', in *A Companion to Eighteenth-Century Britain*, ed. by Harry Thomas Dickinson (Oxford: Blackwell, 2002), pp. 431–46.

21 Notably Conway's *War, State and Society* and *British Isles*.

22 Erica Charters, 'Disease, Wilderness Warfare and Imperial Relations: The Battle for Quebec, 1759–1760', *War in History*, 16.1 (2009), pp. 1–24.

23 Roger Wells, *Wretched Faces: Famine in Wartime England, 1793–1801* (Gloucester: A. Sutton; New York: St. Martin's Press, 1988).

24 For example, Lawrence Stone (ed.), *An Imperial State at War: Britain from 1689 to 1815* (London: Routledge, 1994).

binary separations between 'war and society' and 'war and peace' have been overcome to some extent by studies of the armed forces as institutions, such as J. A. Houlding's *Fit for Service*, which examines the constant process of training and inspection within the army.[25] Such studies are more prevalent in the history of the Royal Navy, however, perhaps because the navy had a much bigger fiscal and physical presence during peacetime.

In both 'war and society' and 'military institution' studies there is a danger of marginalising, if not losing, the history of the people involved. In this context, Mary Jo Maynes' thoughts on social history are apposite:

> For most historians influenced by social science, the use of memoirs or eyewitness accounts and the like has served primarily to flesh out or add a human dimension to essentially structural arguments and models derived by inference from aggregate data. Many of the models so derived, for example, the family economy model, are of unquestionable value for our understanding of the lives of ordinary people in the past. Still, the cost of this emphasis has been substantial. While social science history has provided us with a valuable critique of traditional histories, it nevertheless has often tended to leave the experiences of identifiable people as historical agents by the wayside as it reconstructed the powerful historical processes that contextualized individual lives.[26]

Social histories of the armed forces are particularly liable to prioritise the institution or the model over the individual. That is not to say that excellent work has not been done on the social history of the redcoat: witness the growing body of work on the British soldier in North America, for example.[27] But social history's desire to do 'history from below' necessarily has to contend with the availability and form of the sources upon which to base such a study. Although common soldiers wrote far more than is often supposed, and more has survived than is often indicated in the literature, such personal material is always going to be limited and potentially untypical, and so we need to look for new ways of recreating individuals as historical agents in

---

25 Houlding, *Fit for Service*; Alan J. Guy, *Oeconomy and Discipline: Officership and Administration in the British Army 1714–63* (Manchester: Manchester University Press, 1985).

26 Mary Jo Maynes, 'Autobiography and Class Formation in Nineteenth-Century Europe: Methodological Considerations', *Social Science History*, 16.3 (1992), p. 518.

27 Sylvia Frey, *The British Soldier in America: A Social History of Military Life in the Revolutionary Period* (Austin: Texas University Press, 1982); Stephen Brumwell, *Redcoats: The British Soldier and the War in the Americas, 1755–1753* (Cambridge: Cambridge University Press, 2001); Matthew Spring, *With Zeal and with Bayonets Only: The British Army on Campaign in North America, 1775–1783* (Norman: Oklahoma University Press, 2008).

the process of becoming and being a soldier. To discover the history of those involved, historians need to go beyond potentially anecdotal personal records.

A subdiscipline of social history that has been particularly successful in this regard is the history of crime, not least because so many of our sources about the lower orders emanate from the institutions that sought to police them. The analogy with military discipline is worth pursuing, since the military courts produced voluminous and often detailed records that shed light on the common soldier's experience. Just as historians of crime have shed light on the operation of power within disciplinary institutions,[28] so there is an opportunity to explore the military in this regard. In this volume, chapters 5 and 6 explore the military justice system of the eighteenth century. William Tatum highlights the range of tactics used by soldiers to exert influence upon their officers' execution of justice, and Ilya Berkovich explores how military discipline operated in practice, by considering the case study of Gibraltar: even in this enclosed and apparently governable location, orders appear to have been carried out very imperfectly. Contrary to the stereotype of a brutal and arbitrary system, both chapters therefore emphasise that the military justice system sought to achieve its ends through negotiation and compromise. This parallels recent work on the civilian courts in this period, which emphasises the role of judicial discretion and popular agency.[29] Looking at the system from the soldier's point of view, the humble redcoat comes across as an assertive and well-informed agent rather than an oppressed victim.[30] To borrow another concept from social history, there is a clear sense of a 'moral economy' among soldiers, regarding their rights and the limits of authority.[31] Arguably, this was a shared feature of armies in this period, further supporting Conway's case for 'military Europe' in chapter 1.

Social history drew its methods from across the social sciences, and historians who have sought to understand the nature of human societies, mentalities and behaviours have often been influenced by anthropology. This has the potential to shed light on the military experience, since the military is an enclosed society with specific values and codes of conduct. In his chapter, Matthew McCormack seeks to explore the nature of interpersonal conduct

28 Michel Foucault, *Discipline and Punish: The Birth of the Prison*, trans. Alan Sheridan (London: Penguin, 1991).

29 Peter King, *Crime, Justice and Discretion in England, 1740–1820* (Oxford: Oxford University Press, 2003); Drew Gray, *Crime, Prosecution and Social Relations: The Summary Courts of the City of London in the Late Eighteenth Century* (Basingstoke: Palgrave, 2009).

30 Brumwell, *Redcoats*, ch. 1.

31 E. P. Thompson, 'The Moral Economy of the English Crowd in the Eighteenth Century', *Past & Present*, 50 (1971).

in the military by focusing on relations between the regular army and the militia. He develops Christopher Duffy's remark that officers in eighteenth-century armies were particularly 'rancorous and touchy', and tries to explain why this should be so.[32] By focusing in detail on two incidents where relations broke down spectacularly, he seeks to shed light on the normal expectations of behaviour in this context. Cultural historians are often drawn to incidents where people appear on the face of it to be acting bizarrely: a cat massacre or (in the case of chapter 6) an order to kill dogs can offer a window on a world that is radically different to our own, and can give the historian an insight into how that world worked.[33]

A key growth area within social and cultural history has been the study of gender. The history of masculinity would appear to be particularly apposite to the study of a homosocial institution like the army, but this line of enquiry has been slow to emerge. Military historians have rarely conducted dialogues with gender scholars; and gender historians have tended to emphasise the 'private sphere' of home, family and relationships. The big exception to this in British studies always used to be the First World War, where women's experience of wartime service and men's experience of the trenches provided a fertile meeting-point for historians of war and gender.[34] It is only more recently that the late eighteenth and early nineteenth centuries have been catching up in this respect, often by emphasising how the wars of revolution were concerned with building nations around a highly gendered notion of the citizen soldier.[35] Even here, however, there has been relatively little work on the men who did the actual warring. (Ironically, the handful of female soldiers who disguised themselves to fight in these wars have received more attention from gender scholars than their male counterparts.[36]) Much of this work on gender has epitomised the 'war and society' tradition, by telling us more about society than war, and more about civilians than soldiers.

---

32 Christopher Duffy, *The Military Experience in the Age of Reason* (London: Routledge, 1987), p. 76.

33 Robert Darnton, *The Great Cat Massacre and Other Episodes in French Cultural History* (London: Vintage, 1984); John Tosh, *The Pursuit of History*, 4th edn (Harlow: Longman, 2006), p. 297.

34 Joanna Bourke, *Dismembering the Male: Men's Bodies, Britain and the Great War* (Chicago, MI: Chicago University Press, 1996).

35 Stefan Dudink, Karen Hagemann and John Tosh (eds), *Masculinities in Politics and War: Gendering Modern History* (Manchester: Manchester University Press, 2004); Alan Forrest, Karen Hagemann and Jane Rendall (eds), *Soldiers, Citizens and Civilians: Experiences and Perceptions of the Revolutionary and Napoleonic Wars, 1790–1820* (Basingstoke: Palgrave, 2008).

36 The bibliography on the 'female Marine' Hannah Snell alone is extensive: <http://www.hannahsnell.com/library.htm> [accessed 7 February 2012].

A history of combatant masculinities is beginning to emerge for this period, however.[37] In this volume McCormack thinks about relationships between soldiers in terms of masculine honour codes, and Cicely Robinson and Louise Carter explore the gendered representation of soldiers in visual media and popular culture. Both McCormack and Robinson emphasise the importance of 'polite' manners where the British Army is concerned, suggesting that historians need to pay attention to the influence of social mores upon the military sphere. In contrast to recent surveys of masculinity, which tend to emphasise that militarism was the 'hard' counterpoint to 'soft' civilian life,[38] these chapters suggest that officers placed a great onus on cultivation and civility. In particular, Robinson proposes that the public exhibition of military paintings further helped to reconcile martial and polite masculinities. Carter's chapter examines soldiers' attractiveness to women during the French Wars, which came to be known as 'scarlet fever'. This supposed desire for martial men was no transhistorical phenomenon, she argues, but rather sheds light on the anxieties and enthusiasms of an era that was as turbulent for gender relations as it was for the military.

Carter and Robinson focus on visual representations of soldiers, and much recent work on the cultural history of war on this period has come from the direction of art history. The best of this work has gone beyond a focus on 'war painting' to think about war's impact on the wider culture, and vice versa.[39] Similarly, work on theatre and war has emphasised not only the ways in which war became a subject for theatre, but that war itself was highly theatrical in this period.[40] In this volume Kevin Linch emphasises the important roles of public display and performance in constituting the period's novel paramilitary initiatives as 'soldiers'. Understanding the contemporary reception and discourse surrounding military display, whether it be in art or through parades and other forms of physical performance, provides an important avenue to understanding contemporary opinions of soldiers, and a way to explore the intricate connection between a society and those who took up arms in its name.

---

37 Karen Hagemann, Gisela Mettele and Jane Rendall (eds), *Gender, War and Politics: Transatlantic Perspectives, 1775–1830* (Basingstoke: Palgrave, 2010), part 2: 'Masculinity, Revolution and War'.

38 Christopher Forth, *Masculinity in the Modern West: Gender, Civilisation and the Body* (Basingstoke: Palgrave, 2008).

39 Douglas Fordham, *British Art and the Seven Years War: Allegiance and Autonomy* (Pennsylvania University Press, 2010); Holger Hoock, *Empires of the Imagination: War, Politics and the Arts in the British World, 1750–1850* (London: Profile, 2010).

40 Gillian Russell, *The Theatres of War: Performance, Politics and Society, 1783–1815* (Oxford: Oxford University Press, 1995).

The following chapters utilise this range of methodological lenses and source types in order to explore Britain's soldiers in new ways. They seek to shed light on the soldier himself, but also on the institution of which he was a part, and on civil-military relations. They explore these men's identities, definitions of honour and professionalism, and the means by which they became soldiers. As such, this volume seeks to re-orientate the study of the military, by suggesting that historians should pay closer attention to those who donned a uniform in this period of frequent and intense warfare.

Part 1

Nationhood

The Eighteenth-Century British Army as a European Institution

Stephen Conway

T HE MOST DIFFICULT IDEAS to challenge are often those that are not explicitly articulated, but operate at the subterranean level of deep-rooted assumption. For all the recent emphasis on the need to free ourselves from the distortions of the narrowly national narrative, and recognise the intertwined, entangled, transnational, or even plain old-fashioned international dimensions of every society's past, the default setting for most historians seems to be the national perspective. Armies are perhaps particularly prone to this national approach. We tend to associate them with the nation state, national sentiment, and national identity. They act, especially in wartime, as a symbol of the nation. Historians of the British Army, over many generations, have reflected the general tendency to regard the British state's professional military forces as the embodiment of the nation and therefore as distinct and different from those of other states and nations.[1]

---

1 This is most obvious in older studies: see, e.g., Sir John Fortescue, *A History of the British Army*, 13 vols (London: Macmillan and Co., 1899–1930), 1, Preface, where he refers to 'our old Army' (p. vi) and 'our regiments' (p. xii); the Preface, written by Lt.-Col. Sir Arthur Leetham, to the first issue of the *Journal of the Society of Army Historical Research*, 1 (1921), pp. 1–2, which takes as its inspiration 'the past history of our army, its achievements and traditions'; Cecil Lawson, *A History of the Uniforms of the British Army*, 5 vols (London: P. Davies, 1940–67), 1, p. 1, which invokes 'our own army with its glorious history and ancient traditions'. But see also Correlli Barnett, *Britain and Her Army* (Harmondsworth: Penguin Press, 1970), described in the Preface as a 'history of the army as a British institution' (p. xx); David Chandler (ed.), *The Oxford Illustrated History of the British Army* (Oxford: Oxford University Press, 1994), the Introduction to which sets out some of the distinctive features of its subject.

Yet in the eighteenth century, at least, the British Army was as much a European as a British institution. It had much in common with, and was closely connected to, other European armies. Furthermore, in the right circumstances, its officers and men had little difficulty in appreciating their army's essential Europeanness. Unlikely though it may seem, we can even say that British soldiers possessed a European consciousness, based on occupational solidarity, which sat alongside their other senses of collective belonging. This chapter focuses mainly on the period 1740–93; from the middle of the eighteenth century until the time when Britain became involved in the French Revolutionary War. The case for the British Army's European character would probably be no less strong if earlier decades were examined. Recent work suggests that the argument may also hold good for the years after 1793.[2]

Two important caveats need to be registered before the army's European features are analysed. The first is that the British military had some undeniably distinctive characteristics. Its control by the civil power, while not perhaps as absolute as some accounts suggest, marks it out from other European armies, many of which were clearly not constrained by constitutional limitations.[3] From the middle of the century, the British Army was also more obviously committed to imperial theatres than most of its European counterparts; only the Spanish Army approached the British in terms of the extent of its overseas deployments.[4] The British Army, furthermore, was often overshadowed by the Royal Navy, which attracted substantial and consistent

---

2 John Cookson, 'Regimental Worlds: Interpreting the Experience of British Soldiers during the Napoleonic Wars', in *Soldiers, Citizens and Civilians: Experiences and Perceptions of the French Wars, 1790–1820*, ed. by A. Forrest, K. Hagemann and J. Rendall (Basingstoke: Palgrave Macmillan, 2009), pp. 23–42; Kevin Linch, 'The Politics of Foreign Recruitment in Britain during the French Revolutionary and Napoleonic Wars', in *Transnational Soldiers: Foreign Military Enlistment in the Modern Era*, ed. by B. Collins and N. Airelli (Basingstoke: Palgrave Macmillan, 2012), pp. 50–66.

3 See the venerable, but still unsurpassed, Charles M. Clode, *The Military Forces of the Crown: Their Administration and Government*, 2 vols (London: J. Murray, 1869), 1, chs 5–8 and 2, ch. 21. For more modern emphasis on control of the British Army by the civil power, see John Childs, 'The Army and the State in Britain and Germany during the Eighteenth Century', in *Rethinking Leviathan: The Eighteenth-Century State in Britain and Germany*, ed. by John Brewer and Eckhart Hellmuth (Oxford: Oxford University Press, 1999), esp. 65–70.

4 For the British Army's imperial commitments, see esp. P. J. Marshall, 'Empire and Authority in the Later Eighteenth Century', *Journal of Imperial and Commonwealth History*, 15 (1987), pp. 105–22; John Houlding, *Fit for Service: The Training of the British Army, 1715–1795* (Oxford: Oxford University Press, 1981), pp. 12–13. For the Spanish Army's deployment in America, see D. A. Brading, 'Bourbon Spain and its American

funding that in many continental states would have been devoted to the army.[5] As a result, the British Army was only small or medium-sized in the scale of European militaries. It was only a fraction of the size of the French Army, appreciably smaller than the Austrian, and was eclipsed even by the Prussian, even though Prussia was much less populous than Britain and Ireland.[6] This last point leads naturally to the second caveat: European armies varied considerably, not just in size, but in character. Some might argue that the variations were so great that there was no European norm against which the British Army can be measured. But if variations certainly existed, there were also general European patterns in all the areas explored here; whatever the differences, the similarities between armies are striking, and deserve to be highlighted.

To establish the European credentials of the British Army we will focus first on its functional and structural similarities with other armies. We turn then to its composition, which was also like that of many continental armies. Attitudes and ethos are considered next, and we will see that in important ways they transcended national distinctions. The final part of the chapter tries to explain these various commonalities.

FUNCTIONS

IN FUNCTIONAL TERMS, European armies, including the British, were remarkably similar. They were intended, primarily and most obviously, as the physical coercive power of the ruler for use against external enemies. They defended the territory of the state, and launched offensive operations against the territory of enemy states. Despite the anti-standing army rhetoric that was common in early eighteenth-century England, notwithstanding the enthusiasm (in principle, at least) for a revived militia, and however much faith was expressed in the Royal Navy's role as a bulwark against foreign invasion, even the most populist and parsimonious of governments did not see fit to dispense with the army. When pressed by parliamentary opponents, leading politicians were refreshingly candid on this issue: without a regular

---

Empire', in *The Cambridge History of Latin America, Volume 1: Colonial Latin America*, ed. by Leslie Bethell (Cambridge: Cambridge University Press, 1984), pp. 397–409.

5 For the funding of the navy, see Clive Wilkinson, *The British Navy and the State in the Eighteenth Century* (Woodbridge: Boydell Press in association with the National Maritime Museum, 2004).

6 For comparisons of size of armies, see Peter Wilson, 'Warfare in the Old Regime, 1648–1789', in *European Warfare, 1453–1815*, ed. by Jeremy Black (Basingstoke: Macmillan, 1999), p. 80 (Table 3.1).

military force, both offensive and defensive capabilities would be put in doubt.[7]

Eighteenth-century armies also had important political functions in relation to the subjects of their own governments. The military acted as a prop for the political order. Armies not only used violence or its threat to compel unwilling subjects, but also promoted loyalty to the regime in more subtle ways, through socialising with local elites, parade-ground manoeuvres that entertained (and awed) large crowds of on-lookers, and celebration of royal events.[8] The British Army conformed to this European pattern in many respects. Even though it was meant to withdraw from towns during elections, to avoid the appearance of trying to influence voters, the British Army was by no means politically neutral. It often played a role in encouraging and sustaining loyalty to the government, especially in the first half of the eighteenth century, when the Stuarts offered a dynastic alternative to the Hanoverian monarchy.[9] Troops were stationed much more regularly in communities thought to be potentially disloyal than in towns noted for their support for the Hanoverian regime. More positively, army officers quartered in provincial urban centres encouraged political loyalty by social contact and interaction with local elites. Military parades, a great spectacle for large audiences, perhaps had a similar effect on a broader range of local people.[10] So, too, we can speculate, did the army's participation in the celebration of events that might increase identification with the ruling order, such as royal birthdays, and even military victories abroad.[11]

---

7 See, e.g., the arguments put forward by government speakers in the House of Commons debate on a proposal to reduce the size of the army, 3 February 1738: William Cobbett and John Wright (eds), *The Parliamentary History of England*, 36 vols (London: R. Bagshaw, 1806–20), 10, cols 375–467.

8 For a British tourist witnessing an impressive parade of 2,000 French troops at Strasbourg, see Derbyshire Record Office, Matlock, Gell of Hopton Papers, D 258/17/32/96, Godfrey Meynell to Philip Gell, 4 October [1770].

9 Hannah Smith, 'The Army, Provincial Urban Communities, and Loyalist Cultures in England, c.1714–50' *Journal of Early Modern History*, 15 (2011), pp. 139–58.

10 See, e.g., Henry E. Huntington Library, San Marino, California, Diaries of John Marsh, MS HM 54457/5, 6 May 1776.

11 See, e.g., report in *Adams's Weekly Courant*, 24 June 1760, of Chester's celebrations of George II's accession day, when the North Lincolnshire militia fired volleys and the officers dined with the corporation; and the celebrations in Maidenhead, Berkshire, in June 1761 of the capture of Belle Isle, including 'Troops under Arms to give us a *feu de Joi*': Gloucestershire Record Office, Gloucester, Rooke of St Briavels Papers, D 1833 F1/10.

STRUCTURES

AT A BASIC STRUCTURAL LEVEL, the British Army also had much in common with other European armies. Even when a military officer was serving as its nominal commander-in-chief, the monarch was its recognised head, just as he was in most continental states. George I and George II took very seriously their role as warrior kings, and were particularly committed to their army and solicitous about its welfare.[12] But George III, despite his lack of military experience, was scarcely less proprietorial and just as committed to the minutiae of military affairs. His resistance to the creation of new regiments in the early stages of the War of American Independence demonstrates a commitment to preserving the army as an effective instrument, and avoiding new corps acting as patronage vehicles of very limited military utility.[13] Royal command and control was symbolised by the granting of all officers' commissions in the king's name, and the carrying of royal standards by each of the army's units.

The British Army's fundamental unit of organisation was the regiment, divided into battalions and companies for the infantry and into squadrons for the cavalry. While the number of men in such units might vary from army to army, they were to be found in all European militaries. Different types of soldier were replicated across Europe: each army had its standard infantrymen, and its handpicked grenadiers; light infantry became a feature of more and more armies from the middle of the century. In the cavalry, regiments of horse and dragoons were again common, and light cavalry units came into vogue everywhere from the 1740s – such as hussars and light dragoons, who performed a similar scouting and reconnaissance function to the light infantry.

The rank system was remarkably similar across European armies, too, which made it easier to arrange exchanges of prisoners in wartime.[14] Every European army had private soldiers, non-commissioned officers – corporals and sergeants – and broadly similar officer ranks, from the lowly ensigns and lieutenants to the company and regimental commanders – the captains, majors, lieutenant-colonels, and colonels – and on to the major-generals, lieutenant-generals, full generals, and finally, field marshals. In all

---

12 See Hannah Smith, 'The Idea of a Protestant Monarchy in Britain, 1714–1760', *Past & Present*, 185 (2004), pp. 91–118.

13 Stephen Conway, *The British Isles and the War of American Independence* (Oxford: Oxford University Press, 2000), pp. 14–15.

14 For the exchange of prisoners, rank for rank, see, e.g., Sir Reginald Savory, 'The Convention of Écluse, 1759–1762', *Journal of the Society for Army Historical Research*, 42 (1964), pp. 68–77.

armies, furthermore, the proprietary rights of the company and regimental commanders were under pressure as governments sought to exercise more control over their armed forces, and attempted to mould disparate military units into cohesive armies.[15]

Eighteenth-century armies even looked remarkably similar. Many militaries, to be sure, had distinctively dressed troops. Perhaps the most obvious example is the Russians, whose exotic Cossack and Tartar irregulars so startled one British observer that he described them as 'of a nature different from any which exists in any other Service'.[16] The alarming looking Croatian Pandours attached to the Austrian military attracted similar wonderment.[17] But the same was true of the Scottish Highland regiments in the British Army, who appeared no less outlandish and noteworthy to those who were unfamiliar with their attire.[18] Even so, the bulk of the infantry in every European army was dressed in a strikingly similar fashion. The colour of their coats might distinguish them from soldiers in other armies, but in every other respect they were very similar, usually with lapels and cuffs in a contrasting colour, and the men wore very much the same form of breeches, gaiters, and shoes, topped off with the seemingly ubiquitous tricorn hat.[19]

In their coercive, or military role, European armies all used broadly similar weapons. The cavalry were armed with similar types of swords, pistols, and short muskets or carbines. Amongst the infantry, the pike, originally intended to defend the musketeers from cavalry attack, was abandoned in the early years of the eighteenth century, and the flintlock musket, and socket bayonet, were soon after nearly universal; only in the armies of Russia and the Ottoman Empire, which were both (to varying degrees) seen by many contemporaries as outside the European mainstream, did the older technology of the matchlock handgun persist.[20] The artillery also became an important arm in European armies more-or-less simultaneously. From

---

15 For the situation in the British Army, see Alan J. Guy, *Oeconomy and Discipline: Officership and Administration in the British Army, 1714–1763* (Manchester: Manchester University Press, 1984), esp. p. 162. For contemporaneous developments elsewhere, see Christopher Duffy, *The Military Experience in the Age of Reason* (London: Routledge & Kegan Paul, 1987), pp. 67–8.

16 British Library, London (henceforth, BL), Letter-book of John Ramsay, Additional MS 63,819, fols 4–5.

17 Berkshire Record Office, Reading, Neville Aldworth Papers, D/EN F54, Journal of a Tour of Switzerland and Italy, October 1743.

18 See, e.g., Newberry Library, Chicago, Case MS 0E199. M36 1755, Anon. Diary of French and Indian War, 24 October 1758.

19 For uniforms, see Duffy, *Military Experience*, pp. 105–7.

20 John Childs, *Armies and Warfare in Europe, 1648–1789* (Manchester: Manchester University Press, 1982), pp. 107–8.

the middle of the century, the Austrians formed a fully professionalised and fully militarised artillery corps, followed by the Russians, the Prussians, the French, and the British. Artillery pieces were also increasingly similar in calibre and function, most armies possessing three- or four-pounder guns to support the infantry, medium-weight six- or eight-pounders for use in batteries, and twelve-pounders, the heaviest battlefield cannon.[21]

Common weaponry partly explains common battlefield tactics. Armies deployed in lines to maximise the firepower of inaccurate muskets. Different armies, to be sure, had different tactical approaches; the number of rows in the line might vary, as might the space between soldiers. Some armies were more advanced than others in the development of light infantry, though any temptation to believe that they originated in North America, and were exported to Europe, should be resisted: light infantry emerged on the Continent before they were used extensively by European armies in North America.[22] American experience, admittedly, encouraged the adoption of looser formations; the British Army adapted to local conditions very rapidly in both the Seven Years War and the War of American Independence.[23] Even so, linear tactics were employed everywhere, including by the British Army serving in North America. The drill used to train troops for battlefield conditions, preparing them to carry out manoeuvres under fire, tended to follow Prussian example from the middle of the century, for the simple reason that Frederick the Great's successes in first the War of the Austrian Succession and then the Seven Years War meant that Prussia set the tone that hitherto had been established by the French Army.[24] As an officer in Dutch service noted in 1774, 'the Prussian exercise and discipline has been adopted more or less by almost every army in Europe'.[25] Nor was the British Army an

---

21 See Duffy, *Military Experience*, pp. 230–33.

22 See, e.g., Peter E. Russell, 'Redcoats in the Wilderness: British Officers and Irregular Warfare in Europe and America, 1740 to 1760', *William & Mary Quarterly*, 3rd series, 35 (1978), pp. 629–52. For different views, see Eric Robson, 'British Light Infantry in the Mid-Eighteenth Century: The Effect of American Conditions', *Army Quarterly*, 63 (1952), pp. 209–22; Peter Paret, 'Colonial Experience and European Military Reform at the End of the Eighteenth Century', *Bulletin of the Institute of Historical Research*, 37 (1964), pp. 47–59.

23 See, e.g., David J. Beattie, 'The Adaption of the British Army to Wilderness Warfare, 1755–1763', in *Adapting to Conditions: War and Society in the Eighteenth Century*, ed. by Maarten Utlee (Tuscaloosa, AL.: University of Alabama Press, 1986), pp. 56–83; Matthew H. Spring, *With Zeal and Bayonets Only: The British Army on Campaign in North America, 1775–1783* (Norman, OK: University of Oklahoma Press, 2008).

24 See Houlding, *Fit for Service*, esp. p. 204.

25 [James Cunninghame,] *Strictures on Military Discipline, in a Series of Letters, with a Military Discourse, in which is Interspersed some Account of the Scotch Brigade in the*

exception to this general rule. One of the greatest admirers of the Prussian approach was David Dundas, British Adjutant-General after the American war, who was particularly keen to ensure that his army's tactics conformed with the norms established by Frederick the Great.[26]

Composition

A T FIRST GLANCE, the British Army's composition differed markedly from that of other European armies in one respect. For most of the eighteenth century, it had no foreign regiments as part of its permanent establishment. In the French service, by contrast, German, Swiss, and Irish units were incorporated in the army, and made up about a fifth of the infantry. The Spanish military similarly had Irish and Walloon regiments; while the Dutch Army contained German and Swiss troops as an integral part of the whole.

But, as so often, the impression of British difference turns out to be deceptive. The British Army depended upon foreign manpower as much as other European armies; what distinguished the British service was merely the way in which its foreign component was organised. Soldiers from other European states, and particularly from Germany, served in British regiments alongside British and Irish recruits. The Royal American Regiment, despite its name, relied heavily on men enlisted in Germany.[27] Other British regiments included in their ranks smaller numbers of Germans raised by contractual arrangements with officers of various territories in the Holy Roman Empire, or recruited by British officers while their regiments were fighting in Germany.[28] More importantly, foreign units served as auxiliaries

---

Dutch Service (London: Printed for John Donaldson, 1774), p. 8. For corroboration, see London Metropolitan Archives, London, Jersey Papers, ACC/0510.255, p. 7; BL, Rainsford Papers, Add. MS 23,646, fol. 6.

26 Dundas was the author of *Principles of Military Movements, Chiefly Applied to Infantry: Illustrated by Manoeuvres of the Prussian Troops, and by an Outline of the British Campaigns in Germany, during the War of 1757* (London: Printed for T. Cadell, 1788).

27 See, e.g., Huntington Library, San Marino, California, Loudoun Papers, LO 607, box 34, list of recruits under Baron de Munster; Joseph Redington (ed.), *Calendar of Home Office Papers of the Reign of George III, 1766–1769* (London: Longman, 1879), p. 54; Centre for Kentish Studies, Maidstone, Amherst Papers, U 1350 C41/62-7; BL, Barrington Papers, Add. MS 73,587, fol. 3, Barrington to Capt. [Laurentius] O'Connell, 3 October 1775; Sir John Fortescue (ed.), *The Correspondence of King George the Third from 1760 to December 1783*, 6 vols (London: Macmillan, 1927–8), 3, p. 290.

28 See, e.g., BL, Leeds Papers, Egerton MS 3443, fols 110–11; and the arrangements with a Hanoverian officer, Lt.-Col. Georg Heinrich Albrecht von Scheither, in The

to the British Army, even if they were never institutionally part of the army. Military units from Hessen-Kassel, in particular, acted as British auxiliaries in many eighteenth-century conflicts, perhaps most famously in the War of American Independence. In 1781, auxiliary troops from Hessen-Kassel and other German principalities comprised 37 per cent of the British forces in North America.[29] Hanoverian regiments also acted as British auxiliaries in the same war, serving in the Mediterranean outposts of Gibraltar and Minorca, and as far away as India.

Another seeming difference from other European armies, which becomes less obvious on closer inspection, is the way in which British soldiers were recruited. One mid-century Secretary at War articulated conventional wisdom when he claimed that 'compulsive methods' of enlistment were inappropriate in 'this Country'.[30] On the Continent, by contrast, various forms of conscription were employed to raise the rank and file, ranging from cantonal systems, which compelled defined territories to provide set quotas of men, to wholesale recruitment of able-bodied male criminals. But the British Army was not quite the voluntary body that some contemporaries liked to think. Press acts, authorising the conscription of the unemployed, were in force in 1704–12, 1745–6, 1755–7, and 1778–9. Legislation passed by the Westminster Parliament in 1744 allowed the forcible recruitment of vagrants. Royal proclamations pardoned smugglers, on condition that they joined the army. More generally, male convicts might be offered the option of military service. The degree of choice involved was usually very circumscribed; the alternative was often even less palatable than becoming a soldier. The numbers involved in all these more-or-less compulsory forms of recruitment were probably not very large, relative to the size of the army as a whole; but they demonstrate that the British Army, like many other European armies, relied on both conscripts and volunteers.

The social background of British Army officers was remarkably similar to that of their continental counterparts, though a comparison of titles might suggest otherwise. In many European armies, the officer corps was visibly dominated by the aristocracy. Every single one of the 181 general officers employed in the French Army in western Germany in 1758 was a nobleman.[31] In 1767, nearly 75 per cent of the infantry officers in Piedmont-Sardinia's army

National Archives (henceforth TNA), War Office Papers, WO 43/405 and his papers in the Hauptstaatsarchiv Hannover, esp. Hannover 47 II Nr. 114.

29 Rodney Atwood, *The Hessians: Mercenaries from Hessen-Kassel in the American Revolution* (Cambridge: Cambridge University Press, 1980), p. 257 (Appendix D).

30 BL, Barrington Papers, Add. MS 73,628, fol. 87, undated memo.

31 Lee Kennett, *The French Armies of the Seven Years War: A Study in Military Organization and Administration* (Durham, NC: Duke University Press, 1967), p. 57.

were aristocrats, as were 93 per cent of the cavalry officers. In the Prussian Army in the year of Frederick the Great's death (1786), a mere 3 per cent of the officers ranked major or above were commoners. By contrast, in 1780, only 30 per cent of regular British Army officers had titles.[32] But the British Army was not as out of step as these figures imply. On the Continent, titles were more liberally bestowed on younger members of aristocratic families, who in Britain and Ireland had no outward signifier of nobility.[33] Furthermore, a portion of the titled officers in continental armies acquired aristocratic status only *after* they joined the military. The French Minister of War introduced a *noblesse militaire* in 1750. The hostility of the traditional nobility was so strong that restrictions on entry were imposed in 1758 and the famous four-quartering system of aristocratic exclusivity was eventually introduced in 1781.[34] But if in the French Army ennoblement for military service was short-lived, it became the norm in the Austrian Army, where, from 1757, officers with long and meritorious careers were able to apply for a patent of nobility.[35]

Military ennoblements, and the opposition they provoked, reveal that middle-class penetration of the officer ranks was far from insignificant. Officers from middle-class backgrounds were a rarity in guards regiments and the cavalry, but they were particularly well-represented in the technical branches, such as the artillery and engineers, and to a lesser extent in line infantry regiments. European armies – including the British – even had a small number of officers who had been promoted from the ranks.[36] Not many made it beyond company command, but their presence, and that of the more numerous middle-class officers, demonstrates that the officer corps was not an aristocratic preserve. That said, throughout Europe, officers from middle-class backgrounds, and those who had been promoted from the ranks, were expected to subscribe to an essentially aristocratic honour code and behave like gentlemen.[37]

The common soldiers in all European armies also came from similar

---

32 Christopher Storrs and H. M. Scott, 'The Military Revolution and the European Nobility, *c.*1600–1800', *War in History*, 3 (1996), pp. 15–17.

33 For some of the difficulties in comparing aristocracies, see John Cannon, 'The British Nobility, 1660–1800', in *The European Nobilities in the Seventeenth and Eighteenth Centuries*, 2 vols, ed. by H. M. Scott (London: Longman, 1995), 1, pp. 54–5.

34 Duffy, *Military Experience*, pp. 37, 38, 44; Rauf Blaufarb, *The French Army, 1750–1820: Careers, Talent, Merit* (Manchester: Manchester University Press, 2002), ch. 1.

35 According to Michael Hochedlinger, *Austria's Wars of Emergence: War, State and Society in the Habsburg Monarchy, 1683–1797* (London: Longman, 2003), pp. 305–6, only about half of the officers in the 'German' regiments of the Austrian Army came from the Austrian or Bohemian nobility.

36 For the British case, see Houlding, *Fit for Service*, p. 105.

37 See Duffy, *Military Experience*, pp. 74–80, for the cult of honour.

segments of society. Pardoned criminals, paupers, and vagrants were present in continental European armies, just as they were in the British regiments. At the other end of the scale, all armies had a sprinkling of socially superior men serving in their ranks – the sons of farmers, or merchants, or clergymen; students, teachers, and even upper-class 'volunteers', acting as common soldiers while waiting for an officer vacancy.[38] But by far the most important groups in the rank and file came from two broad occupational backgrounds; unskilled labourers and artisans. In the British 52nd Foot, surveyed in 1756, men described as labourers comprised 47 per cent of the rank and file.[39] The proportion varied in different British regiments, at least partly depending on the terminology used, but other recruiting returns underline the importance of labourers: they formed 70 per cent of the soldiers raised in Ireland for the 46th Foot in the winter of 1775–6;[40] and 52 per cent of the 96th Foot's enlistees between 1779 and 1782.[41] But the same returns show that skilled craftsmen played a significant part in filling the ranks, even though the enlistment of apprentices was forbidden.[42] From shoemakers to weavers, from smiths to tailors and clockmakers, artisans comprised 38 per cent of the recruits for the 52nd Foot in 1756, 28 per cent of the men raised for the 46th in 1775–6, and 48 per cent of those joining the 96th between 1779 and 1782. These proportions are broadly comparable to those found in other contemporary European armies: both labourers and artisans were similarly prominent in the ranks. The number of skilled and semi-skilled men might have been smaller in some militaries; only a little over a quarter of the Austrian Army's soldiers at the time of the Seven Years War 'declared a civilian trade upon being recruited'.[43] In the French Army, however, the share of those with an artisan background was nearer to the British: in 1763 about 40 per cent of French soldiers were craftsmen or the sons of craftsmen.[44]

In many countries, furthermore, urban centres provided a disproportionately large share of recruits, as these were the places to which young

---

38 For the British Army's 'gentlemen volunteers', see Houlding, *Fit for Service*, p. 103.

39 Royal Archives, Windsor, Cumberland Papers, Box 67/X.35.20.

40 TNA, War Office Papers, WO 1/992, 'List of Recruits Rais'd for the 46th Regiment of Foot', Dublin, 9 February 1776.

41 TNA, WO 25/537.

42 For the prosecution of an English apprentice for trying to join the army, see Worcestershire Record Office, Worcester, Quarter Sessions Order-book, V, fol. 87 (7–8 October 1777).

43 Christopher Duffy, *The Austrian Army in the Seven Years War, Volume 1, Instrument of War* (Rosemont, IL: Emperor's Press, 2000), p. 203.

44 See André Covisier, *L'Armée Française de la fin du XVIIe siècle au ministère de Choiseul: Le Soldat*, 2 vols (Paris: Presses universitaires de France, 1964), 1, pp. 449–542 for the social background of French soldiers.

men tended to gravitate in search of work and opportunities. In Britain, this tendency was perhaps more marked than elsewhere, as Britain was the most urbanised European country (apart from the Dutch Republic), and migration from countryside to town increased in the course of the eighteenth century.[45] Birmingham, Bristol, Glasgow, Leeds, Manchester, Dublin and, most importantly, London were favourite haunts for recruiting officers.[46] But the tendency was discernible throughout Western Europe.[47] Even in so rural a country as France, a disproportionate number of recruits were drawn from urban centres, especially Paris: at a time when perhaps no more than a fifth of French people lived in towns and cities, something like a third of the French Army's soldiers had an urban background.[48] Nevertheless, the influence of large landowners was a major factor in recruitment everywhere in Europe, including Britain and Ireland, where leading noblemen played a key role in raising new regiments.[49]

MILITARY ATTITUDES

IN 1755, Lieutenant-Colonel James Wolfe commented on the prevalence of libertarian attitudes amongst the British rank and file: 'they have no idea', Wolfe wrote, 'of a free born English Soldier's marching, working, or fighting,

---

45 For different rates of urbanisation, see Jan de Vries, *European Urbanization, 1500–1800* (London: Methuen, 1984), Table 3.6.
46 See, e.g., Glasgow City Archives, Glasgow, Hamilton of Barnes Papers, TD 589/586 and 630; National Library of Scotland, Edinburgh, Albemarle Papers, MS 3730, fol. 14; Robert Renwick et al (eds), *Extracts from the Records of the Burgh of Glasgow*, 11 vols (Glasgow: Scottish Burgh Records Society, 1881–1916), 7, p. 99; Historical Manuscripts Commission, *Various Collections*, 8 vols (London: Printed for HMSO, by Mackie & Co., 1901–13), 8, p. 414; Historical Manuscripts Commission, *Buccleuch and Queensbury MSS*, 3 vols (London: HMSO, 1899–1926), 1, p. 412; Alan J. Guy (ed.), *Colonel Samuel Bagshawe and the Army of George II, 1731–1762* (London: Bodley Head for the Army Records Society, 1990), p. 234; William Salt Library, Stafford, S. MS 478B, Milo Bagot to --------, 29 November 1760.
47 Duffy argues that the Austrian Army 'had an overwhelmingly rural character' (*The Austrian Army in the Seven Years War*, 1, p. 203). The same was surely true of the Prussian and Russian armies.
48 Duffy, *Military Experience*, p. 92.
49 For the European pattern, see M. S. Anderson, *War and Society in Europe of the Old Regime, 1618–1789* (Leicester: Leicester University Press 1988), pp. 122–3; for the British and Irish case, see Richard Middleton, 'The Recruitment of the British Army, 1755–1762', *Journal of the Society for Army Historical Research*, 67 (1989), p. 235; and Stephen Conway, *War, State, and Society in Mid-Eighteenth-Century Britain and Ireland* (Oxford: Oxford University Press, 2006), pp. 73–5.

but when he thinks proper'.[50] If Wolfe criticised such attitudes, other officers acted as though they accepted that their soldiers had not entirely given up the character of liberty loving Britons when they joined the colours. Volunteer recruits effectively entered into a contract. They would provide military service, and in return their officers would undertake to ensure that they were properly provisioned and not ill-treated. Punishments inflicted on the rank and file, though undoubtedly harsh, were rarely arbitrary; soldiers complained bitterly if they were subjected to penalties imposed by officers acting on their own authority, without the sanction of a court martial.[51] Contemporary depictions sometimes suggested that soldiers in other armies were much less fortunate; one British officer believed Prussian troops were treated 'as so many Slaves and Prisoners'.[52]

British soldiers certainly seem to have regarded their service in contractual terms. As we shall see in more detail in chapters 5 and 6, those who were unhappy with their lot, and assumed that their officers had broken a tacit agreement about how they were to be looked after, might steal from local inhabitants if their rations were cut, or their pay were not forthcoming; desert if they felt that they were being ill-treated; or, in extreme cases, even mutiny if they thought that the imperatives of the military 'moral economy' had been ignored.[53] But if we view these different expressions of dissent as indicative of the soldiers' contractual mindset, then we have to acknowledge that the rank and file in other armies showed similar dissent. Pillaging, desertion, and mutiny were not problems experienced only by the British Army. They were not, of course, attributable simply to a sense that a contract had been broken; they could be caused by entirely different circumstances. But the widespread nature of such problems suggests that even soldiers not blessed with the rights of Englishmen or Britons might see their military service as a form of contract, in which their obligations were removed if their officers failed to live up to their side of the bargain. French soldiers recruited by landowner influence seem to have recognised a bond of loyalty to the officers

50 West Sussex Record Office, Chichester, Goodwood MSS, 223/3/5, Wolfe to the Duke of Richmond, 25 October 1755.

51 See, e.g., two cases from the American war period, TNA, WO 71/89, p. 86; BL, Liverpool Papers, Add. MS 38,214, fol. 323.

52 Hertfordshire Archives and Local Studies, Hertford, Cowper Papers, D/EP F249, Lord De La Warr to Earl Cowper, 16 June 1743.

53 For an instance of mutiny, caused by increasing stoppages to pay, see Peter Way, 'Rebellion of the Regulars: Working Soldiers and the Mutiny of 1763–4', *William & Mary Quarterly*, 3rd series, 57 (2000), pp. 761–92. For the original concept of the 'moral economy', applied more generally, see E. P. Thompson, 'The Moral Economy of the English Crowd in the Eighteenth Century', *Past & Present*, 50 (1971), pp. 76–136.

who brought them into the army, but sometimes felt no longer committed if that officer left their regiment.[54] Frederick the Great's troops, according to one of their historians, 'had very solid ideas of their implied rights'.[55] Even contemporary British observers recognised that contractual thinking was not unique to their own soldiers. In 1775, at the beginning of the American war, when the British government asked a German military entrepreneur to raise soldiers for British service, a British commentator argued that the German recruits would almost certainly desert if the terms under which they had enlisted were changed.[56]

British soldiers were also capable, in appropriate circumstances, of seeing themselves as linked to fellow-soldiers in other armies. We know that they shared their rations with Hanoverian troops after the Battle of Fontenoy in 1745; the year before, a senior British officer reported that the common soldiers were socialising with the Hanoverian rank and file despite the language barrier.[57] Feelings of military solidarity could even extend to enemies. Troops who were suffering the privations of a hard campaign could easily identify with those they were fighting, who might be undergoing similar hardships. Corporal William Todd, who kept a detailed – and invaluable – journal of his military life, recorded a very revealing incident in north-west Germany during the Seven Years War. He was frequently hungry, due to problems encountered by the army's commissaries and contractors in maintaining a regular supply of provisions, and on 31 August 1761 he noted that he and his colleagues bought supplies from French sentries, from whom the British sentries were separated by 'only a small Ditch': 'they are very ready', Todd wrote, 'to Either Buy, sell or Exchange anything they have with [us] as Bread, Liquor etc.' As Todd explained, 'the Enemy seems very agreeable'.[58]

Officers were perhaps even more inclined to see themselves as members of a military fraternity that transcended national boundaries, or what we might describe, in a useful shorthand phrase, as 'military Europe'.[59] The club's

---

54 Anderson, *War and Society*, p. 123.

55 Denis Showalter, *The Wars of Frederick the Great* (London: Longman, 1996), p. 6.

56 TNA, Treasury Papers, T 1/514, fol. 131, 'Remarks on Lieutenant Colonel S[c]heither's Plan for raising Men in Germany for the Service of Great Britain'.

57 John M. Gray (ed.), *Memoirs of the Life of Sir John Clerk of Penicuik* (Scottish History Society, 13, Edinburgh: Printed at the University press by T. and A. Constable for the Scottish history society, 1892), p. 191; Historical Manuscripts Commission, *Stopford Sackville MSS*, 2 vols (London: Printed for HMSO by Mackie & Co. Ltd, 1904–10), I, pp. 289, 290.

58 Andrew Cormack and Alan Jones (eds), *The Journal of Corporal Todd, 1745–1762* (Army Records Society, 18, Stroud: Sutton Pub. for the Army Records Society, 2001), p. 187.

59 See Stephen Conway, 'The British Army, "Military Europe", and the American War of Independence', *William & Mary Quarterly*, 3rd series, 67 (2010), pp. 69–100.

membership might extend to include officers in all other armies, including those of the enemy, but its boundaries were not limitless. Non-Europeans were rarely regarded as part of this professional association. Very occasionally, a particularly skilled native warrior might elicit professional respect; some British officers showed a grudging regard for the martial abilities of Tipu Sultan, the prince of Mysore who inflicted embarrassing defeats on British arms.[60] But not even Tipu truly qualified as a member of the fraternity. Racial and cultural prejudice no doubt partly explains his exclusion, but it hardly accounts for the similar British reluctance to admit colonial Americans. They might in exceptional circumstances be viewed as associate members if they played by the rules – George Washington is perhaps the most obvious example of such a special case – but usually they were denied access to the club on the grounds that they lacked the professional qualities required.[61] In the War of American Independence, the rebels' Continental army was usually dismissed by British officers as a glorified militia. Small wonder that British commanders, when obliged to surrender at Yorktown in 1781, tried to give their swords to the French auxiliaries of the Americans; to surrender to fellow-European professionals was one thing, to have to humiliate themselves in front of the amateurish Americans was quite another.[62]

As with all professional fraternities, 'military Europe' used its own language. The terms of art employed by European officers were largely French, or at least French in derivation.[63] British officers, despite the rhetorical gallophobia prevalent in eighteenth-century Britain, were familiar with these terms, and appear to have used them without awkwardness or inhibition. Indeed, many British officers saw acquaintance with the French language more generally as important, partly because it was the means by which they could communicate with officers in other armies, but also because they continued to regard past generations of French generals as the font of military wisdom even after Frederick the Great had become the contemporary source of martial inspiration.[64]

---

60 Alexander William Crawford Lindsay, Lord Lindsay, *Lives of the Lindsays*, 4 vols (Wigan: Printed by C. S. Simms, 1840), 3, p. 319.

61 For British respect for Washington, see, e.g., E. Stuart-Wortley, *A Prime Minister and His Son: from the Correspondence of the 3rd Earl of Bute and of Lt. General the Hon. Sir Charles Stuart, K.B.* (London: Murray, 1925), p. 99.

62 For the surrender, see John D. Grainger, *The Battle of Yorktown, 1781: A Reassessment* (Woodbridge: The Boydell Press, 2005), p. 149.

63 See the glossary in Childs, *Armies and Warfare in Europe*, pp. 208–11: the dominance of French terms is striking.

64 See, e.g., Robert Donkin, *Military Collections and Remarks* (New York, 1777), pp. 33, 39, 46, 59, 66, 110, 158, 159.

The rules of 'military Europe', well understood by the initiated, but strange and impenetrable to outsiders, derived from a common etiquette – the knowledge of what to do in certain situations. The British Army shared with other European armies of the time a commitment to defending the regimental flags or colours; to allow these to fall into enemy hands was regarded as a disgrace, and extraordinary efforts were made by both officers and men in all militaries to defend the colours to the uttermost, and, if all else failed, to destroy or hide them rather than permit them to be displayed as trophies by victorious foes.[65] British soldiers – like their continental counterparts – were equally familiar with what was expected of both sides in a siege. The formalities of offering terms, turning them down, and resisting until further defiance was hopeless, were followed even by armies fighting beyond Europe. Indeed, punctilious observance of the ornate choreography of siege warfare was perhaps still more obvious when Europeans were locked in conflict in America or Asia than when they fought each other in Europe itself.[66]

EXPLANATIONS

How can we account for all these commonalities? We have glimpsed some explanations already, in passing, but now we need to consider the question more systematically. On a general level, war was an obvious and pervasive influence. It acted as a major homogenising agent, promoting best practice and providing the stimulus for many of the specific explanations relating to the movement of ideas and personnel that we will now examine. On a more specific level, an international professional literature was surely important. Officers read about the methods used by their predecessors and contemporaries in other armies. British officers, despite their reputation for rejecting book-learning, and placing more emphasis on experience, were not backward in this respect. We have a few direct indications of the reading of professional works, such as Earl

---

65 See, e.g., Joachim Miggelbrink, 'The End of the Scots-Dutch Brigade', in *Fighting for Identity: Scottish Military Experience, c.1550–1900*, ed. by Steve Murdoch and Andrew Mackillop (Leiden: Brill, 2002), p. 86.

66 See, e.g., Stephen Conway, 'Scots, Britons and Europeans: Scottish Military Service, c.1739–1783', *Historical Research*, 82 (2009), pp. 129–30; and, for India, the comments of Hector Munro on the 'gallant defence' of Pondicherry in 1778 by his French opponent, Oriental and India Office Library, London, Home Misc./142, Munro to Lord Weymouth, 27 Oct. 1778.

Percy's desire to immerse himself in the military memoirs of the Marquis de Feuquières at Boston during the winter of 1774–5.[67] We also know that officers subscribed to help pay the publication costs of works of military literature. In 1757, William Faucett, a British officer, produced *Regulations for the Prussian Cavalry*, an English translation of the original German.[68] The subscription list for the publication contains the names of more than 300 of his army colleagues, junior and senior, many of them in infantry regiments. Whether the subscribers actually read Faucett's translation is, of course, a moot point. But by paying a subscription to cover the costs of publication they were at the very least indicating a commitment to the enterprise, and demonstrating a desire to be seen to be keen to learn from the Prussian example.

The education of at least some British officers also fostered a European perspective. A small number of officers attended continental universities or academies.[69] In the first half of the century, before Prussia established its military reputation, French academies attracted British students, many of whom were already young officers, or were destined for a career in the army.[70] From the mid-century onwards, while French academies continued to draw British students,[71] Germany increasingly became the destination for ambitious British officers in search of training and connections. Brunswick academy attracted a steady flow of British students; and Göttingen, in Hanover, had a fair number of military recruits from Britain and Ireland after the Seven Years War.[72] As one of Göttingen's British students put

---

67 Boston Public Library, Boston, Massachusetts, Letters of Hugh, Earl Percy, MS G 31.39.4, Percy to Dr Thomas Percy, 25 November 1774.

68 Faucett (or Faucitt as he often appears) had earlier translated *Regulations for the Prussian Infantry*, and in 1757 was also responsible for the English translation of Marshal de Saxe's *Reveries*. For Faucett's unacknowledged role in the translation of Saxe, see Calderdale District Archives, Halifax, Lister of Shibden Hall MSS, SH 7/FAW/47.

69 For two examples from the time of the American war, see TNA, State Papers Ireland, SP 63/445, fol. 7, and SP 67/14, fol. 173.

70 See, e.g., Nottingham University Library, Nottingham, Mellish of Hodsock MSS, MeC 24/3/8, for evidence relating to 1731; and Tyne and Wear Archives, Newcastle, Ellison MSS, bundle A30, esp. letter from Henry Thomas Carr to Henry Ellison, 24 September 1749.

71 See, e.g., BL, Pelham Papers, Add. MS 33,126, fol. 299; National Archives of Scotland, Edinburgh, Shairp of Houston Muniments, GD 30/1590/3, 4, 5, Thomas Shairp to his grandfather, 3 December 1767, 25 March and 18 May 1768; Library of Congress, Washington, DC, Peter Force Collection, Journal of Richard Augustus Wyvill; TNA, SP 63/445, fol. 7, Viscount Harcourt to the Earl of Rochford, 7 January 1775.

72 For Brunswick, see BL, Althorp Papers, Add. MS 75,571, Anna Maria Poyntz

it, 'As I had resolved on being a soldier, a German education was the best suited to the profession I had chosen.'[73] Even the small number of officers who enrolled at military academies at home might be exposed to continental influence. The Royal Military Academy in London was run by Lewis Lochée, a native of Brussels, and schooled its students in 'the Modern Languages, and all the Military Sciences'.[74] Larger numbers of British officers went on the Grand Tour, which sometimes involved brief attendance at a continental university or academy, but had a broader educative function. While travelling, they visited old battlefields, saw military manoeuvres and met officers of other armies, as well as learned, or improved, competence in French, the international language of the age.[75]

Commonalities across the European armies almost certainly owed something to the movement of personnel between armies. British soldiers were involved in this military migration. Early in 1749, just after the end of the War of the Austrian Succession, a report from France suggested that 'some hundreds' of discharged British marines were crossing the Channel to join the Scots regiments in French service.[76] Nearly thirty years later, during the American war, a newly raised Highland regiment probably secured some of its recruits from Scotsmen who had been soldiers in the Scots brigade in Dutch pay, a unit originally formed in the sixteenth century.[77] As usual, we know more about the officers. The 1st Duke of Marlborough, famous victor of Blenheim, received his military training as a young officer in the French Army.[78] The Earl of Crawford, killed in action while leading British troops at the Battle of Dettingen in 1743, had earlier been an officer in the Austrian

to Countess Spencer, 11 October 1766; Cornwall Record Office, Truro, Diary of Thomas Hawkins, DD J 2245; [John Moore,] *A View of Society and Manners in France, Switzerland, and Germany: With Anecdotes relating to Some Eminent Characters* (London: Strahan & Cadell, 1779), p. 2; for Göttingen, see Gordon M. Stewart, 'British Students at the University of Göttingen in the Eighteenth Century', *German Life and Letters*, 33 (1979), pp. 24–41.

73 George Hanger, *The Life, Adventures, and Opinions of Col. George Hanger*, 2 vols (London: J. Debrett, 1801), I, p. 14.

74 J. E. O. Screen, 'The "Royal Military Academy" of Lewis Lochée', *Journal of the Society for Army Historical Research*, 70 (1992), p. 146.

75 See the advice tendered by John Burgoyne in E. B. De Fonbanque, *Political and Military Episodes in the Latter Half of the Eighteenth Century: Derived from the Life and Correspondence of the Right Hon. John Burgoyne* (London: Macmillan and co., 1876), p. 19.

76 TNA, State Papers France, SP 78/232, Pt. I, Joseph Yorke to the Duke of Bedford, 30 January/10 February 1749.

77 BL, Hamilton and Greville Papers, Add. MS 42,071, fol. 205.

78 Anderson, *War and Society*, p. 86.

and Russian armies.[79] But the most important foreign military seminary for British officers was surely the Dutch Scots brigade. Even after the Seven Years War, when its rank and file became increasingly cosmopolitan, the brigade's officers continued to be overwhelmingly Scottish. In that same war, when the Dutch Republic remained neutral, significant numbers of Scots brigade officers applied to transfer into the British Army, partly perhaps from a sense of patriotic duty, but primarily, one suspects, because they recognised that promotion was always easier in an army that was likely to see battle. The same process was repeated in the early stages of the American war, when the Dutch again were neutral.[80] A similar desire for professional advancement encouraged British officers, especially at the end of wars, when the army was reduced in size, to seek their fortunes in foreign armies. The Portuguese service attracted a number of British officers at the end of the Seven Years War;[81] one of them, Francis McLean (who had earlier served in the Scots brigade), rose to become a general in Portuguese pay before rejoining the British Army in 1778.[82] At the end of the American war, at least one junior officer in a disbanded British regiment sought new employment in the Russian Army.[83]

The traffic was two-way. The British Army also provided a military home for continental Europeans. As we saw earlier, the ordinary soldiers of the Royal Americans were drawn in significant numbers from Germany, and the same was true, though to a lesser extent, of other British regiments. The officer ranks were theoretically closed to foreigners; the Act of Settlement of 1701 stipulated that public office, civil and military, must be confined to the crown's subjects. But at the end of the seventeenth century, and the beginning of the eighteenth, large numbers of Huguenot, or French Protestant, refugees became officers in the British Army.[84] Their male descendants tended to follow in their footsteps; officers from Huguenot families continued to be well represented in the army for many decades after the main Huguenot migration.

---

79 Thomas A. Fischer, *The Scots in Germany: Being a Contribution towards the History of the Scots Abroad* (Edinburgh: O. Schulze & Co., 1902), pp. 119–20.

80 See, e.g., Stephen Conway, 'The Scots Brigade in the Eighteenth Century', *Northern Scotland*, 1 (2010), pp. 30–41.

81 See BL, Loudoun Papers, Add. MS 44,069, fols 20, 144.

82 For McLean, see Conway, 'Scots, Britons and Europeans', pp. 126–8.

83 BL, Leeds Papers, Egerton MS 3500, fol. 15.

84 Robin Gwynn, 'The Huguenots in Britain, the "Protestant International" and the Defeat of Louis XIV', in *From Strangers to Citizens: The Integration of Immigrant Communities in Britain, Ireland, and Colonial America, 1550–1750*, ed. by Ralph Vigne and Charles Littleton (Huguenot Society of Great Britain and Ireland; Brighton: Sussex Academic Press, 2001), p. 413.

In 1770, the year of his death, Lord Ligonier, or, to use his original French name, Jean-Louis Ligonier, was commander-in-chief.[85] Special legislative dispensation was given for other Protestant foreigners to serve in the Royal Americans; German and Swiss Protestants dominated its officer ranks.[86]

The British Army not only contained continental Europeans, and British-born soldiers who had served in continental armies; it also fought alongside European allies and auxiliaries. The role of auxiliaries has already been mentioned, but the importance of working with allies merits a few words. British troops campaigning in the Low Countries and western Germany in every major war from 1689 to 1762 did so as part of an allied force, brought together to resist French ambitions. In the Seven Years War, admittedly, when the Prussians were the British Army's main ally, direct contact between the two was very limited.[87] But British troops co-operated much more closely with the Austrians and the Dutch in the War of the Spanish Succession at the beginning of the century, in the War of the Austrian Succession in the 1740s, and again in the early 1790s in the Low Countries campaigns at the beginning of the French Revolutionary War.[88]

Friction between British soldiers and troops in allied armies, or auxiliary forces, was a feature of all Britain's eighteenth-century wars. The targets of British disdain often attributed it to national prejudice.[89] But the disdain was usually professional rather than national; it focused on allies' or auxiliaries' perceived military deficiencies, such as their being too slow to advance, or too quick to retreat. When, on the other hand, allies or auxiliaries displayed military qualities, British soldiers tended to treat them as comrades and equals, rather than look down on them as 'foreigners'. In 1709, for example, after the bloody Battle of Malplaquet, a private soldier in the Foot Guards

---

85 See Rex Whitworth, *Field Marshal Lord Ligonier: A Story of the British Army, 1702–1770* (Oxford: Clarendon Press, 1958).

86 Such as Augustine Prevost, a Swiss who had earlier served in the Dutch Army: see his commissions in National Army Museum, London, MS 6106-48. For the Royal Americans more generally, see Alexander V. Campbell, 'Atlantic Microcosm: The Royal American Regiment, 1755–1772', in *English Atlantics Revisited: Essays Honouring Ian K. Steele*, ed. by Nancy L. Rhoden (Montreal: McGill-Queen's University Press, 2007), pp. 284–309.

87 See Sir Reginald Savory, *His Britannic Majesty's Army in Germany during the Seven Years War* (Oxford: Clarendon Press, 1966).

88 See the description of the allied forces in Kenneth Garlick and Angus Macintyre (eds), *The Diary of Joseph Farrington, 1793–1796*, 2 vols (New Haven, CT: University of Yale Press, 1978), 1, p. 24.

89 See, e.g., William L. Stone (ed. and trans.), *Journal of Captain Pausch, Chief of the Hanau Artillery during the Burgoyne Campaign* (Albany, NY: J. Munsell's Sons, 1886), p. 107.

regretted the death of an 'abundance of good old experienced souldyers belonging to the severall countreys concerned in this confederacy'.[90] Similarly, in 1793, a British officer described the Austrian soldiers he had encountered in Flanders as 'the very best troops I ever saw'.[91] Both negative and positive British comments suggest that the army's officers, and perhaps even its rank and file, were thinking less as Britons and more as soldiers.

A sense of international military solidarity was probably also promoted by the Laws of War, part of the Law of Nations, or what we would now call international law. Based on the essentially European concepts of Christianity and chivalry, and the more modern ideas of enlightened proportionality, these Laws laid down what was acceptable, and unacceptable, in the conduct of war, with particular emphasis placed on protecting non-combatants and limiting the business of fighting to professional armed forces. By stressing the distinction between soldiers and civilians, the Laws of War encouraged military men in all European armies to think in terms of what united them in a professional comradeship that transcended national boundaries.[92]

But the most fundamental explanation for the significant similarities and connections between European armies reminds us that armies are products of societies and not hermetically separated from them. This chapter began with the observation that historians of the British Army have tended to see it as the embodiment of the nation and therefore as different from other armies. The same kind of reflective logic – armies are representative of society – can lead to a very different conclusion. European armies were similar in many ways for the simple reason that European societies were themselves broadly similar. The Laws of War operated on the assumption that there was a European club of nations, sharing many values and norms.[93] That assumption was sound. Despite their manifest local peculiarities, European states shared a great deal in terms of political structures, social organisation, culture, religion and law.[94] Eighteenth-century Britain, whatever exceptionalist narratives might

---

90 John Marshall Deane, *A Journal of Marlborough's Campaigns during the War of the Spanish Succession, 1704–1711*, ed. D. G. Chandler (Society for Army Historical Research, Special Publication No. 12, London, 1984), p. 94.

91 Sir Harry Verney (ed.), *The Journals and Correspondence of General Sir Harry Calvert* (London: Hurst and Blackett, 1853), p. 83.

92 For the Laws of War, see Stephen C. Neff, *War and the Law of Nations: A General History* (Cambridge: Cambridge University Press, 2005), Pt. II.

93 See, e.g., Robert Ward, *An Enquiry into the Foundation and History of the Law of Nations in Europe, from the Time of the Greeks and Romans, to the Age of Grotius*, 2 vols (Dublin: Printed by P. Wogan, P. Byrne, W. Jones, and J. Rice, 1795), esp. 1, p. 98.

94 See Stephen Conway, *Britain, Ireland, and Continental Europe in the Eighteenth Century: Similarities, Connections, Identities* (Oxford: Oxford University Press, 2011).

suggest, was essentially a European state, so we should not be surprised that its army displayed many of the characteristics to be found in other European armies of the time.

My thanks are due to the owners and the custodians of the manuscript material used in this study, particularly to Her Majesty the Queen for permission to use documents in the Royal Archives at Windsor.

2

Soldiering Abroad

The Experience of Living and Fighting among Aliens during the Napoleonic Wars

Graciela Iglesias Rogers

B RITANNIA, proverbial land of freedom, tolerance and safe-haven for political refugees, has long found it difficult to deal with strangers. It is no accident that the English language has a word for foreigners that in modern parlance has become associated with everything that is weird and even extra-terrestrial: aliens. As early as 1712, Joseph Addison noticed that the conviction that Britons could stand proud and alone among nations, disdainful of and impervious to foreign influences was among the many 'honest prejudices which naturally cleave to the heart of a true *Englishman*'.[1] Keeping this conceit among the military could not have been easy in the long eighteenth century. The vast majority of the conflicts in which British soldiers were involved during the period 1750–1815 took place abroad, bringing them into unprecedented contact with foreign cultures and manners. This encounter with 'the other' presented a wide range of challenges and dilemmas, more noticeable among those who took the decision to serve in foreign armies – a step by which they joined, perhaps more consciously than others, 'Military Europe', the international occupational fraternity outlined by Stephen Conway in chapter 1.[2]

This chapter will examine some of the experiences of British soldiers who

---

1 *The Spectator*, Volume 5, Nr. 383, 20 May 1712, p. 259.
2 See also: Stephen Conway, *Britain, Ireland, and Continental Europe in the Eighteenth Century: Similarities, Connections, Identities* (Oxford: Oxford University Press, 2011), pp. 266–78; Christopher Duffy, *The Military Experience in the Age of Reason* (London: Routledge, 1987), p. 3.

joined the Spanish and French forces as volunteers during the Napoleonic Wars. They constituted a small number of men, mainly officers: forty-two in the case of those Britons who fought under the Spanish flag from 1808 to 1814,[3] and perhaps less than a hundred in the Irish Legion, created by a decree of Napoleon on 31 August 1803 and disbanded on 28 September 1815. Indeed, despite its name, it appears that less than half of the Legion was ever able to claim any Irish connection.[4] So we are not here confronted by a phenomenon of large-scale emigration to volunteer for war abroad. The British Army remained the first employer of choice in the military, particularly in the case of the Irish, who made up 28 per cent of the British Army during the Peninsular War, a figure that had risen by 1830 to 42.2 per cent of British recruits.[5] Nonetheless, there is much to be learnt from the study of the experiences of those who could be considered the exception that confirms the rule. Their personal journeys into a foreign and often hostile world provide an opportunity to look at the way British subjects (which at the time also included all Irish-born soldiers) managed to navigate through different cultural contexts. They also offer us a chance of a transnational view of a period in history and of particular conflicts that have been studied from national perspectives, often leading to mutually exclusive historiographies.

---

3 Graciela Iglesias Rogers, '"British Liberators": The Role of Volunteers in the Spanish Forces during the Peninsular War (1808–1814) … and Far Beyond,' (DPhil, University of Oxford, 2011), pp. 2, 261–7. This thesis produced the study *British Liberators in the Age of Napoleon: Volunteering under the Spanish Flag in the Peninsular War* (London and New York: Bloomsbury, 2013).

4 The exact number of those men who could claim to be Irish by birth or blood remains unclear. At one stage, the Legion comprised five battalions and managed to recruit 2,363 men, but the proportion of Irish soldiers appears to have been minimal. For Marianne Elliott, the figure never exceeded sixty-seven officers and twenty-four men. Many departed after plans for an Irish invasion were dropped, leading the historian John Gallaher to assert that as from 1805 it had become a 'Foreign Legion' in everything but name. It appears that in October 1806 only 46 per cent were Irish, 37 per cent were French, while the rest had no declared country of origin. See Marianne Elliott, *Partners in Revolution: The United Irishmen and France* (London: Yale University Press, 1982), p. 333; John G. Gallaher, *Napoleon's Irish Legion* (Carbondale, IL: Southern Illinois University Press, 1993), pp. 156, 221; Nicholas Dunne-Lynch, 'The Irish Legion of Napoleon, 1803–1815', in *Franco-Irish Military Connections, 1590–1945*, ed. by Nathalie Genet-Rouffiac and David Murphy (Dublin: Four Courts, 2009), p. 192.

5 K. B. Linch, *Britain and Wellington's Army: Recruitment, Society, and Tradition 1807–15* (Basingstoke: Palgrave Macmillan, 2011), p. 60; E. M. Spiers, 'Army Organization and Society in the Nineteenth Century', in *A Military History of Ireland*, ed. by Thomas Bartlett and Keith Jeffery (Cambridge: Cambridge University Press, 1996), p. 337.

This is certainly the case with the Iberian contest which in the English-speaking world has been labelled the 'Peninsular War', but in Spain, and to an extent also in France, is known as the 'Spanish War of Independence'. This difference in nomenclature reflects divergent interpretations of the conflict that have been largely echoed by the historiography.[6]

The methodology and framework adopted here is part of a wider research agenda that seeks to explore military service in a much more holistic way by breaking free of purely nationally orientated studies of the military, particularly the phenomenon of transnational volunteering in war.[7] Despite the stereotypical hostility to foreigners outlined in the introduction, since at least the 1690s there had been a well-established tradition of men leaving the British Isles to fight in foreign armies, particularly in the case of Irish and Scottish Catholics, who served French and Spanish kings. They fought in all major wars and enjoyed a high reputation as soldiers.[8] But there is something that distinguished these men from those who volunteered abroad after 1776. The latter fought for a cause, not for a monarch. This is not to deny that many Jacobite exiles pledged loyalty to Catholic monarchs out of a desire to take revenge against their English foe, but this was by proxy and there was no guarantee that such vengeance would ever materialise. Many spent their whole careers without ever crossing swords with their ancestral enemy. As dynastic conflicts gave way to revolutionary and national wars, a shift in the terms of engagement is also evident. This necessarily had an impact on the way volunteers approached the whole experience. Many of those who joined the Irish Legion did so only in the belief that Napoleon would invade Ireland to free it from English oppression. If they dreamed of glory, it was less for imperial Napoleonic France than for Irish civil and religious liberties.[9] Yet the Napoleonic Wars also produced a schism among Catholics, including in the Irish diaspora, evidenced by the British volunteers' awareness of Spaniards of

---

6 Charles J. Esdaile, 'Recent Works of Note on the Peninsular War (1808–1815)', *The Journal of Military History*, 74 (2010), pp. 1243–52 (esp. p. 1251); José Luis Martínez Sanz, and Emilio de Diego (eds), *El comienzo de la Guerra de la Independencia - Congreso Internacional del Bicentenario* (Madrid: Actas, 2009), *passim*; Jean René Aymes, *La guerre d'indépendance espagnole, 1808–1814* (Paris: Bordas, 1973), *passim*.

7 For a collection of case studies covering the period from the Napoleonic wars to the late twentieth century, see: Nir Arielli and Bruce Collins (eds), *Transnational Soldiers: Foreign Military Enlistment in the Modern Era* (Basingstoke: Palgrave, 2012).

8 See, for example, Harman Murtagh, 'Irish Soldiers Abroad, 1600–1800', in *A Military History of Ireland*, ed. by Thomas Bartlett and Keith Jeffery (Cambridge: Cambridge University Press, 1996), pp. 297–312; Grant G. Simpson (ed.), *The Scottish Soldier Abroad 1247–1967* (Edinburgh: Rowman & Littlefield, 1992); Mark G. McLaughlin, *The Wilde Geese – the Irish Brigades of France and Spain* (London: Osprey, 1980).

9 Elliott, *Partners in Revolution*, pp. 331–5; Gallaher, *Napoleon's Irish Legion*, pp. 72–5.

Irish descent serving on both sides of the conflict.[10] At one point, General Juan O'Donojú (O'Donohue) headed the Patriots' War Department at Cádiz while General Gonzalo O'Farrell served King Joseph Bonaparte as War Minister in Madrid, aided by Irish veterans of the Rebellion of 1798.[11] In Spain, British volunteers, including many Irish, fought for the 'Spanish cause', which they considered to be a people's war against the juggernaut of Napoleon's expansionism.[12] Both groups were ready to give their lives for a cause of national liberation through engagement in very international settings.

When we consider their experiences and the lives of these individuals, many of these men shared something in common, although they were on opposing sides of the conflict: they had acquired a grounding in military fundamentals in the British regular army, the Royal Navy, the Royal Marines, the militia, local volunteer forces, and sometimes a mixture of many of these. Such knowledge could range from simply having learnt how to load and cock a pistol to matters as serious as authoring manuals of instruction for junior officers in the infantry.[13] Thirty of the forty-two British officers in the Spanish forces received some degree of formal military training in Britain prior to arriving to Spain. They had been sergeants, second lieutenants, captains, majors and lieutenant-colonels in various British regiments. Many joined the Spanish Army without relinquishing their British commissions.[14] In the Irish Legion, a good number were professional men, merchants and ex-students who got mixed up in the movement for Irish autonomy in the late 1790s through membership of voluntary forces and local yeomanry regiments. Thomas and William Corbet, for example, had been lieutenants of the Trinity College Dublin Yeomanry in 1798.[15] William Aylmer, before becoming a United Irish commander, had been a lieutenant in the Kildare militia.[16]

---

10 Archivo General Militar de Segovia, Segovia, Spain, (AGMS), P-541 *Expediente Guillermo Parker Carrol*: Report on Carrol's proclamation calling Irish soldiers to desert the French forces, undated.

11 Murtagh, 'Irish Soldiers Abroad, 1600–1800', pp. 297, 310.

12 Iglesias Rogers, *British Liberators*, pp. 43–58.

13 See, for example, Major [Charles William] Doyle, *The Military Catechism for the use of Covering or Supernumerary Sergeants* (London, 1804); Major [Charles William] Doyle, *The Military Catechism for the use of Young Officers* (London, 1804).

14 Iglesias Rogers, *British Liberators*, pp. 1, 30, 178–80.

15 James Quinn, 'Corbet, Thomas', in *Dictionary of Irish Biography*, ed. by James McGuire, James Quinn (Cambridge: Cambridge University Press, 2009), <http://dib. cambridge.org/viewReadPage.do?articleId=a2036> [access date: 13 February 2012].

16 C. J. Woods, 'Aylmer, William', in *Dictionary of Irish Biography*, ed. by James McGuire, James Quinn (Cambridge: Cambridge University Press, 2009), <http://dib. cambridge.org/viewReadPage.do?articleId=a0288> [access date: 13 February 2012].

Edward Masterson, William O'Meara, Alexis de Couasnon and John Mahony had all served in the British Army between 1794 and 1802.[17] Couasnon fought against the French in the Low Countries while Mahony, who was to be appointed chief of the third battalion of the Napoleonic Irish Guards in Burgos, started his military career in England, joined the campaign in Egypt against the French, and only after the peace of Amiens in 1802 did he sell his captain's commission in the British service to travel to France and join the Irish Legion.[18]

Basic skills acquired during their time in the British military system proved to be easily transferable to the service of their host country. In Spain, no requirement was made to adapt their military expertise. Recruitment tended to be immediate, but previous training was highly valued and tended to guarantee rapid promotion. Samuel Ford 'Santiago' Whittingham, a lowly captain in the 13th Light Dragoons despite having graduated with honours from the Military Academy of High Wycombe, enjoyed meteoric progress to the rank of *mariscal de campo* (approaching the rank of major-general on the British scale) in less than a year.[19] In France, the situation was different. The first men recruited into the Irish Legion were assembled at Morlaix, a village on the coast facing the Channel, to receive instruction in French infantry and artillery tactics.[20] It is said that many made the journey on foot to accustom themselves to the long winter marches they expected to make after their arrival in Ireland.[21] Training appears to have consisted mainly in maintaining that fitness. A few basics were also imparted, such as adjusting to 'the position of a soldier without arms, marching in quick and ordinary time' and 'learning the manual exercise with the musket'.[22] Nonetheless, after almost a year of daily practice, the area commander at Brest, General Francois-Xavier Donzelot, considered that the instruction had been rather

17 Gallaher, *Napoleon's Irish Legion*, p. 60; Dunne-Lynch, 'The Irish Legion of Napoleon', p. 200.

18 Fanny Byrne (ed.), *Memoirs of Miles Byrne: Chef De Bataillon in the Service of France, Officer of the Legion of Honour, Knight of Saint-Louis, Etc.*, 3 vols (Paris: G. Bossange, 1863), 3, pp. 72–3.

19 AGMS, V-43 *Expediente* Santiago Whittingham; Bristol Central Library, Bristol, R1 Pr 2pb Biog. U-Z - B 4120: Extract of biographical notes of Samford Whittingham published by the *Bristol Mercury*, 15 January 1870, with handwritten notes; C. B. Major-General Ferdinand Whittingham (ed.), *A memoir of the Services of Lieutenant-General Sir Samuel Ford Whittingham, K.C.B., K.C.H., G.C.F., Colonel of the 71st Highland Light Infantry, derived chiefly from his own letters and from those of distinguished contemporaries* (London: Longmans, Green and Co., 1868), p. 561.

20 *Memoirs of Miles Byrne*, 2, p. 11.

21 Elliott, *Partners in Revolution*, p. 331.

22 *Memoirs of Miles Byrne*, 3, p. 267.

deficient.[23] Such a rudimentary induction to the military was not exclusive to foreigners. French junior officers and the rank and file received little if any theoretical preparation. A school, the *École spécial militaire*, had been established at Fontainebleau for 1,000 students (500 recruits per year) in 1802. But as war began, the one-year courses were progressively reduced to six months, two and even less than one.[24] The state of affairs in Morlaix did not fit any recognised pattern. For Napoleon, the Legion was a training school for future political leaders in a French-friendly Ireland. Military experience was undoubtedly an advantage, at least from the perspective of the personal safety of each recruit, but offered no great advantage regarding promotion. Those who came straight from the 1803 rebellion in Ireland or were unknown in France because of imprisonment were left in subordinate positions. Superior rank was awarded to those Irishmen of known local standing or with proven qualities of political leadership.[25] Yet if they had in the past made a career in the British military forces, as had been the case with the Kildare leader John Mahony, this was not considered a disadvantage, provided that their commitment to the Irish cause was not in doubt.[26] For some it was even believed ultimately to have played in their favour, as the changing circumstances in Europe demanded their transformation – for many, never fully accomplished – from Irish national liberators to Napoleonic professional soldiers.[27]

The first and more serious challenge in the experience of soldiering abroad was not so much the need to acquire or adjust to foreign military practices, but the more prosaic one of breaking the language barrier. For many in the Irish Legion, this was far from an insurmountable challenge. It was common for upper-class Irish Catholics families – and the majority of these men belonged to that group – to send their children to be educated in the Irish College in Paris or to have at least visited France as part of the Grand Tour.[28] But not all did. For his first encounter with a French officer after, literally, jumping ship at Bordeaux, the most famous member of the Irish Legion, the republican Miles Byrne, had to engage the services of a translator – himself an Irishman named Brown.[29] The life of an interpreter in the French Navy

---

23 Gallaher, *Napoleon's Irish Legion*, pp. 57–61.

24 See Jean Morvan, *Le soldat impérial 1800–1814*, 2 vols (Paris: Plon-Nourrit, 1904), 2, pp. 80–95; Rafe Blaufarb, *The French Army, 1750–1820: Careers, Talent, Merit* (Manchester: Manchester University Press, 2002), p. 176.

25 Elliott, *Partners in Revolution*, pp. 334–5.

26 *Memoirs of Miles Byrne*, 3, pp. 72–3; Elliot, *Partners in Revolution*, pp. 303, 310.

27 *Memoirs of Miles Byrne*, 3, pp. 72–3; Gallaher, *Napoleon's Irish Legion*, p. 222.

28 Patrick Fagan, *Catholics in a Protestant Country: The Papist Constituency in Eighteenth-Century Dublin* (Dublin: Four Courts, 1998), pp. 1–53.

29 *Memoirs of Miles Byrne*, 1, pp. 390–2.

must have been hard. Even when Byrne wanted us to believe that Brown was 'quite contented with his situation because the officers were very kind to him',[30] he recalled in this memoirs that, before leaving for the French capital, he felt compelled to leave the man his jacket and trousers and one of six pounds received from a lady friend in Dublin. As soon as he arrived in Paris, the Wexford leader dedicated the next three months, from September to November 1803, to teach himself French by reading a grammar book and a dictionary, with just a little guidance from veteran Irish exiles on matters of pronunciation.[31] One can only wonder how, on that basis, he managed to make himself understood by the French, but he certainly did. Many of his compatriots found it more difficult. After ten months of intense training at Morlaix, only 45 per cent of the fifty-five Irish officers for whom data is available could read and write in the language, while 16 per cent were still unable to do either.[32]

The situation was far more challenging in Spain, a country rarely included in the Grand Tour and one that remained among the least-known countries in Western Europe.[33] At first, only eight of the British volunteers could master more than a few words in Spanish.[34] The rest grasped the basics of the language by trial and error in the short time they had available, listening, watching and learning from the communities they encountered along the way. This often hampered the learning process because of the diversity of regional language and dialects already existing at the time in Spain. Although a bewildering number of Spanish generals had Irish surnames on account of being second- or third-generation descendants of the 'Wild Geese' who had quit Ireland after the Battle of the Boyne (1690), only a few, such as Joaquín Blake and Pedro Sarsfield, could communicate in English.[35] More often than

---

30 Ibid., p. 392.

31 Ibid., pp. 23–4.

32 Service Historique de la Défense, Vincennes (SHD), X^h 14, 'Legion Irlandaise – État Nominatif des Officiers de la Legion', signed by General Donzelot, 11 October 1804; Gallaher, *Napoleon's Irish Legion*, p. 56.

33 W. E. Mead, *The Grand Tour in the Eighteenth Century* (New York: Ayer, 1972), p. 252.

34 AGMS, A-2104 *Expediente* Jaime Arbuthnot; AGMS, P-541 *Expediente* Guillermo Parker Carrol; AGMS, D-1177 *Expediente* Juan Downie; AGMS, D-877 *Expediente* Carlos Guillermo Doile [*sic*]; AGMS, Q-1 *Expediente* Juan Quearney [*sic*] Donnelan; AGMS, R-1365, *Expediente* Daniel Robinson; AGMS, Q-1 *Expediente* Felipe Qeating [*sic*] Roche; AGMS, V-43 *Expediente* Santiago Whittingham.

35 See Archivo General Militar de Madrid, Madrid (AGM), *Fondo* Blake, Microfiche 1, Caja 2, correspondence sent to General Joaquin Blake in English Nrs. 21, 22, 23, 24, 34, 36, 39, Microfiche 2, Caja 2, Nr. 21; Bodleian Library, Oxford (Bod. Lib.), North Collection, c. 16, fol. 381, General Sarsfield to General Doyle, Calatayud, 6 February 1813.

not the British volunteers had to rely on Spanish *aide-de-camps* to act as their spokesmen or,[36] worse, they had to use French as, literally, the *lingua franca* in their correspondence with Spanish colleagues – a practice that they knew left them vulnerable to the prying eyes of the enemy.[37] A second lieutenant in the Royal Marines, Robert Steele spent several weeks learning 'indefatigably' the language prior to the opening of the campaign of 1813, the moment when he decided to join the Spanish Army with the rank of captain. The effort, he said in his memoirs, proved worthwhile not just for the obvious benefits of being able to understand commands and act immediately when addressed by colleagues and superiors, but also to broaden his cultural horizons:

> to be able to read Don Quixote in the original (and from having mixed with the chivalrous and romantic Spanish people, so as to really comprehend and enjoy that racy and incomparable work) would of itself be a sufficient harvest for all the toil and danger I passed in Spain, and for any pains I took to acquire what they themselves call *la Lengua de Dios*, the language of Heaven![38]

Learning the local language was a prerequisite for, as well as a much desired by-product of, the integration in the host communities. The volunteers' status within the Spanish forces afforded opportunities – often denied to the regular British soldiery – to become immersed in Iberian society. For example, in Cádiz, British regiments were confined to cantonments beyond the city walls, while most of the volunteers enjoyed the hospitality of Spanish high society. They were welcome guests, whereas British troops were feared as potential occupiers. It was not until late 1811, nearly four years after the war started, that the local authorities designated a complete block (20 Calle de la Carne) to be exclusively 'occupied by the English'.[39] In contrast, British volunteer officers were regular attendants of *tertulias*,[40] the Spanish version of

---

36 See, for example, British Library, London (BL), Additional Manuscripts, Add. MS 15675 fol. 10, General Doyle to governor of Tortosa, 14 June 1810.

37 Bod. Lib., North, c. 13, fol. 57, Copy of letter Major Edwin Rowlandson Green to Marquess de Palacio, undated, apologising for a clumsy attempt at writing in Spanish to avoid doing it in French.

38 Sir Robert C. Steele, *The Marine Officer; or, Sketches of Service* (London: William Clowes and Sons, 1840), p. 272. A more accurate translation of the phrase 'la lengua de Dios' is 'the language of God', probably a reference to Emperor Charles V's alleged assertion that 'to God I speak Spanish, to women Italian, to men French, and to my horse – German', see Angela Partington (ed.), *The Oxford Dictionary of Quotations*, Rev. 4th edn (Oxford: Oxford University Press, 1998), p. 191.

39 Archivo del Ayuntamiento de Cádiz, Cádiz (AAC), Census 1812: *Padrón* 1055 (Calle de la Carne), p. 1.

40 Gatherings held at private homes and considered as the first and foremost example of modern sociability in Spain, similar to that of the *salons* in France. See Francois-

salon meetings, such as those organised by María 'Mariquita' Strange, wife of the Irish merchant Pedro Strange, which attracted guests of all political persuasions and from all corners of the Spanish world.[41] They also patronised the theatre and even found time to organise their own private sessions of *bolero, fandango* and other popular Spanish dances, where they socialised with rich and humble members of society alike.[42]

The Irish Legion also had the chance to mingle with the local community. While stationed in the west coast of Brittany, many officers were lodged in family homes, and frequented balls and evening entertainments given by the prefect of Finisterre.[43] Byrne's memories are full of references to dinners, breakfasts and *déjeuners* enjoyed in Parisian restaurants while on extended leave.[44] On at least one occasion, he also attended the *Salle du variétés*. He recorded his excitement at being able to understand the French language – and French humour – well enough to enjoy the performance there of the celebrated comedian Brunet.[45] Yet the Irish volunteers' relations with the French, and indeed with any foreigner, were often strained. The intensity of their national self-awareness made them distrust anybody who was not a member of their Irish circle. This was a serious problem because the initial commitment to recruit only Irishmen in their ranks could not be met, so soon the Legion was swarmed with outsiders, mainly Prussians and Polish who, to make matters worse, often spoke neither English nor French. The appointment of an Italian commander, Lieutenant-Colonel Eduardo Antonio Petrezzoli, a little over a year after the Legion's creation was particularly objected to. In the five years he remained in the post, the Irish Legion became a by-word for disobedience among the sixty-eight foreign regiments serving with Napoleon.[46]

Xavier Guerra, *Modernidad e independencias: ensayos sobre las revoluciones hispánicas* (Madrid: Editorial Mapfre, 1992), p. 93.

41 Special Collections, King's College, Aberdeen University, Aberdeen (AB), MS 3175/1410/3 Messages Strange family to viscount Macduff, 1809–1813; Bod. Lib., North, c. 17, fol. 362, List of Doyle's Spanish acquaintances.

42 Codrington Library, All Souls College, University of Oxford, Oxford (ASL), Vaughan Papers, uncatalogued, reel 7, British envoy Charles Stuart to Vaughan, Lisbon, 6 May 1810 and 26 August 1810; AB, MS3175/2296. William Miller to the fourth Earl of Fife, Canterbury, 29 June 1827 in which Miller mentioned an entry in his journal for 27 October 1812, 'Cadiz, re. meeting MacDuff at the theatre'; Jorge Campos, *Teatro y sociedad en España (1780–1820)* (Madrid: Editorial Moneda y Crédito, 1969), p. 163.

43 *Memoirs of Miles Byrne*, 2, pp. 18–20.

44 Ibid., 1, p. 129; 3, pp. 23–4, 59, 227.

45 Ibid., 3, pp. 23–7.

46 Ibid., p. 162; Elliott, *Partners in Revolution*, pp. 335–40; Dunne-Lynch, 'The Irish Legion of Napoleon', pp. 205–6.

Hurt national pride caused a serious incident with French civilians early on in the life of the regiment. Captain Patt MacSheehy had a dispute that almost ended in a duel with the son of the mayor of the small town of Lesneven, where many officers of the Legion had been lodged for almost a year. The mayor's son wanted to fight with swords; the seconds prevailed and settled the matter. Unfortunately, on returning to town, the boy told some of his friends that the Irish officers could only fight with pistols. This reached the ears of a Lieutenant Osmond, who immediately challenged him to a duel with small swords in which the mayor's son received a desperate wound and was carried, in what appeared a fatal state, to his father's house. If ever proof is needed that the Irish are capable of understatement, Miles Byrne's memoirs provide an excellent example. He said that this incident had 'caused a painful sensation'.[47] It did more than that. An order came from the general in chief at Brest for the Legion to quit the town that very night and move to Quimper, almost a 100 kilometres away.[48]

On the other side of the Pyrénées, the British volunteers' status as subjects of a country long considered Spain's staunchest enemy, added to the harsh realities of war, occasionally generated antagonism, but never to the point of manifesting itself in acts of physical violence. Only on one occasion did a volunteer send summons to a duel. However, this was not directed at a Spaniard, but an English Guardsman who was believed to have uttered some expressions insulting to the Spanish officers.[49] Indeed, the biggest challenge for the British volunteers in Spain was not dealing with their hosts, but with their own compatriots, particularly those in the high command. On 18 November 1808, the British agent and volunteer in the Spanish army, Charles William Doyle received an order from the British Secretary of War, Lord Castlereagh, to abandon Saragossa, the capital of Aragón, travel immediately to Catalunya, and to remain there. This was an order that Doyle felt he could not obey.[50] Saragossa was preparing itself for a second siege that was to end with 54,000 civilian dead,[51] the worst war tragedy in the history of Spain before that of Guernica in 1937.[52] Sir John Moore had just arrived in

---

47 *Memoirs of Byrne*, 2, p. 19–20.
48 Ibid.
49 Whittingham (ed.), *Memoir*, p. x, Lord Fife to Major Ferdinand Whittingham, Duff House, 28 March 1845.
50 National Archives of the United Kingdom, London (TNA), War Office Papers, WO 1/227 fols 527–8: Doyle to Lord Castlereagh, Saragossa, 18 November 1808.
51 Raymond Rudorff, *War to the Death: The Sieges of Saragossa, 1808–1809* (London: Hamish Hamilton, 1974), p. 227.
52 Immortalised by Picasso's eponymous painting, the number of dead in Guernica, estimated at over 1,600, was smaller than that of Saragossa, but the plight of these

Salamanca and was believed to have been given authority over British military agents. Doyle asked a friend, the Oxford academic Charles Vaughan, who was due to meet Moore in a few days, to intercede to enable him to remain with the hard-pressed Spanish forces in Saragossa. In reply, Vaughan warned him that Moore had 'displayed much asperity against all employed with Spanish armies, calling them the Partizans [sic] of the Spaniards'. He promised his friend: 'If I am permitted to talk with this tyger [sic, i.e. Moore] I shall feel my way about [concerning] you.'[53] Yet he also tempered any hint of success in his mission with the remark that he would rather stay in Spain as Doyle's *aide-de-camp* 'than feeding upon the dull prejudices of our own countrymen at home'.[54] In the event, Vaughan had no chance to intercede with Moore and Doyle chose to ignore his orders for two weeks, during which he helped to build up defences at Saragossa, called for assistance from the *Junta Central* – the first Spanish national government – and gathered a regiment under his command from dispersed troops.[55] Spain's liberation was the volunteers' primary concern. For those with the dual status of volunteers and British agents, this often entailed responding to events as they unfolded, regardless of instructions drafted weeks earlier by British superiors with little knowledge of the country and even less of the evolving circumstances. In this respect, they appeared to have adopted an old Spanish formula, that of '*obedezco, pero no cumplo*' (I obey, but I do not comply), which allowed generations of Spanish bureaucrats, particularly in Latin America, to delay the application and sometimes completely circumvent royal directives for the local good.[56] By exercising their own discretion they became free agents – and they saw no reason to abandon this position as long as it benefited the common cause.

---

towns turned into ruins by foreign attack similarly shocked the world, see Leonardo Romero Tobar, 'Los "Sitios de Zaragoza", tema literario internacional (1808–1814)', in *El comienzo de la Guerra de la Independencia: Congreso Internacional del Bicentenario, Madrid, 8–11 de abril 2008*, ed. by Emilio de Diego García (Madrid: Editorial Actas, 2009), pp. 571–89; Herbert Rutledge Southworth, *Guernica! Guernica! A Study of Journalism, Diplomacy, Propaganda, and History* (Berkeley, CA: University of California Press, 1977), pp. 362–70.

53 Bod. Lib., North, c. 16, fol. 97, Vaughan to Doyle, Madrid, 25 November 1808.

54 Ibid.

55 Archivo Histórico Nacional, Madrid, Spain, (AHN), Estado Nr. 43, *Legajo* 184, Report on activities of Carlos Doyle, Seville, 1 October 1809.

56 Brian R. Hamnett, *The Mexican Bureaucracy before the Bourbon Reforms, 1700–1770: A Study in the Limitations of Absolutism* (Glasgow: Institute of Latin American Studies, 1979), p. 3; Patricia H. Marks, *Deconstructing Legitimacy: Viceroys, Merchants, and the Military in Late Colonial Peru* (London: Pennsylvania State University Press, 2007), p. 178; David Ringrose, *Spain, Europe, and the 'Spanish Miracle', 1700–1900* (Cambridge: Cambridge University Press, 1996), p. 256.

Relations became particularly difficult with Wellington, a man not known for his ability to delegate responsibilities or to assimilate other people's ideas.[57] After the Battle of Talavera in 1809, Anglo-Spanish co-operation foundered: the commander of the British forces blamed the poor results of the campaign on the perceived pusillanimity of the Spanish Army led by General Gregorio de la Cuesta, while the Spaniards considered Wellington's persistent demands for supplies, accompanied by threats of immediate retreat to Portugal, as signs of prevarication. Antipathy peaked when Wellington made his co-operation with the Spanish Army conditional upon several points: the removal of Cuesta; the establishment of a reliable supply system; admission of a British garrison to Cádiz; and his own appointment as commander-in-chief of the allied forces.[58] Volunteer James Duff, Lord Macduff (later 4th Earl of Fife), who acted as liaison officer during and after the battle, was caught in the verbal crossfire. In a letter to his elder brother, Marquis Wellesley, dated 21 September 1809, Wellington sardonically referred to an encounter with 'Lord Macduff, who has taken the Spanish cause under his protection'.[59] The Scottish volunteer had arrived at his camp with a letter from General Francisco de Eguía quoting correspondence with the British ambassador (another of Wellington's brothers, Richard Wellesley) instructing the commander to take up a particular defensive position. The Spaniards proposed acting in concert with the British in this deployment. Wellington refused outright. When Macduff exclaimed: 'What! will you not carry into execution an arrangement settled by the British ambassador?',[60] the British commander sent him back to Spanish headquarters with the message that his brother knew perfectly well that any of his suggestions would only be executed if Wellington's terms for remaining in Spain were met. As Wellington judged that they had not, 'the proposal must be considered as never having been made'.[61] Such a reaction left the British volunteers in the Spanish Army in an unenviable position because to the Spaniards it seemed to confirm the duplicity of their ally.

Somehow, the volunteers managed to avoid the wrath of their Spanish brothers-in-arms. Relations with Wellington, however, hardly improved

---

57 Hew Strachan, *Wellington's Legacy: The Reform of the British Army, 1830–54* (Manchester: Manchester University Press, 1984), pp. 6, 8, 14.

58 John Gurwood (ed.), *The Dispatches of Field Marshall the Duke of Wellington during his various campaigns in India, Denmark, Portugal, Spain, the Low Countries, and France from 1799–1818*, 13 vols (London: J. Murray, 1838), 5, pp. 34–5, 62–4; Charles J. Esdaile, *The Peninsular War: A New History* (London: Allen Lane, 2002), pp. 212–15.

59 Gurwood, *Dispatches*, 5, p. 165.

60 Ibid., p. 166.

61 Ibid.

when he was appointed *generalísimo* of the Spanish Army on 22 September 1812. Whittingham, Doyle and their fellow volunteer and agent Philip Keating Roche were at times authorised to draw money from the British treasury to fund military operations and the activities of Spanish military training establishments of their own creation.[62] As funds from Spanish sources dried up due to the effects of war and the *de facto* loss of control of the Spanish Latin American colonies after 1810, English subsidies became the only official lifeline. The British volunteers used their contacts with merchants in Gibraltar, Cádiz, Catalunya and Valencia, as well as the fortunes of family and friends to supplement resources, but even these efforts were often insufficient.[63] In February 1812, known as the 'famine year',[64] Whittingham's troops in Majorca began to show clear signs of starvation; some officers even fainted for want of food.[65] Supplies received from the mainland offered short-term relief, but the drama was compounded by letters from Wellington (8 January 1813) addressed to Roche in Valencia, and to Whittingham in Majorca, instructing that British funds should not be used for hospitals, food provisions, means of transport or salaries, but limited to cover costs of clothing, arms and accoutrements.[66] In a further letter, dated 28 January 1813, Wellington told Roche that if he could not find subsistence, he should remove himself with a detachment to Majorca and leave the rest of his troops under the command of the British-Sicilian army in Alicante.[67] The situation facing Roche was dire: some officers of his division were accused in the *Cortes* of taking hostage the authorities of four Valencian towns (Elche, Gijona, Novelda and Aspe) in search of supplies.[68] Perhaps fearing mutiny, Roche protested. Wellington tersely replied that if he disliked the situation or should 'make any further difficulties' he must resign his command.[69] That is precisely what Whittingham did on

---

62 Ibid., p. 245; Whittingham (ed.), *Memoir*, pp. 182–4; Bod. Lib., North c. 13, fols 27–8; Iglesias Rogers, *British Liberators*, pp. 121–6.

63 Bod. Lib., North c. 16 fol. 314: Banker Juan Fortaleza Ross to Doyle, 6 April 1811, re. loan granted for defensive operations; AGMS, R-1496 *Expediente* Felipe de la Roche [*sic*], Letter from members of the municipality of Alicante re. supplies for Roche's division, 30 March 1811; Whittingham (ed.), *Memoir*, pp. 149, 156, 169, 184.

64 Ronald Fraser, *Napoleon's Cursed War: Spanish Popular Resistance in the Peninsular War, 1808–1814* (London: Verso, 2008), p. 18.

65 Whittingham (ed.), *Memoir*, pp. 173–4, Whittingham to H. Wellesley, Palma, 21 February 1812.

66 Gurwood, *Dispatches*, 10, p. 24.

67 Gurwood, *Dispatches*, 10, p. 57–8.

68 *Diario de Sesiones y Actas de las Cortes Generales y Extraordinarias*, 23 vols (Cádiz 1810–1813), 20, pp. 49–50.

69 Gurwood, *Dispatches*, 10, p. 184, Wellington to Roche, Frenada, 12 March 1813.

6 August 1813.[70] He had been deeply hurt by Wellington's earlier attempt to remove him from the position of Inspector General of his division, a move that, although later retracted, Whittingham felt had undermined his standing in the Spanish Army.[71] His resignation took Wellington by surprise and seems to have opened his eyes to something that his brothers Richard and Henry, as diplomatic envoys, had already realised: to undermine the volunteers' position in the Spanish Army offered no benefit to the prosecution of the war. More importantly, their services were needed. Wellington, therefore, relented. On 20 September 1813 he asked Whittingham to withdraw his resignation, in return for authorisation to access British stores to feed his troops.[72] On these terms, the Spanish divisions of Whittingham and Roche played a crucial role in the liberation of the eastern provinces and in the Pyrenean campaign.[73] Nevertheless, to British eyes, the volunteers would always remain those compatriots who had 'gone native' by simply understanding, and sometimes also embracing, the codes, mores and lifestyle of the Spaniards.

It may easily be assumed that relations between members of the Irish Legion and the leadership of the British regular army were invariably hostile. Byrne told us, after all, that Napoleon gave the Irish volunteers commissions as French officers so that in the event they might 'fall into the hands of the English they should be protected; or, should any violence be offered them, he should have the right to retaliate on the English prisoners in France'.[74] A full study of the fate of the Irish prisoners of war captured by the British and their allies on the Continent is still waiting to be written, but there are indications

---

70 Whittingham (ed.), *Memoir*, pp. 234–5, Whittingham to Wellington, 6 August 1813. In this edited version of correspondence left by Samuel 'Santiago' Ford Whittingham, his resignation is attributed to a quarrel with the Spanish authorities. Whilst it is true that Whittingham was unhappy with the treatment received from the government in Cádiz, no mention of the episode has been found in his record of services (*Expediente*) at the Spanish military archives. It is possible that the editor of the *Memoir*, Whittingham's first son, Ferdinand (his real name was Fernando Santiago Antonio Nicolas Whittingham), who was at the time of publication a Major in the British Army, may have found it embarrassing to show his father in direct confrontation with the by then much-admired Wellington.

71 Whittingham (ed.), *Memoir*, pp. 187–9.

72 Whittingham (ed.), *Memoir*, pp. 237–9, Wellington to Whittingham, Lesaca, 20 September 1813, p. 287, Wellington to Clinton, St. Pé, 14 November 1813.

73 ASL, Vaughan Papers, OB. No. 25 (reel 12), 'Relación de los Cuerpos de Infantería existentes en los Exercitos Nacionales hoy día de la fecha con expresión de los Jefes y fuerza que cada uno contiene, enero 1813'; Charles J. Esdaile, *The Duke of Wellington and the Command of the Spanish Army, 1812–14* (Basingstoke: Macmillam, 1990), pp. 141–2, 161.

74 *Memoirs of Byrne*, 2, p. 8.

that not all were cruelly mistreated. While fighting in Spain, in 1811, Captain John Allen of the 2nd Division of the Irish Legion received four sabre wounds and was taken prisoner by the *guerrillero* Don Julián Sánchez. He spent eighteen months in a prison in Cádiz. His past as an Irish rebel was well known, yet the British never asked the Spaniards to turn him over to them, and he was eventually exchanged.[75] More remarkable was the case of another victim of Sánchez, the *Chef de Bataillon* Jerome Fitzhenry. Four months after capture, he was seen at liberty, and carrying a sword, at Wellington's headquarters. Reports soon followed that placed him back with his family in County Wexford. He was charged with desertion and court-martialled *in absentia* during the summer and autumn of 1811. But Fitzhenry had been a much admired member of the Legion; his colleagues simply refused to believe what turned out to be accurate information. So he was acquitted.[76]

Soldiering under a foreign flag appears to have been an experience full of surprises. Loyalty to a common cause in an uneasy alliance, such as that of Britain and Spain during the Napoleonic Wars, fostered tensions, not so much with 'the other' but with compatriots. It could also be taken for granted that a degree of cosmopolitanism was inherent to the experience of volunteering abroad. This was certainly the case for those who left homes and careers behind to fight for the Spanish cause. Yet we have seen that exclusive national loyalties, such as those professed by many officers in the Irish Legion, could make relations with non-compatriots equally difficult. Living and fighting among aliens was not war tourism. It did not necessarily amuse, improve manners and expand the mind – although for men like Robert Steele such opportunities undoubtedly constituted part of the attraction of enlistment. Wearing a foreign uniform demanded high levels of personal drive, stamina and flexibility. Volunteers had to confront challenges perhaps not very dissimilar to those faced by most short-term emigrants, such as breaking the language barrier, but war left them little time to find coping mechanisms. Military skills acquired at home were easily transferable to other settings; a factor that reinforces the view of the British Army as a European institution outlined in chapter 1.[77] But theoretical martial training and experience, while highly valued, did not constitute a *sine qua non* for recruitment. British and Irish volunteers were often enlisted not so much on account of proven abilities, but for their wholehearted support for a particular cause. In the period of the Revolutionary and Napoleonic Wars, military professionalism often had to play second fiddle to political fervour

---

75 *Memoirs of Byrne*, 2, pp. 137–9; Gallaher, *Napoleon's Irish Legion*, p. 142.
76 *Memoirs of Byrne*, 3, pp. 72–3, 80–1; Gallaher, *Napoleon's Irish Legion*, p. 144.
77 Conway, *Britain, Ireland, and Continental Europe*, pp. 266–78.

and commitment. This added onus would have easily deterred men for whom soldiering was just an occupation like any other. It may also come to explain why British and Irish volunteers remained few in numbers during this period, and perhaps unusual within the context of the mass armies that operated in continental Europe during the Napoleonic Wars.

Part 2

Hierarchy

3

Effectiveness
and the British Officer Corps,
1793–1815

Bruce Collins

I T HAS LONG BEEN ARGUED that the British officer corps was typically ineffective or at best unscientific during the protracted wars against France. At the beginnings of his scholarly history of the British Army, John Fortescue accounted for the failings of the British campaign in the Netherlands by deploring the amateurism of the battalion officers, as well as many on the staff.[1] Among modern historians, David Gates has argued that the army 'sank into dereliction' between 1783 and 1793, characterised by poor organisation and inadequate training. When wartime expansion followed, the officer corps increased in size too quickly to improve in quality. Only with the Peninsular War did continuous service foster qualitative improvements and raise the status of the army sufficiently high to attract better recruits as privates and later NCOs.[2] Such an interpretation has been restated by Antony Clayton in his general history of the British officer corps.[3] Yet, although reforms introduced at home by the Duke of York, including the establishment of the Royal Military Academy, whose cadets began entering active service during the Peninsular War, may have helped, expert contemporaries such as William Napier and A. H. Jomini saw a newly celebrated professionalism as

---

1 J. W. Fortescue, *A History of the British Army*, 13 vols (London: Macmillan, 1899–1930), 4, p. 4.

2 David Gates, 'The Transformation of the Army, 1783–1815' in *The Oxford History of the British Army*, ed. by David Chandler (Oxford: Oxford University Press, 1996), pp. 132–60, esp. pp. 132–3, 140, 142–3, 146–8, 160.

3 Anthony Clayton, *The British Officer. Leading the British Army from 1660 to the Present* (Harlow: Pearson, 2006), pp. 55–71.

the outcome not of 'superior tactics or better armament but endurance and discipline'.[4]

The case for enhanced effectiveness in war fighting remains contested. For example, Rory Muir attributed victory at Salamanca to excellent management in detail by Wellington and his army's high level of general competence in discharging orders and manoeuvring units.[5] But, in a recent study of Waterloo, Alessandro Barbaro offers a more mixed assessment. While the long experience of fighting by 1815, and especially the rigours of the Peninsular War, meant that the British army at Waterloo was 'more middle-class and more meritocratic than one might suppose', Barbaro also argues that the more meritocratic composition of the officer corps 'did not make it more professional'. Traditional values and the supremacy of adherence to a code of honour continued to apply: 'The worth of a good officer was determined by the physical courage with which he led his men, and by nothing else.'[6] The obvious question – how then did the British perform so well at Waterloo? – has been answered by Russell Weigley: 'The professional competence of Napoleon's officer corps was inadequate to the requirements that the expansion of the army and the empire after 1806 placed upon it.'[7] This, of course, expands upon David Chandler's earlier criticisms of defective French staff work and Napoleon's declining capacity to manage a large battle.[8] Thus, the British got no better; the French simply got worse.

Allowing that technical and organisational advances occurred, how far did success in 1815 result from declining French competence or improved British performance? The first point to be stressed is that the transformative effect of the Peninsular War can be exaggerated if it is assumed that a new generation of officers emerged during that campaign. There was instead identifiable and probably considerable continuity in the British officer corps over time. This phenomenon may be illustrated by reference to three major episodes in the conduct of war: the surrender at Yorktown in 1781, the dismal campaign in the Netherlands in 1793–5, and then the triumph at Waterloo.

An initial expectation might be that the first two episodes, as failures,

---

4 Hew Strachan, *From Waterloo to Balaclava. Tactics, Technology, and the British Army, 1815–1854* (Cambridge: Cambridge University Press, 1985), p. 16.

5 Rory Muir, *Salamanca 1812* (New Haven, CT: Yale University Press, 2001), pp. 208, 211–18.

6 Alessandro Barbaro, *The Battle. A History of the Battle of Waterloo* (London: Atlantic, 2005), pp. 30–1.

7 Russell F. Weigley, *The Age of Battles: The Quest for Decisive Warfare from Breitenfeld to Waterloo* (London: Pimlico, 1993), pp. 499, 511–12.

8 David G. Chandler, *The Campaigns of Napoleon* (London: Weidenfeld and Nicolson, 1966), pp. 1021–2, 1026, 1091–2.

would have terminated military careers. In fact, there were marked continuities. The *Oxford Dictionary of National Biography* provides details of nineteen officers who surrendered at Yorktown, a good sample from among about 200 officers present there. Of those nineteen men, sixteen became major-generals or rose higher in rank; nine went on to become commanders-in-chief, governors, lieutenant governors, and an adjutant-general of the army. The commander at Yorktown, Cornwallis, went on to positions of power and authority, as governor-general in Bengal and as viceroy and commander-in-chief of Ireland, far exceeding those positions attained by any of his opponents, including George Washington. While his impetuous strategy in plunging into North Carolina and then Virginia has been roundly criticised by military historians – Fortescue called it 'mad'[9] – his generalship was typically competent and his perspicacity in selecting subordinates was favourably commented upon by contemporaries. As Arthur Wellesley noted in 1802, 'to have been selected by Lord Cornwallis for any situation is strong presumptive evidence in a man's favour that he is fit for it'.[10] Of the eighteen other officers, ten were employed in the Netherlands or in the West Indies in 1793–6, a clear indication that involvement in Yorktown cast no shadows on military careers. In 1806, twenty-five years after the surrender, eleven of the nineteen were on active service; four others had died by then and one was too old for military duties. Only one of these prominent officers was scarcely deployed at all during the long wars of 1793–1815: Banastre Tarleton, one of the most notorious of all British commanders in the American war. He was side-lined as much for his political postures, his scandalous private life, and his personal turbulence as for his reputation for brutality in America.[11]

This level of continuity contrasted with the turmoil experienced by the French. The French had to replenish their officer corps in the early 1790s because the Revolution expunged the *ancien régime* officer class. Of 500 officers who served in America during the entire period 1780–3, only thirty-eight were still in the French Army in 1794.[12] The French simply had to rely on promotion from the ranks of NCOs in order to sustain their armies. Paddy Griffith argued that the process of replenishment also brought forward upper-middle-class junior officers. Both they and, by implication, the promoted NCOs were better educated than their opponents and more capable of adapting

---

9 Fortescue, *History of the British Army*, 3, pp. 395–6.

10 Duke of Wellington (ed.), *Supplementary Despatches and Memoranda of Arthur, Duke of Wellington*, 15 vols (London, 1858–72), 3, p. 499.

11 *Oxford Dictionary of National Biography* entries.

12 Alan Forrest, 'The French Revolutionary and Napoleonic Wars' in *Early Modern Military History, 1450–1815*, ed. by Geoff Mortimer (Basingstoke: Palgrave, 2004), pp. 196–211, esp. p. 210 citing S. F. Scott's work.

their operational practice to new circumstances. Griffith has stressed the importance of operational innovation, with the French launching waves of attacks by battalion to exhaust and break down their opponents and deploying strong reserves to maintain the flow of attacks and to safeguard their rear positions from counter-offensives.[13] In contrast, the British officer corps remained intact in 1792, the product of long service and slow promotion.[14]

Entries in the *Oxford Dictionary of National Biography* necessarily represent some degree of personal success or notoriety, but the continuity of service evidenced by the Yorktown officers is corroborated by looking back from the Peninsular War and Waterloo. During 1812–14, a new and substantial monthly journal, the *Royal Military Panorama*, published biographies of twenty leading generals. Seven of them had served during the wars of 1776–83 and thirteen had served in the Netherlands at some point in 1793–5, while three had served elsewhere in those years.[15] The biographical sketches went to great lengths to demonstrate deep connections with the past, both in social standing and in service records. These generals were persistently linked with families of long and socially elevated lineage, even though the biographies sometimes had to go back to the seventeenth century to find distinguished ancestors for their subjects. The entries underscored how traditional elites continued to furnish the military leadership associated with the ruling establishment. But these articles also denied any radical break in the professional development of the officer corps. These men had acquired their basic military skills long before the Royal Military Academy had been established or reforms associated with the Duke of York had been effected.

The careers of middle-ranking and senior officers in action at Waterloo confirm this journalistic impression. Of the fifteen lieutenant-colonels who led their battalions at Waterloo, excluding lieutenant-colonels on the staff, nine had served overseas in the 1790s or in Egypt in 1801. Their professional formation as subalterns therefore long preceded organisational reform. Of the twenty-one generals who were on the field at Waterloo, ten had served in the Netherlands, West Indies or Toulon in 1793–6, and some were deeply involved in campaigning.[16] Three were *aides-de-camp* to generals: Lord Hill,

---

13 Paddy Griffith, *The Art of War of Revolutionary France 1789–1802* (London: Greenhill, 1998), pp. 280–3. For more on the French officer corps, see: Rafe Blaufarb, *The French Army, 1750–1820: Careers, Talent, Merit* (Manchester: Manchester University Press, 2002).

14 J. A. Houlding, *Fit for Service. The Training of the British Army, 1715–1795* (Oxford: Clarendon Press, 1981), pp. 109–10, 115.

15 Bruce Collins, *War and Empire. The Expansion of Britain 1790–1830* (Harlow: Pearson, 2010), p. 474.

16 See appendix A for details.

at Toulon in 1793, to Charles O'Hara, the second-in-command at Yorktown; Sir Henry Clinton, whose father commanded in North America in the 1780s, to the Duke of York in 1793; George Cooke to Major-General Samuel Hulse in 1794–5. None of this is to gainsay the importance of the experience of the Peninsular War. Of the twenty-one generals, only one had not served in the Peninsula. Of seventy-seven majors and lieutenant-colonels fighting with their regiments on 18 June, at least forty-one had served there. But the shared experience of the Peninsular War should not disguise the continuity of service, stretching back twenty years, which affected significant numbers of middle-ranking and senior officers. Overlapping service from Yorktown to the campaigns of 1793–6 and from those latter campaigns to 1815 demonstrates a degree of continuity that has been ignored.

Mere presence indicates nothing about effectiveness. But if we accept that the army had become efficient by 1815, this suggests that the officers who commanded it in the field had acquired such competence through experience. J. A. Houlding has argued that the dispersal of the eighteenth-century army in overseas garrisons and in activities in support of the civil power meant that it was unprepared for fighting in the early stages of major wars. Only with practice in actual campaigning were British soldiers able to gain the experience necessary to engage in significant battles.[17] That experience may not have been translated into any new science of war, but it developed in senior and middle-ranking officers those qualities of calmness, patience and determination which proved so vital in fighting a battle. If Napoleon did indeed believe that luck was a decisive attribute of successful generalship, then Wellington would presumably have responded by emphasising the importance of 'character' and resilience in managing an army on a complex battlefield, a subject which remains understudied.

Despite the revisionism of recent years, whereby numbers of soldiers and controlling the supply of troops and reinforcements are seen as central factors in explaining victory,[18] the use of those numbers effectively in battle remained vital. Senior British officers were as committed as their French counterparts to managing their men in battle, as demonstrated by the high casualty rates suffered by generals on both sides at, for example, Salamanca.[19] At Waterloo,

---

17 Houlding, *Fit for Service*, pp. 390–1, 394–5.

18 Griffith, *The Art of War*, pp. 201–2, 230–4, 276–84; Randolph G. S. Cooper, *The Anglo-Maratha Campaigns and the Contest for India: The Struggle for Control of the South Asian Military Economy* (Cambridge: Cambridge University Press, 2003). Griffith argues that it was efficient and very focused political and administrative mobilisation for war which distinguished the French republic in 1793–5, while the opponents of France failed diplomatically to forge a coalition against their enemy.

19 Muir, *Salamanca 1812*, pp. 210–11.

two British generals were killed and eight were wounded, and 50 per cent of the majors and lieutenant-colonels present were killed or wounded. The highest casualties, at two-thirds, were suffered by lieutenant-colonels leading their battalions into action.[20] Although senior officers' minor injuries were more likely to be reported than those suffered by privates, it still represents a significant proportion of the group, and exceeds the 34 per cent casualties suffered by the entire officer corps. Such a level of casualties did not simply represent courage, or indifference to danger, under fire. It was symptomatic of engagement in depth in managing the battle.

Calm and determination, demonstrated by a readiness and capacity to take heavy casualties, were not the only qualities sought and found among senior officers. Horse Guards and the monarch kept a close eye on the calibre of the officer corps as well as on the condition of the army more generally. Monitoring the officer corps fell to the commander-in-chief, a position held for most of this period by George III's second son, the Duke of York. He performed inspections personally and through a system of staff work organised by a range of generals. During wartime, or at least in periods of threatened invasion, the commander-in-chief sent weekly returns on the state of the army in Britain and recommendations for vacant commissions to the king. Thus, for example, the Duke of York spent over a week touring Kent and Sussex in August 1804, when a French invasion was at least possible, inspecting 8,000 troops at Rochester and then smaller units at five other places, including Maidstone, Dover and Deal.[21] This inexorable process of inspection enabled Horse Guards to make judgements on the readiness of individual battalions to serve overseas and to assess middle-ranking and senior officers. York reported that the troops were 'in general in a very advanced state of discipline, and with very few exceptions perfectly fit for service'. John Moore's brigade at Shorncliffe took pride of place; the Duke had never seen such 'perfect' regiments in any service as the brigade's 4th (King's Own) and the 52nd. He also commented on the high intelligence of the officers of the King's German Legion.[22]

The steady flow of such information enabled the king to comment on and make recommendations about military appointments, promotions and rewards. On receiving proposals for honouring overseas service in June 1804, George III, recollecting 1801–2, added John Moore to the suggested recipients

20 All information on officers at Waterloo is drawn from Charles Dalton, *The Waterloo Roll Call* (London: Arms and Armour Press, 1971).

21 A. Aspinall (ed.), *The Later Correspondence of George III*, 5 vols (Cambridge: Cambridge University Press, 1968), 4, pp. 126, 224 (n).

22 Ibid., p. 226.

of a knighthood, because Moore 'ha[d] by the unanimous testimony of the troops that served in Egypt the greatest share in the brilliant successes in that part of the globe'. In considering senior officers' achievements, the king at least saw service in Egypt as a significant qualification. A command in Ireland went to an Irish peer 'whose services in Egypt g[a]ve him the fairest claim for that situation'. Major-General John Stuart was recommended to Grenada for his record in Egypt, especially for 'the able and judicious manner in which he conducted himself when in the command at Alexandria'. More generally, when a new commander for the Windward and Leeward Islands was considered, William Myers' previous knowledge of the islands and his past ability to withstand the climate and disease there proved decisive arguments in his favour.[23]

Informal comment on individual commanders' capabilities inevitably brought out personal, political and professional rivalries and differences in the assessment of attributes and accomplishments. Thus in 1803, the Duke of York recommended Lord Cathcart for the post of commander-in-chief in Ireland since he was the only general officer of 'rank and reputation [...] against whom there was no political objection'.[24] Yet the notion that the difficulties in finding competent senior commanders betokened a peculiar inefficiency in the army needs to be qualified by reference to similar challenges experienced by the Royal Navy in selecting senior commanders.

Despite the fact that the leadership of the Royal Navy has received far less severe criticism than has that of the army, there were considerable reservations about senior admirals' competence for high command. In August 1796, Sir John Jervis informed the Secretary of the Admiralty, 'You and I, and in truth the whole profession are Hero-Makers, and nothing so common among us, as to say, this, that, and t'other man is a great officer, when we really have few officers on the list of Admirals.'[25] Finding officers suitable for senior command, with its numerous, varied and often taxing demands, remained challenging, even though the list of flag officers expanded appreciably during the 1790s. In 1801, Lord St Vincent, as Jervis had become, reported to George III his 'extreme difficulty in pointing out to your Majesty an officer in all respects fitted for such an important command' as that of the Baltic fleet, given both the 'critical situation' in diplomatic affairs and 'the objections which occur to different people'.[26]

---

23 Ibid., pp. 200–1, 228.
24 Ibid., p. 126.
25 Roger Knight, *The Pursuit of Victory: The Life and Achievement of Horatio Nelson* (London: Allen Lane, 2005), p. 551.
26 Aspinall (ed.), *Later Correspondence*, 3, p. 545.

Appointing officers to senior command therefore differed little between the services by the 1810s. Horse Guards informed Wellington in June 1813 that 'No brevet has occurred for many years which includes the promotion of so many useful officers to the rank of M[ajor] General.' It cautioned that the promotion of so many colonels currently serving under Wellington might create 'some embarrassment', since the ambitions of those serving elsewhere had not been so generously satisfied. But three of the twelve colonels promoted were deemed to be among the best officers in the service.[27] Although Wellington periodically complained of his officers' abilities, he did so most obviously when seeking to attribute blame for failing to achieve objectives. His criticism in July 1813 after the Battle of Vitoria – 'The officers of the lower ranks will not perform the duty required from them in order to keep the soldiers in order and it is next to impossible to punish any officer for neglects of this description'[28] – has been taken as indicative of a lack of consistent professionalism.[29] But such comment reflected the way in which Wellington's army, following a demanding and prolonged advance and a physically challenging battle, was distracted by plundering once the great victory had been secured. Wellington had to explain to the responsible minister in London why he was not pursuing the retreating French. It might have been more honest to state that no army can sustain marching and fighting without some relief from intense pressure on performance. More generally, the relative efficiency of Wellington's army in the peninsula depended upon attracting, and retaining, competent middle-ranking officers from the existing officer corps who could effectively manage battalions.

Such competence was assessed as a prominent part of annual battalion reviews. Inspections reported on the overall competence of battalion commanders and the administrative abilities of adjutants and quarter-masters. Captains were not commented upon individually, but generalisations were made about their attentiveness to duty and their efficiency; the attention they paid to educating subalterns was also noted. The troops' state of health, cleanliness, and skill in drill were taken as evidence of a battalion's efficiency. Battalions based in the UK were often in the process of training their men, and this was reflected in reports noting improvement rather than high levels of efficiency.

Relatively few battalion commanders in June 1815 were in place during the winter inspections of 1812–13, but reports on those who were indicate sound

---

27 University of Southampton Special Collections, Southampton (Sou. SC), Wellington Papers, WP1/371, folder 1, Torrens to Wellington, 3 June 1813.

28 Sou. SC, WP1/373, Wellington to Earl Bathurst, 2 July 1813.

29 Barbaro, *The Battle*, pp. 30, 187.

battalion management. Lieutenant-Colonel William George Harris of the 73rd was in charge of a battalion where 'great harmony seems to prevail and all seem willing to support and forward the wishes of their commanding officer'. The privates were a 'fine body of men', partly because 'No man is kept on the strength [...] that does not do his Duty as a soldier.' Neither of these two assessments were commonplace judgements. In February 1813, Andrew Barnard, as a brigade commander, inspected the 95th, which he was to command at Waterloo. He found a battalion 'perfect in its field exercises'. The officers were 'active[,] intelligent and zealous in the performance of their duties', creating a unit in which 'the greatest unanimity prevails'.[30] Colin Campbell, commanding the third battalion of the Royal Scots, was described as 'an intelligent, steady officer'. The battalion's officers, who were 'intelligent and extremely zealous', including 'a most intelligent and zealous' adjutant 'very fit for his situation', ensured that 'Unanimity and a good understanding prevail in the Corps and they afford the commanding officer every support.' Meanwhile, the fourth battalion of the Royal Scots was commanded by Major Robert Nixon, who was to lead the 28th at Waterloo; the inspecting general emphasised that 'I cannot say too much in his praise for the marked improvement' in the battalion since he took command.[31] Efficient organisation and unit cohesion, partly reflected in the troops' health, appearance and skills in drill, shaped reports on the condition of battalions. But there were more informal and personal checks on senior officers' military competence.

The informal assessment of officers' performance occurred through extensive social networks which resulted from the systemic intermingling of the country's political and military leadership. The extent of wide-ranging familial links between political leaders and military, and naval, officers may be illustrated very simply by the associations connecting the armed services with the seventeen prime ministers who served in the years from 1762 and 1834. Only three had been army officers and only Wellington served in high rank. But three others were enthusiastic volunteers, Pitt the Younger and Lord Liverpool both commanding volunteer battalions; Spencer Perceval was the third. As a young MP the future Lord Liverpool became a colonel of fencible cavalry in 1794; he took his regiment to Dumfries in 1796 and in 1798 wrote that 'my military duties make it difficult for me to obtain leave of absence from My Regiment this Summer'.[32] Another seven had brothers or

---

30 The National Archives, London (TNA), War Office papers, WO 27/112, Confidential Reports on: 2nd battalion 73rd; 51st regiment; 1st battalion 95th.

31 TNA, WO 27/111, Confidential Reports on: 3rd battalion Royal Scots; 4th battalion Royal Scots; 2nd battalion 28th.

32 Norman Gash, *Lord Liverpool* (London: Weidenfeld & Nicolson, 1985).

sons who were officers. George Canning had a son serving as a naval captain while he was prime minister, as well as a cousin who, as a lieutenant-colonel, was killed at Waterloo; Robert Peel's father-in-law was General John Scott. Earl Grey had four brothers who were army or naval officers, and his father was a general; one of his own sons, then a lieutenant-colonel, acted as his private secretary when Grey was prime minister. It is quite striking that the fourteen members of the Whig cabinet of 1830 included three men whose fathers had been generals and one who had a grandfather who attained that rank. In addition, Lord Palmerston had been an eager volunteer officer in the 1800s and Lord John Russell had trained as a militia officer and had visited a brother serving in the Iberian Peninsula in 1813.[33]

This intermingling of political and military elites within families created a far-reaching network through which information and judgement on fellow officers' aptitudes and performance could be communicated. For example, Sir John Moore, a general from a professional rather than an establishment background, was accompanied to the Iberian Peninsula in 1808 by eleven brigadiers and generals. Seven of them had aristocratic connections, including three who were related to members of the cabinet in London: Lord William Bentinck was a son of the prime minister, Charles Stewart was half-brother of the Foreign Secretary, Lord Castereagh, and Henry Fane was a nephew of Lord Westmoreland.[34] The possibility of detailed checks on generals' performance through such connections did not guarantee against incompetence. But it meant that scrutiny could be intense and continuous, and feedback went straight to the top.

This aspect of how commanders' performance was monitored reinforces an image of the senior officer corps as being embedded within the ruling establishment rather than being driven by professional standards and ambitions. But the officer corps' relationship to civil society varied considerably, depending on officers' career motivations and the type of force in which they served. In effect, there were three armies in existence by the 1800s – the regulars, the militia and volunteers, and the East India Company army – and each was subdivided into distinctive elements.

The regular regiments were, of course, at the heart of the state's military apparatus. Allowing for the separate existence of its specialist artillery and engineer branches, where officers became more technically qualified during the eighteenth century, the regiments provided three quite different career paths for their officers. They offered a species of semi-occupation for amateurs who needed, or were required by their families to undertake, some formal

33 *Oxford Dictionary of National Biography* entries.
34 Collins, *War and Empire*, pp. 427–8.

duties as an alternative to idleness or dissipation. Military participation among the landed elite was very high; in 1830 about 70 per cent of aristocratic households had at least one member who had served in the army or navy.[35] This first group were essentially 'court' officers who wanted access to London society and to royal and governmental circles. Not all such officers were amateurs. The Duke of York argued that the Guards regiments enabled scions of the ruling classes to fulfil some military duties while also remaining in touch with family responsibilities from their base in London. Because these units did not normally serve for long overseas, to 'young men of high rank and fortune […] the Guards offer an opportunity of honorably pursuing the military profession without subjecting themselves to those inconveniences which would otherwise preclude their belonging to the service'.[36]

Another group of regular officers were men of financial means and/or very high social standing who wanted to forge a military career. Wellington and Lord William Bentinck are obvious examples. These officers had serious intentions, but were impatient for advancement. They progressed rapidly through the lower and middle ranks by purchase, changing regiments frequently in their twenties as they pushed themselves up the promotion ladder. This second general group of affluent, fast-track officers tend to be the ones we know most about. The third group, of which we know least, were the regimental officers who could not afford purchase and who did not exchange between regiments. These men might secure one, or possibly two, promotions without purchase, but progress was glacial, even in periods of sustained warfare.

Within the UK, the militia and volunteers formed the second type of army. Called upon for defensive duties in periods of national crisis, the militia depended for its management on local elites and their readiness to accept some degree of military discipline and the overall command of regular, district generals. But local political and socio-economic elites maintained their power within and through the militia, which was even more dominated by the political authorities than was the regular army. Members of the government might also serve as commanding officers of militia, as Pitt did in his second term as prime minister. The Secretary at War in 1803, Charles Yorke, commanded the Cambridgeshire Militia, while also seeking election to parliament for the county.[37] The organisation of the militia was the

---

35 I took a large sample from 1830 of 247 peers whose titles began with the letters A–G. Some 181 of them had an immediate family member who had served in the army or navy. In eighteen families a relative had been killed or died of wounds. *Sharpe's Genealogical Peerage of the British Empire*, 2 vols (London: Sharpe, 1830), 1, *passim*.

36 Aspinall (ed.), *Later Correspondence*, 3, p. 623.

37 Ibid., 4, pp. 114, 124.

responsibility of the county lords lieutenant, reporting to the Home Secretary, not Horse Guards and the commander-in-chief of the Army. Thus in 1794, when the Duke of Portland joined the government as Home Secretary, he gained further patronage for his Whig political faction by securing the appointment of his eldest son and heir, the Marquess of Titchfield, as Lord Lieutenant of Middlesex, the county covering much of north and west London. George III saw the appointment of a mere 26-year-old as a 'highly advantageous' way 'of bringing a young man of quality into a line the most useful to himself as well as the public if he zealously turns his attention to the police of the county and capital'.[38]

Leadership of the militia was an important attribute of social rank. When a vacancy arose in the colonelcy of the North Mayo militia, Lord Tyrawley asked that his illegitimate son be appointed or that he himself be nominated to the position. The deceased incumbent, Tyrawley's nephew, had betrayed a family understanding about the succession. Citing his thirty-nine years of supporting the government and his thirty years of holding public office, the peer claimed he was the most prominent county figure who did not then command a regiment. Clearly seeking to maintain his standing in County Mayo on a par with Lord Sligo and Lord Dillon, who each commanded a battalion, he indicated that, if his son were appointed, he would place 2,000 freeholders in Mayo at the government's command and furnish all the additional assistance he could.[39] Another example of the importance of family, loyalty and the need to reward past services arose when Lord Clarina, the son of a general, pleaded for a post on the regular staff supervising the militia in Ireland. Sir Arthur Wellesley as Chief Secretary for Ireland recommended that Horse Guards appoint Lord Clarina as a brigadier on the staff, partly to help bind Protestants to the cause of Union. He added:

> I don't know much of him as an officer, but he has produced testimonials of his good conduct [...] he belongs to a family much respected in this country and this appointment would give very general satisfaction.[40]

Well below lords lieutenant and colonels in the social order, even modest commands in the militia could be subject to considerable discussion. When a vacancy arose in the County Fermanagh militia, Lord Enniskillen recommended for militia captaincies two men who enjoyed excellent standing in the county. But his argument against a third, apparently a retired regular

---

38 Ibid., 2, p. 226.
39 Sou. SC, WP1/170/17, Lord Tyrawley to Wellesley, 4 June 1807.
40 Sou. SC, WP1/167/53, Wellesley to Lt Col J. W. Gordon, 9 May 1807.

infantry captain, was summarised as being that the latter was 'a good and loyal man, but not of that situation in life to command a body of men'. The earl regretted that there were few men of property in the county to form an acceptable leadership cadre.[41] Militia appointments, and other military appointments related to them, were part of a large cluster of patronage, including civil government posts and nominations to positions in the established church, which enabled governments to maintain their power and sustain their authority. Political factors probably played a far greater role in militia appointments than they did in appointments in the regular forces, and contributed to a widespread sense that military leadership had more to do with the possession of habits of command, and social acceptability, than with military professionalism, a cultural and social distinction that could lead to disputes between services, as we shall see in chapter 4.

Yet beyond the UK there existed a third 'British' army, that of the East India Company. As with the regulars and the militia and volunteers, many further distinctions can be made between and within the armies of the three presidencies in India. But if we consider only its officer corps, then those differences may be of lesser importance. By the standards of the period 1790–1819, this army was the most successful in the world, in that it secured enormous territorial gains which remained in British hands for over a century. Campaigns were generally won at low cost in manpower losses and through a dynamic political process of incorporating conquered or annexed peoples into the Company's own armies. This officer corps had little of the 'court' amateur about it. One long-range analysis of British officers in India indicates that some 77 per cent were from middling and professional backgrounds, compared with only 47 per cent of regular officers in the British Army.[42] Company officers could not purchase promotion, but pay was good and there were many opportunities for employment on secondment to allied Indian princes' armies and to an array of posts in the political and administrative service. As a result, 65 per cent of the Bengal Army's officers in 1820 were on secondment from their regiments.[43]

Although this group of officers was less aristocratic than the officer corps in the regular army and although some officers became distinguished administrators and accomplished writers, the group as a whole was not any more

41 Sou. SC, WP1/170/14, Earl of Enniskillen to Wellesley, 3 June 1807.

42 P. E. Razzell, 'Social Origins of Officers in the Indian and British Home Armies, 1758–1960', *British Journal of Sociology*, 14 (1963), pp. 102–39.

43 Douglas M. Peers, *Between Mars and Mammon. Colonial Armies and the Garrison State in India 1819–1835* (London; Tauris, 1995), pp. 75–9. It is symptomatic of the historiography that the Indian Army is omitted from, for example, Edward M. Spiers, *The Army and Society 1815–1914* (London: Longman, 1980).

meritocratic or professional. Cadets were often selected through the patronage of influential men back home. In 1808, for example, the Lord Lieutenant of Ireland received four cadetships to which he could make nominations.[44] These slots were awarded to the relations and friends of political or business contacts or those who worked for patrons in senior capacities, such as solicitors or estate stewards. Despite coming from less privileged backgrounds, Company officers indulged in outdoor pursuits unencumbered by advanced study, and certainly not military studies.[45] The more serious and ambitious among them applied themselves to civil governance.

The influence of this group of officers outside India and the East was limited too. About half the officers in the Company army died in India. This may be demonstrated by examining three cohorts of officers in the Bengal Army. Sampling those cadets whose names began with C and who joined the Company army in the years 1770–1815, 55 per cent had died in the East by 1838. Even for those who attained senior rank, the chances of dying overseas were high. Of the 353 officers in the Bengal Army who rose to become lieutenant-colonels by 1820, some 42 per cent had died in India, elsewhere in the East, or in transit by 1838. Examining a cohort of cadets who joined in 1807 confirms these statistics. By 1830, 46 per cent of those 138 cadets were dead, even though their age range was probably in the low forties. Once those who had retired, resigned or been removed are accounted for, only fifty-five of the intake of 138 remained in the Bengal Army by 1830; twenty-two of them became majors and two became lieutenant-colonels by 1837 (see Appendix B). This British officer corps was plentiful, middle-class and contributed to a successfully expansionist empire, but it was essentially exiled, serving and dying well out of sight of the inhabitants of the United Kingdom. And it was undistinguished in its contribution to military science or practice. Ironically, in the mid-1850s, when public opinion in Britain argued for the incompetence of the British aristocratic generals and called for an infusion of Indian officers into the Crimean high command, there were those in India who decried the calibre of the Indian Army's officer corps.[46]

During the wars of 1793–1815, however, these different kinds of army enjoyed military success at quite different times and in different military circumstances. In India, the war against Mysore in 1790–2 saw a degree of co-ordination between the presidency armies not attained earlier and an

---

44 Sou. SC, WP1/187/62, J. Meheux to Duke of Richmond 9 Jan 1808.

45 John Blakiston, *Twelve Years of Military Adventure*, 2 vols (London: Henry Colburn, 1829).

46 Sir Henry Lawrence, *Essays, Military and Political, Written in India* (London: W. H. Allen, 1859), pp. 452, 473–4, 478–81.

advance in the concentration of military effort. The attack on Seringapatam in 1799 was completed far more quickly and effectively than expected. Vigorous planning and logistical preparation were the keys to success. But energy and single-mindedness in implementing a demanding timetable were also important. By the Maratha wars of 1803–5, the Company armies commanded enough resources and momentum to out-recruit and out-march their opponents. But the Maratha princes were woefully divided and it is possible to argue that their political divisions assisted the British in those years as much as the divisions among the coalition powers assisted France in 1793–5. For the militia and the volunteers, the great test came not against a French invasion but against the Irish rising of 1798. As usual with Irish affairs, the pieties of our own age interfere with historical explicitness. Militia, volunteer and fencible forces raised and deployed plentiful numbers and then, albeit with grim excesses of blind brutality, crushed the uprising.

Thus, by the end of 1799 two of the three officer corps delineated here had conducted effective campaigns, if through the extensive and sometimes ruthless application of force. While 'regular' officers were involved in those military successes, they came into their own only in the Iberian Peninsula because it was only there that they operated a sizeable regular army in a sustained campaign. Although the campaigns of 1790–2 and 1799 in India and in Ireland in 1798 were headed and managed by regulars, the Peninsular War differed in scale and tied down a large regular force for five years. This gave time for local expertise to accumulate and fighting experience to unfold. The regulars had had no similar continuous exposure to campaigning since the war in America in 1776–82, and that, for the most part, had not been against a large regular force. Combatting French armies in the Iberian Peninsula did more for morale and a sense of self-worth than much of the campaigning in America did a generation earlier.[47]

Assessing the efficiency of the officer corps thus depends upon a variety of perspectives. For many historians, the defects of the pre-Peninsular army were epitomised by the disasters of the winter of 1794–5 in the Netherlands. Yet the losses and failings there were mere bagatelles compared with the French defects in planning and logistics during the Russian campaign of 1812. Those failings, as David Chandler long ago stressed, occurred well before the worst ravages of the Russian winter set in, as staff work failed to take account of the condition of Polish and Russian roads, overestimated the availability

---

47 Americans' experience of Vietnam offers a parallel, by deflating the army officer corps' self-confidence and sense of efficiency, which were restored through a 'regular' war against a regular enemy in 1991.

of local food supplies for men and horses, and miscalculated the speed with which cattle could be brought to the army. The French command system, despite the ample and apparently distinguished presence of Napoleonic marshals, could not cope with the magnitude of the tasks it faced.[48] So, too, the defensive operations in eastern France in January 1814 demonstrated a chronic lack of co-ordination in the high command and in staff work. There were tactical lapses, particularly in a failure to destroy bridges, and the troops suffered from shortages of pay, clothing and food.[49]

By contrast, concern for logistics strongly shaped British military grand strategy. For the most part, except for the Walcheren expedition, which was devastated by sickness, the British learned the lessons of 1794–5. The main priority was to produce fit, disciplined and cohesive battalions, a task for which the officer corps was judged perfectly capable, well before the Peninsular War.[50] This focus – often implicitly regarded as traditionalist regimentalism – is fully consonant with modern notions of the centrality of effective unit command, unit autonomy, and control and certainty at the unit level.[51] Although battlefield decision-making was centralised, training and a good deal of operational activity were devolved to battalions and ad hoc brigades formed from a number of battalions. The real problem facing the British in launching continental expeditions was not the efficiency of the battalions but the availability of supplies and the reliability of continental allies. When an expedition into Germany was mooted in September 1805, the Duke of York warned George III of the lesson 'from the experience of all former wars'. British forces attached to an allied (Prussian) army 'would be immediately exposed to the most hazardous service and sacrificed to save the troops of the Sovereign with whom they would be destined to cooperate'. Moreover, they would compete for local supplies, including horses, with their Prussian putative allies.[52] In November, he firmly advised the prime minister, William Pitt, against any winter expedition to Germany, since success depended on uncertain support from the Prussian authorities and from the local population. York underscored the risks for the army:

> great loss must unavoidably be expected among them by sickness, from the season of the year, the damp and deep country in which they are to act, and the great fatigues they must have to undergo, without having the means of

48 Chandler, *The Campaigns of Napoleon*, pp. 848–60.
49 Michael V. Leggiere, *The Fall of Napoleon. The Allied Invasion of France 1813–1814* (Cambridge: Cambridge University Press, 2007), pp. 463–4, 468–9, 479, 487–91.
50 Aspinall (ed.), *Later Correspondence*, 4, p. 357.
51 Martin van Creveld, *Command in War* (Cambridge, MA: Harvard University Press, 1985), p. 307; Vincent, *Nelson*, pp. 5, 324–6.
52 Aspinall (ed.) *Later Correspondence*, 4, pp. 357–8.

taking with them any of those comforts which are essentially necessary for the health of the soldier.[53]

The British military challenge emerges as not so much the creation of a well officered army, but how to support it logistically on campaign and how to deploy it where reliable allies would enable it to function effectively. Thus performance in war fighting had more to do with sustaining logistical support and securing reliable allies than with overcoming officers' inefficiency. The officer corps in Britain's three types of army played distinctive roles according to the expectations their societies placed upon the different kinds of army, and interacted differently with their societies. Militia and volunteers were deeply influenced by social and political elites, subject to detailed local control and tied closely into civil society. Militia battalions were typically mobile within the UK once they were embodied, serving away from their original recruiting grounds. But officer appointments remained linked to county social establishments and the militia had to work closely with local leaders wherever they were stationed. At the other extreme, the armies of the East India Company provided an officer corps which spread outwards to become a prominent part of the governing class of India, providing the personnel who watched over and advised subsidiary princes and who filled numerous administrative positions in expanding the realm under direct Company control. The dynamic, unprecedented extension of Company territorial rule from 1790 to 1819 transformed the officer corps in India from an uncertain and sometimes inglorious cadre into the essential arm of British government in the sub-continent. Only later, after the upheaval of the Mutiny-Rebellion of 1857–9, were senior administrative positions assigned to a civil service differentiated from the officer corps.

The experience of regular officers might be located somewhere between these extremes. Political influence was important, but appointments to senior commands also reflected extensive monitoring of officers' capabilities within the high command, which encompassed the commander-in-chief and, until 1810, the king. In addition, the role of the regular army expanded in this period as further colonies were acquired and the empire grew. Some senior officers became involved in governing colonies on the lines experienced far more widely by the East India Company officer corps. This may have been resented by radical critics of the establishment, but it provided further evidence of the governing class' reliance on the officer corps' general competence. From training and managing battalions to organising campaigns and battles, and in responding to and shaping the distinctive societies in which it operated, the officer corps performed effectively during the wars of 1793–1815.

---

53 Ibid., pp. 367–9.

Appendix A: Middle-Rank Officers at Waterloo

Table 3.1   Majors and lieutenant-colonels in battalion command roles
and not detached for staff duties

Total	77	of whom Lt-Cols	15
In the Peninsula	39 (+2)*		7 (+2)
Overseas but not in Peninsula	7 (+1)		3 (+1)
Overseas in 1790s or in Egypt in 1801	16 (+2)		7 (+2)
In Egypt in 1801	9 (+2)		6 (+2)
Reported involvement in battle	15 (+2)		
Casualties at Waterloo			
wounded	40		7
killed	6		3

No prior experience was reported for five of the fifteen Lt-Cols.

Date of commission as Lt-Col	
1810 or earlier	5
1811–12 inclusive	6
1813–14	4

In addition, nineteen majors were on the staff, of whom five were wounded and two killed. At least eleven of them served in the Peninsula; no information on early careers of eight. Twenty-three Lt-Cols were on the staff, of whom five were wounded and one was killed. Of the twenty-three, at least sixteen had served in the Peninsula and two had other, pre-1808 overseas service. Eight of the twenty-three held the KCB by Waterloo.

119 officers in these two ranks: nine killed, fifty wounded

* No biographical background was provided for five Lt-Cols. The *ODNB* was used to add basic details for three of them – Sir Andrew Barnard, John Cameron and William Elphinstone. Further information is needed on Charles Morice and Sir Robert Macara, both killed.

Source: Charles Dalton, *The Waterloo Roll Call* (London: Arms and Armour Press, 1971 reprint of 1904 edn).

Appendix B: Officers in the Bengal Army

Table 3.2   Sample of cadets who joined the Bengal Army, 1770–1815

The data report their careers to 1838.
Sample of officers whose surname began with C:

Total	retired	died	died in India	at sea/ on passage	elsewhere in East	in duels	in action
284	20	160	133	14	4	2	7

For these cadets, there was a 55 per cent chance of dying in India, the East or in transit.

Total	reached rank of Lt-Col	Major	brevet Major by 1838
284	44	70	6

Retirement came for 75 per cent of retirees after twenty years or more of service; for 65 per cent it was after twenty-five years. Promotion was therefore slow.

Table 3.3   Lieutenant-colonels in in the Bengal Army to 1820

Total attaining rank	died	died in India/ East	at sea/ on passage	retired/ removed	invalided
353	150	133	17	84	2

Only three Lt-Cols are recorded as having been killed in action.
Even for Lt-Cols, there was a 42 per cent chance of dying in India, the East or in transit.

Table 3.4   Cadets who joined the Bengal Army in 1807

Total attaining rank	resigned/ retired/ removed	dead	Major (by 1837)	Lt-Colonel
138	20	63	22	2

Of promotions to major, twenty occurred in 1832 or later, after twenty-five or more years' service.

Source: Messrs. Dodwell and Miles (eds), *Alphabetical List of the Officers of the Bengal Army* (London: Longman, Orme, Brown, 1838) reprinted in 3 vols as *Alphabetical List of Officers of the Bengal Army* (Uckfield: Naval and Military Press, 2007; reprint of 1838 edn), pp. 56–70 and *passim*.

4

Stamford Standoff

Honour, Status and Rivalry
in the Georgian Military

Matthew McCormack

Anyone who has studied military history will be familiar with soldiers' acute sensitivity to questions of precedence and honour. Most military historians take this for granted, although there is a growing appreciation that this type of phenomenon in the military is worthy of study, since institutional cultures can have a crucial operational significance.[1] Armies are hierarchical organisations wherein formal rank is only achieved at great personal cost – be it by purchase, qualification or service – and where individual reputations are hard won and easily lost. These organisations have usually been all-male, and questions of status in the military have commonly been articulated in terms of masculine honour, creating further potential for rivalry and offence.[2] Christopher Duffy has noted that the officers of European armies in the eighteenth century were particularly 'rancorous and touchy'.[3] In the Georgian military, disputes between officers over apparently trivial matters routinely escalated into exchanges of insults, blows and challenges to duel. Recourse was made with surprising frequency to the formal military authorities to resolve disputes, whether by courts martial[4] or via the personal intervention of senior officers, the Secretary at War or even the king himself.

---

1 Jeremy Black, *Rethinking Military History* (Abingdon: Routledge, 2004), p. 55.
2 David Morgan, 'Theater of War: Combat, the Military and Masculinities', in *Theorizing Masculinities*, ed. by Harry Brod and Michael Kaufman (Thousand Oaks, CA: Sage, 1994), pp. 165–82.
3 Christopher Duffy, *The Military Experience in the Age of Reason* (London: Routledge, 1987), p. 76.
4 Arthur Gilbert, 'Law and Honour among Eighteenth-Century British Army Officers', *The Historical Journal*, 19.1 (1976), pp. 75–87.

Nowhere was this truer than in England's militia. Reformed in 1757 as a parallel establishment to the regular army, it was officered by civilians who qualified by virtue of their social rank and landed property, and who thus provided 'natural' leaders to the civilian men who were balloted to serve in the county regiments. This equation of social with military rank may have simplified relations between militia officers – 'Sir *John* or Sir *Thomas* must not be commanded by Squire *any thing*' – but there was potential for tension when militia and regular officers came into contact with each another. Militia officers were at once aware of their social superiority to their regular counterparts, and were sensitive to accusations of military inferiority. As a correspondent to the *Gentleman's Magazine* complained: 'The present method taken for chusing the officers, and ascertaining their rank, has no regard to the necessary qualifications or abilities of the person to be commissioned.'[5] In general, the militia was from the outset vulnerable to comparison with the regulars. Although they were dressed and armed alike, the militia were by definition part-timers who were usually inexperienced in combat, and who often relied on NCOs from the regulars to conduct their training. The army slang terms 'parish soldier' and 'tame army' give a flavour of the standing in which the militia was held by the rank and file in the army,[6] and, arguably, the feeling was mutual.

Historians of the Georgian militia have had little to say about its relationship with the regular army. Although J. R. Western explains how the militia was born out of political hostility to the 'standing army', he does not consider whether this manifested itself in practice after 1757: he notes one incident at Stowmarket barracks in 1801 where a 'big fight' took place between regulars and militia.[7] Stephen Conway argues that, in the camps of the American War, 'contact between officers of the various militia and regular units was both frequent and largely amicable'.[8] A few examples will suffice to illustrate that this was not always the case. The *Morning Chronicle* reported that 'there was but little union between the regulars and militia' encamped near Portsmouth in 1778: the Cornish Militia and the 13th Regiment 'heartily, I believe, hated each other'.[9] Meanwhile, at Coxheath, General Keppel acquired a reputation for hostility towards militia officers. He objected to

---

5 *Gentleman's Magazine*, XXX, February 1760, p. 86.
6 Francis Grose, *A Classical Dictionary of the Vulgar Tongue* (London: S. Hooper, 1785), cols. PAW, TAP.
7 J. R. Western, *The English Militia in the Eighteenth Century: The Story of a Political Issue 1660–1802* (London: Routledge, 1965), p. 428.
8 Stephen Conway, *The British Isles and the War of American Independence* (Oxford: Oxford University Press, 2000), p. 193.
9 *Morning Chronicle*, 28 October 1778.

their habit of taking absence without leave, and clamped down upon it by means of courts martial and ordering them to their tents. When Mr Joliffe, an officer in the Hampshire Militia and an MP, complained about the quality of the men's bread, Keppel's reply was so high-handed that 'he immediately threw up his commission, ordered a chaise and four, and drove to town'. 'If Government was anxiously desirous of disgusting the militia,' mused the *Gazetteer*, 'they could not fix on any Lieutenant-General better calculated for that service.'[10]

This antipathy continued into the French Wars. A private letter of October 1801 reported a 'terrible fray' at Colchester, when 'some of the 29th Regt who being intoxicated chose to abuse the Militia in the Barracks of 2d York': 'their men coming to extreme disorder & blood must have been shed but unexpected & most fortunate General Balfour arrived in the midst of this Business, ordered every Man to keep in his Quarters & the 29th to d'bark early next Morning'.[11] Unfortunately, bloodshed was not always avoided. On Christmas Eve 1808, some militiamen of the North Lincolns were drinking in a public house in Colchester when a party of the 4th Regiment of Foot arrived. The regulars demanded their place by the fire, which was granted them, and then proceeded to abuse the militiamen as 'feather-bed soldiers'. One of the regulars, Richard Costello, then became violent and struck William Wrach with a poker. He died from a fractured skull, and Costello and two other soldiers were tried at the Essex Assizes, receiving death sentences that were later respited.[12] The tragic outcome of this dispute sets it apart, but the dispute itself revolved around familiar issues of precedence and very gendered evaluations of what constituted a soldier.

This chapter will explore relations between the army and militia, and in particular their officers, by focusing on one regiment, the Lincolnshire Militia. Disputes of this kind appear to have dogged the regiment in its early years. In particular, it was involved in two related incidents in 1761 where minor questions of decorum escalated into major disputes that drew in the War Office and the king. By focusing on these two affairs in detail, this chapter will think about interpersonal conduct in the military more widely. Whilst Arthur Gilbert is right to characterise the Georgian officer corps as 'an exclusive club with its own distinctive values',[13] I will show how

---

10 *Morning Post and Daily Advertiser*, 29 June 1778; *Gazetteer and New Daily Advertiser*, 29 September 1778.

11 Dorset History Centre, Dorchester, D29/F20F, Surtees to Fanny Hoare, 24 October 1801.

12 *The Morning Chronicle*, 18 March 1809; *The Bury and Norwich Post*, 22 March 1809. I am grateful to Joseph Cozens for this reference.

13 Gilbert, 'Law and Honour', p. 75.

military discourse and honour codes were also indebted to civilian codes such as politeness, gentility and sensibility – and how their slightly different inflections on the parts of the army and militia could lead to conflict between these two branches of the service.

Stamford, April 1761

T HE CREATORS OF THE MILITIA anticipated that the social rank of its officers could create 'jealousy and complications' between regiments, and so devised clear rules of precedence.[14] There remained confusion, however, about relations within regiments and with the regulars. Lincolnshire was one of the first counties to comply with the Militia Act, but was beset by conflicts of precedence from the off. Given the size of the county, the Lord Lieutenant divided the regiment in two. Sir John Cust was Colonel of the Southern Battalion: an MP for Grantham and later Speaker of the House of Commons, he had been an active supporter of the Militia Bill in parliament.[15] He was anxious to resolve which battalion should be shown favour, since 'many Difficulties were likely to arise at their meeting'.[16] In May 1760 he wrote to the Secretary at War for clarification, who judged that the Earl of Scarborough's Northern Battalion would take precedence due to the earlier date of his commission. Relations between the two battalions remained tense. After being stationed in Manchester, the regiment was ordered to return to the county for the winter. Cust raced the Southern Battalion back in order to obtain quarters at Lincoln, 'the only good Town in the County'. Scarborough upbraided Cust for this 'ungenteell' action and, following an acrimonious correspondence, the South Lincolns were eventually quartered in Stamford instead.[17]

---

14 From September 1759, regiments would take precedence according to their arrival in camp or garrison; from June 1760, it was decided that regiments would draw lots when serving together; and from June 1778, they would rank according to an annual ballot. W. Y. Baldry, 'Order of Precedence of Militia Regiments', *Journal of the Society of Army Historical Research*, 15 (1936), p. 5.

15 Lewis Namier, 'Cust, Sir John, 3rd Bt. (1718–70), of Belton, Lincs', *The House of Commons 1754–1790*, 3 vols, ed. by Namier & Brooke (London: HMSO, 1964), 3, pp. 290–1. Cust attended a meeting of friends of the Militia Bill on 7 April 1759: Western, *English Militia*, appendix C.

16 *Records of the Cust Family. Series III. Sir John Cust, Third Baronet*, ed. by Lionel Cust (London: Mitchell, Hughes & Clarke, 1927), p. 303, John Cust and Captain Vyner to Lord Barrington, 10 May 1760.

17 *Records of the Cust Family*, pp. 306–7, Earl of Scarborough to John Cust, n.d. [October 1761].

It was at Stamford that the South Lincolns were involved in a dispute with the 72nd Regiment, known as the Duke of Richmond's. Such a dispute may well have been amplified by the fact that they were stationed in their own county: militia regiments were more usually stationed away from home in wartime, so they may have felt more hostile to outside soldiers when on home territory.[18] We know about the incident in detail because the War Office created a letter book copying all sides of the subsequent correspondence between the Secretary at War Charles Townshend and the various protagonists. The existence of this letter book suggests that the War Office considered the dispute to be significant: as the militia was in its early days, it was an indication of likely further disputes, and a precedent for how to resolve them.[19] In addition, further letters in the Cust papers and in Lincolnshire Archives mean that over forty letters survive that relate to the affair. It was not reported in the press at the time, although two of Townshend's letters were widely reprinted after his death, as an example of how he was capable of handling 'a very delicate Occasion'.[20]

On 14 June 1761, the 72nd Foot marched towards Stamford, following a route prescribed by the War Office from their winter quarters in Yorkshire to a new posting on the south coast. The First Division under Major Thomas Troughear marched straight into town, without acknowledging that the South Lincolns were already quartered there. Lieutenant-Colonel William Welby took umbrage at this, since it disregarded the convention that a body of troops entering a garrison should send an officer ahead to seek permission to do so. As he explained to Townshend: 'I thought I had a right as Commanding officer of the Garrison to have leave asked, before any Troops entered the Town; for I apprehend it is the rule of Discipline, and for the safety of the Garrison that those Ceremonies are always complied with.' Welby chose to overlook this, and ordered that they be granted all the civilities due to another regiment, including the parole and details of the town duty, and provided a sentry at Troughear's door and ordered the 'Centinels to rest [arms] to him'. Major Troughear sent his adjutant to explain that, 'he had no right to the Compliments paid him as being of a different Corps'. The Major himself then arrived, who insisted that, 'there was no sort of Connexion between us & them,' and that he would provide his own parole. As the Major left, he passed the sentry, who rested arms:

---

18 I am grateful to Stephen Conway for this observation.

19 TNA, WO43/404. WO43 comprises in-letters to the Secretary at War on a wide range of subjects, illustrating the variety of issues with which he had to deal. As most of these are bound in-letters only, the letter book is unusual.

20 *Gentleman's Magazine*, November 1767, pp. 758–9, Townshend to Major Troughear and Townshend to Lieut. Col. Welby, 12 June 1762.

'the Major told him not to do it to him, the Militia man told him it was the order, but he said he had no right to rest to him, unless he (the Sentry) had been a soldier, the man replied he *was* a soldier'.[21]

Welby saw this as 'a great Slight to the Corps, and the Militia in general' and so took the unusual step of posting sentries at the entrances to Stamford, 'to prevent any armed Troops entering the Town for the future without my knowledge and consent'. So when the pioneers of the Second Division tried to enter the town on 17 June without sending advance word, the militia sentries stopped them at the point of their bayonets.[22] The militia corporal in charge of the guard approached Captain Morris of the 72nd and asked that they send an officer to Welby, but Morris cursed the corporal and the militia, and replied that 'he would not be stoped by him, or anybody else'. The pioneers rushed forward and Morris attempted to brush away a sentry's bayonet with his espontoon, which grazed the sentry and would have stabbed him had it not hit his cartridge box. At length, Morris went to see Welby, where he explained that his regiment never had anything to do with the militia. By way of justification, he claimed that George II had once explained to Richmond that, 'they were the King's soldiers, & the Militia the Country's'. Welby replied that since they both received the king's pay, the militia 'were to be treated as much Soldiers as the Regulars'.[23] As they could not come to an agreement on this point, Welby resolved to write to the War Office.

Thus began a bad tempered correspondence that would preoccupy the Secretary at War for the following two months. Townshend wrote to Troughear, expressing that he was 'very seriously concern'd to find that any distinctions have been made between the different Corps of His Majesty's Army'. He enclosed a copy of Welby's account and invited the Major to comment upon it.[24] Troughear denied that he had made any remarks to the sentry and insisted that the militia had acted aggressively: Morris 'saw the Centinels present their Bayonets to the breasts of the Pioneers & refuse them admission into the town, without giving any reason'. But he made no attempt to disown the remarks that he or Morris had made about the respective positions of the army and militia, and indeed insisted that 'no officer who bears the King's Commission, should be under the orders of those who have not the King's Commission'. He furthermore lodged a complaint about Welby's attempt to halt the 72nd regiment, given that they were marching

---

21 TNA, WO43/404, fol. 4, Welby to Townshend, 4 May 1761. My emphasis.
22 TNA, WO43/404, fol. 10, Troughear to Townshend, 16 May 1761.
23 TNA, WO43/404, fol. 5, Welby to Townshend, 4 May 1761.
24 TNA, WO43/404, fol. 6, Townshend to Troughear, 12 May 1761.

a route prescribed by the War Office.[25] Townshend's reply suggests that he took exception both to Troughear's tone and his claims.[26] It furthermore emerged over the course of the investigation that the 72nd Regiment had form in this regard, since complaints about their behaviour towards the militias of Leicestershire and Essex came to light.[27]

Meanwhile, Welby wrote to Sir John Cust, detailing his view of the affair and alleging that the regulars had 'behaved unbecomingly'. Cust reassured Welby that he approved of his conduct, and proceeded to draft a letter for Welby to send to Townshend, wherein he pressed the militia's claims:

> I beg leave to assure you, Sir, I have made it my particular study to cultivate Harmony and a good understanding between the two Corps, being sensible how very prejudicial any dispute must be to His Majesty's Service, I should not do justice to the Gentlemen of the army, if I did not take this opportunity of acknowledging that they have uniformly shown the same good disposition, and that I have been treated with the greatest Politeness and Civility from the officers of the several Corps we have met, till Major Troughear came into Stamford with the first Division of the 72nd Regiment.

Rather theatrically, he begged the Secretary at War to point out where he had been at fault: 'It is very natural for a gentleman who has liv'd upon his Estates without making Arms his profession, but who has taken them up occasionally to shew his zeal for His Majesty's Family, person & government to fall into Mistakes.' He concluded by requesting that a special court martial be convened, composed of both militia and regular officers, to settle the case.[28] His request was not granted, and never could have been granted given that such a court would not have been possible under either the Articles of War or the Militia Act.

At length, Townshend sought to conclude the case by writing letters of censure to both Troughear and Welby on 12 June. In both cases he explained how he had reported the facts of the case to the king, and that the judgement therefore proceeded from him. Welby received the lighter censure: the king reaffirmed that he had a right to receive notice from an approaching regiment, and that he had a right 'to receive & pay those reciprocal marks of Civility & respect which in the course of Service usually pass'. On the other hand, Welby was informed that he had exceeded his duty in posting sentries and preventing the 72nd from entering an open town: 'the consequences

---

25 TNA, WO43/404, fols 8–12, Troughear to Townshend, 16 May 1761.
26 TNA, WO43/404, fols 13–14, Townshend to Troughear, 18 May 1761.
27 TNA, WO43/404, fols 51–2, Townshend to Morris, 27 June 1761.
28 TNA, WO43/404, fols 20–7, Welby to Townshend, 28 May 1761. The draft, which is identical, is dated 27 May: *Records of the Cust Family*, pp. 313–14.

of the measure you took might have been extensive, and very fatal to the Regiments concerned'.[29] Townshend clearly intended this to be the end to the matter, but Welby wrote further letters contesting the verdict and pressing his request for a court martial.[30] Furthermore, Cust took up Welby's case. In a series of letters he took great exception to the censure aimed at Welby, which he perceived 'as a douceur to the Army or a sort of salvo to their Honour'.[31] His persistence on this point clearly irritated the Secretary at War: his brother Peregrine encountered Townshend in London, where he 'flew into a very great passion' and claimed that the actions of the South Lincolns 'wou'd in his opinion be a means of putting an end to ye Militia in this Country'.[32] Peregrine had subsequently to smooth things over with Townshend by thanking him for the trouble they had given him.

The censure sent to Major Troughear was more comprehensive. The king judged that he acted contrary to the practice of the army in refusing to accept the South Lincolns' marks of civility. He furthermore expressed his 'entire disapprobation of all distinctions' made between the army and militia, contrary to 'that Equality and harmony in Service which is so much to be wished & cultivated, both upon the grounds of private satisfaction and of public utility'.[33] In contrast to the militia officer, the regular officer appears to have accepted the judgement. (The affair did not appear to do his career any harm, since he was shortly promoted to Lieutenant-Colonel and Deputy Governor of the Isle of Wight.[34]) Indeed, Townshend wrote to Welby reporting a conversation with Troughear, whereby he 'expressed to me in the strongest terms, his sense & conviction, of the impropriety of his conduct'.[35] This *mea culpa* helped to bring the matter to a close, since Welby expressed his satisfaction with it and hoped that it would 'effectually prevent all misunderstandings for the future' between the army and militia.[36] As we will now see, his optimism on this point was to be short lived.

29 TNA, WO43/404, fols 31–2, Townshend to Welby, 12 June 1761.

30 TNA, WO43/404, fols 35–6, 57–60, Welby to Townshend, 20 June 1761; Welby to Townshend, 29 June 1761.

31 *Records of the Cust Family*, p. 316, Cust to Townshend (draft).

32 *Records of the Cust Family*, p. 314, Peregrine Cust to Sir John Cust, 25 June 1761.

33 TNA, WO43/404, fols 33–4, Townshend to Troughear, 12 June 1761.

34 *St James's Chronicle*, 3 February 1763.

35 TNA, WO43/404 fols 47–8, Townshend to Welby, 24 June 1761.

36 TNA, WO43/404, fols 57–60, Welby to Townshend, 29 June 1761.

LINCOLN, DECEMBER 1761

LATER IN THE YEAR, the South Lincolns' other Lieutenant-Colonel, Philips Glover, was involved in a comparable dispute with regular soldiers at Lincoln. According to Welby, Philips Glover was known for his 'hasty temper and inconsiderate conduct'.[37] His correspondence with Cust reveals disputes with other militiamen and a quarrel over a bet.[38] Indeed, when the Lincolns had been stationed at Manchester the previous year, he been involved in a petty dispute in a theatre that had got out of hand. An apothecary named Jackson struck him on the back in jest, but Glover objected in the strongest terms so a duel with swords was arranged. Glover ran him through and killed him, for which he was tried at the assizes, but was discharged due to lack of evidence.[39] Glover found himself on trial again in February 1762, this time a general court martial for 'having behaved in a Manner unbecoming an Officer and a Gentleman'. The published *Proceedings* provide a detailed account of an incident that again sheds light on the relationship between the army and militia.

On Christmas Eve 1761, Philips Glover was lodging at the Angel Inn in Lincoln. The Marines had been recruiting in the town, and their recruiting sergeant had a new recruit named Coupland with him. A militiaman from the South Lincolns recognised the recruit as a deserter from his company and clapped his hand on his shoulder declaring, 'You are my prisoner.' They could not find any militia officers to confirm this – they were 'gone out a Sporting' – so they took Coupland to Captain James Gardiner of the Marines. Later that day, Gardiner, Glover and various other gentlemen were at the Angel Inn, where the dispute apparently occurred. Lieutenant Edward Willes of the South Lincolns suggested that the deserter be taken to a Justice of the Peace so that the Corporal who enlisted him could swear to him being a deserter. Gardiner objected to this: the civilian authorities handled militia recruiting, and to do so would have been to forfeit his recruit, so he insisted that he remain under military authority. Glover said that he would write to the War Office, and Gardiner replied that he would not give up the prisoner until their answer was received. It was at this point that Glover uttered the words that prompted Gardiner to request a court martial: 'By God, he would not be bilked by him or any Regular.'[40]

---

37 *Records of the Cust Family*, p. 320, Welby to Cust, 19 January 1762.
38 *Records of the Cust Family*, pp. 310–12, 321.
39 J. Conway Walter, *Records Historical and Antiquarian, of Parishes around Horncastle* (Horncastle: W. K. Morton, 1904), pp. 244; *The London Chronicle*, 30 August 1760.
40 *Proceedings of a General Court-Martial, upon the Trial of Lieutenant-Colonel Glover, of*

The language that Glover used, and the tone that he employed, was exhaustively examined by the court martial. The term 'bilk', meaning to defraud or swindle, was deemed language 'which ought not to pass between one Officer and another'. He was asked whether he had also used the expressions, 'That he would shew the Regulars what their duty was' and 'That he would trust no Regular', both of which he denied.[41] Willes deposed that Glover 'seemed rather warm' and Gardiner was 'cool' at the point at which the prisoner was delivered to them. Other witnesses were questioned regarding Glover's tone. Reverend Moreton deposed 'That Lieutenant Colonel Glover has not the softest Manner of expressing himself; but at the Time spoke with more than his ordinary Vehemence.' And Gardiner added that Glover, 'puts a greater Stress upon his Words, than other People do'.[42]

The most revealing aspect of the trial was the publication of letters that had passed between Glover and Gardiner. Both were aware that these letters would become matters of public record: indeed, Gardiner published them in advance of the trial, which Glover alleged was an attempt to prejudice its outcome. In the first letter, Gardiner insisted that he would only release the prisoner on production of sufficient proof. Glover replied that he could provide ten men to swear to that effect, whereupon Gardiner claimed that Glover did not understand 'what sufficient Military Proof of a Deserter is', namely his attestation. He then launched into a diatribe about the respective mastery of military matters by army and militia officers:

> In the Army, superior Rank implies superior Knowledge of Discipline, because it supposes superior Experience: but in the Militia, where Officers Rank merely from their Fortune, and where, from the Lieutenant Colonel to the Ensign, the Experience is all equal, I flatter myself common Candour will at least allow me to have as true and just an Idea of Military Discipline, as any Field Officer in your Service, who themselves have been instructed in what they know of it by Officers of my Rank, or inferior to it.[43]

Glover replied: 'I can assure you, we are obliged to no Regulars for our Knowledge in Military Affairs; and what we have acquired by constant Application and Reading, the latter of which many in your Rank have not in their Power to do.'[44] In order to emphasise his point that the army are capable of making mistakes regarding military conduct, he referred the regular to

---

the South Battalion of Lincolnshire Militia. By Virtue of His Majesty's Special Warrant, bearing the date the 16th February 1762 (London, 1762), pp. 22–5, 7–8.

41 Ibid., pp. 8, 11.

42 Ibid., p. 47.

43 Ibid., pp. 28–9.

44 Ibid., p. 31.

Troughear's acknowledgement of fault in the Stamford affair: this was also offered to the court martial, but was deemed inadmissible.

After five days of trial, the court found the militiaman 'guilty of having used some Expressions towards Captain Richard Gardiner not strictly becoming an Officer, which appear to have proceeded from Warmth, occasioned in Part by some Provocation on the part of Captain Gardiner'. Glover was ordered to receive a reprimand from his colonel. Ironically, a later ruling from the Judge-Advocate's office revealed that Gardiner was not answerable to a court martial, as he was not actually an officer at the time of the offence. The king nevertheless expressed his disapprobation at his making 'odious and unjustifiable Distinction between the Militia and his Majesty's other Regiments', and the Judge-Advocate trusted that this royal admonition was punishment enough.[45]

Honour, Status and Rivalry

THESE TWO CASES suggest the importance of interpersonal conduct in the Georgian military. By studying disputes that occurred when things went wrong, the historian can get an insight into the normal expectations of civility, precedence and honour that structured everyday interactions in the military. These disputes also show the sheer amount of time and effort that was expended on these matters by senior officers and the military authorities, suggesting how seriously they were taken. As we conclude this chapter with reflections on the nature of these disputes and what they tell us about the culture of the military, it is first worth considering the mechanisms that were used to resolve them.

Primary among these mechanisms was the court martial. Although the court martial ostensibly existed to maintain military law and discipline, the vague charge of 'conduct unbecoming an officer and a gentleman' could cover a wide range of interpersonal issues. As Alan Gilbert has argued, the military's honour code could come into conflict with military law, so it was useful to have a charge flexible enough to encompass this.[46] What is striking about the court martial for 'conduct unbecoming' was that it was often requested by the protagonists themselves. As we have seen, Gardiner was granted one, and Welby was probably only refused because of his unusual request about how it should be composed. There is a parallel here with recent work on the civilian courts, which has shown how Georgians 'used'

---

45 Ibid., p. 69.
46 Gilbert, 'Law and Honour', pp. 76, 78.

the law to their own ends. Robert Shoemaker has suggested that Londoners had recourse to the courts to resolve public insults, although in the period when this was declining in the civilian sphere it showed no sign of doing so in the military.[47] It might seem surprising that soldiers should wish to do this, given the court martial's rather negative historical reputation for the apparent arbitrariness of its verdicts and brutality of its punishments. But, as we saw in the Glover–Gardiner dispute, the court took its time to hear evidence from a number of witnesses, and the punishments that it delivered were 'honour' punishments – reprimand from superiors and royal admonition – that arguably befitted the charges. The prospect of being tried by one's peers was attractive to soldiers, and especially so in the case of honour disputes. On the other hand, there appears to have been a wider public perception that soldiers were too quick to go down this route. One commentator on the Glover–Gardiner case suggested that it 'affords a caution to officers, not to be too precipitate in demanding courts-martial upon every frivolous altercation, the issue of which seldom redounds to the honour of either party'.[48]

Nevertheless, the court martial remained a useful means of resolving honour disputes between military men. This was particularly the case when a dispute was in danger of escalating into a duel, which was forbidden under the Articles of War: a court martial for 'conduct unbecoming' was a useful way of heading this off. Duelling is of course highly relevant to issues of masculine honour: it is a large subject in its own right, although some points are worth making here. Gender scholars have demonstrated how the duel was central to elite male notions of honour, as a means of demonstrating one's refinement and courage.[49] Soldiers were disproportionately given to duelling, comprising around a third of all duellists in the mid-century and more towards its end.[50] This was an aspect of elite masculinity that was peculiarly accessible to military men, so their willingness to duel was in a sense socially aspirational. Militia officers may have felt under even more pressure than their regular counterparts to go down the duelling route – as Phillips Glover did in Manchester – in order to prove their soldierly credentials. One prominent gentleman of the 1760s famous for duelling was the radical politician John Wilkes: he was a Lieutenant-Colonel in the Buckinghamshire Militia, an organisation that reinforced his claims to being a patriot and a

---

47 Robert Shoemaker, 'The Decline of Public Insult in London 1660–1800', *Past & Present*, 169 (2000), pp. 97–131.

48 *The Critical Review* 14, July 1762, p. 19.

49 Pieter Spierenburg (ed.), *Men and Violence: Gender, Honor and Rituals in Modern Europe and America* (Columbus, OH: Ohio State University Press, 1998).

50 Robert Shoemaker, 'The Taming of the Duel: Masculinity, Honour and Ritual Violence in London, 1660–1800', *The Historical Journal*, 45.3 (2002), p. 540.

classical warrior-citizen. By fighting duels, he was proving his martial *virtus* and virility, as well as making a claim to equality with the aristocrats he fought, by proving that he too possessed gracious courage and gentlemanly accomplishments.[51] The duel therefore serves to illustrate the overlap of military and civilian honour codes.

A further mechanism for resolving disputes was requesting the intercession of the Secretary at War. War Office in-letter books show that a significant proportion of their correspondence concerned disputes between individuals. In June 1778, Lord Hardwicke wrote to Viscount Barrington in anticipation of problems when the militia was called out, asking what the procedure for settling disputes would be, 'sh[oul]d any Regimental Differences arise, either ab[ou]t the Discipline of the Corps, or Behaviour of Officers to each other'.[52] Often these concerned issues of precedence: cases that hinged on dates of commission could usually be settled easily by the Secretary at War.[53] As the king's minister, he was also the conduit for issues that had to be resolved by the commander-in-chief himself: the king personally got involved in both of the disputes studied here, even though they concerned the minutiae of everyday military interaction. The king was anxious in both cases to intervene where a dispute served to disrupt the 'equality and harmony' between the branches of the service.[54]

Although Peregrine Cust sought an audience with Townshend in person, the Secretary at War usually conducted this kind of business by letter. The conventions of polite correspondence therefore structured the way in which these disputes were resolved. The deferential conventions of letter writing, with its sensitivity to questions of honour and personal sincerity, were peculiarly apt for these kinds of dispute. The polite letter also blurred the distinction between public and private correspondence: Sir John Cust begged Townshend that he might 'speak my mind freely to you upon this occasion, & to do it with more freedom I address myself to you in a private letter', but the tone and content of this letter were in fact little different to his others.[55] The personality and epistolary style of the Secretary at War therefore had a significant impact on how issues such as this were handled. Barrington's business-like approach contrasts with that of Townshend, who had a reputation for being difficult and emotional. His biographer Sir Lewis Namier notes that his letters had a habit of finding fault 'by putting forced

---

51 John Sainsbury, *John Wilkes: The Lives of a Libertine* (Aldershot: Ashgate, 2006), pp. 70–80.

52 TNA, WO1/1000, fol. 92, Hardwicke to Barrington, 11 June 1778.

53 TNA, WO1/1000, fol. 31, James Barker to Barrington, 6 October 1778.

54 TNA, WO43/404, fols 33–4, Townshend to Troughear, 12 June 1761.

55 TNA, WO43/404, fols 37–41, Cust to Townshend, 20 June 1761.

constructions on what the other has said'. This is certainly perceptible in some of his correspondence on the Stamford affair and may partly be to blame for why it subsequently got out of hand.[56]

More generally, the code of politeness informed military behaviour. Politeness had come into vogue at the beginning of the eighteenth century, with the aim of softening male manners, moderating behaviour and easing social interaction.[57] This might seem incompatible with the masculinity of the soldier, but Philip Carter has shown how even the 'man of war' was expected to embrace polite manners.[58] Indeed, given the formality of military manners and the importance in the army of such 'polite' practices as bodily comportment, fine dress and heterosexual gallantry, soldiers took to the culture of politeness in a big way, and it continued to be important in the regular army even after it was losing vogue in civilian society.[59] Disputes could therefore occur where behaviour was perceived to be impolite: Welby complained that the 72nd Regiment acted 'very contrary to [...] polite behaviour' when they entered Stamford.[60] And much of Glover's trial hinged on his failure to live up to the polite standards of military interaction, from his choice of words to the tone of his voice. 'Civility' was a hugely important standard in military life, and the Stamford affair fundamentally concerned the 72nd's failure to observe 'reciprocal marks of civility and respect', those rituals and courtesies that ensured the smooth running of military life.

Other aspects of civilian manners are perceptible in these disputes. The cult of 'sensibility' prized emotional expression and sincerity, and in the second half of the century it began to inform male manners, in part as an antidote to the potential falsity of politeness.[61] In contrast with the army, where politeness had such an enduring hold, I have argued elsewhere that the creation of the New Militia had been justified along sentimental lines, in terms of harnessing the patriotic and protective feelings of the male citizen.[62] It is perhaps significant, then, that it is in the correspondence of militia

---

56 Sir Lewis Namier and John Brooke, *Charles Townshend* (London: Macmillan, 1964), p. 3.

57 Lawrence Klein, 'Politeness and the Interpretation of the British Eighteenth Century', *The Historical Journal*, 45.4 (2002), pp. 869–98.

58 Philip Carter, *Men and the Emergence of Polite Society: Britain, 1660–1800* (Harlow: Longman, 2001), p. 75.

59 Matthew McCormack, 'Dance and Drill: Polite Accomplishments and Military Masculinities in Georgian Britain', *Cultural and Social History*, 8.3 (2011), pp. 315–30.

60 *Records of the Cust Family*, pp. 312, Welby to Cust, 19 April 1761.

61 G. J. Barker-Benfield, *The Culture of Sensibility: Sex and Society in Eighteenth-Century Britain* (Chicago: Chicago University Press, 1992).

62 Matthew McCormack, 'The New Militia: War, Politics and Gender in 1750s Britain', *Gender & History*, 19.3 (2007), pp. 483–500.

officers that we see regular recourse to the culture of feeling. Sir John Cust informed Townshend that Welby was 'excessively affected' by the censure in his letter: 'such a reproof must lie very heavy upon a Gentleman who is conscious of his own good intentions'.[63] His whole corps was apparently 'very sensibly affected' by the way Welby had been treated.[64] Militia officers often had recourse to the language of feeling when pursuing a complaint with the War Office. George Buck, Lieutenant-Colonel of the North Devonshire Militia, complained to Barrington that he had been wronged by his fellow officers: 'Thus situated, superseded, and calumniated, I cannot express, being conscious of innocence, of integrity of conduct, and of zeal for the service, nor can any one, but an officer of sensibility, under similar circumstances, conceive the anguish of my mind!'[65]

Finally, these disputes give us an insight into the identity of the soldier, and in particular the different ways in which the regular army and the militia perceived themselves and each other. The officers of the 72nd sought 'no connexion' with the militia since they did not regard them as proper soldiers: as 'the Country's' soldiers rather than the king's, who did not hold proper commissions, and therefore should not be obeyed nor shown marks of respect. The contempt between Gardiner and Glover was mutual. Glover was adamant that he would not be 'Bilked [...] by any Regular', a group of people he regarded as impoverished and illiterate. In the appendix to the printed *Proceedings*, the two antagonists took the opportunity further to explain and defend their conduct. Here, Glover revelled in the militia's self-identity as the constitutional force that patriotically defended Britain against invaders. He provoked Gardiner by characterising the job of the militia as defending liberty and property – 'the latter of which you can have no Idea of'.[66] This prompted a lengthy reply from Gardiner, in which he reflected upon the identity of the regular soldier:

> I must confess, I am no Man of Property, it is my Misfortune, not my Crime, that I am not; but there have been Officers who, with as little Property as I have, have fought nobly and gallantly for the Property of others; and though it never fell to my particular Duty to expose my Life at Home, for the Estates and Patrimonies of my Countrymen, [yet] I have ventured it in Action with our enemies Abroad [...] In regard to my Liberty, my Lord, I do from my Heart believe, that the Liberties of this Kingdom are as dear to the Soldiers of Great Britain, as to the Inhabitants of it.[67]

63 TNA, WO43/404, fols 37–41, Cust to Townshend, 20 June 1761.
64 *Records of the Cust Family*, p. 316.
65 TNA, WO1/1000, fol. 37, Buck to Barrington, 11 December 1778.
66 *Proceedings*, p. 32.
67 Ibid., p. 82.

While the critique of 'standing armies' would have it that regular soldiers were unpatriotic mercenaries and a danger to liberty, they did not appear to have imbibed this identity, and indeed saw themselves in quite the opposite light.[68]

In conclusion, then, it is hardly surprising that the Georgian army and militia had an antagonistic relationship. Set up as parallel establishments, they inevitably came into conflict in their day-to-day interactions. In a practical sense, they became rivals in recruiting, as we saw in the Glover–Gardiner case. The army was not permitted to recruit from the militia, and the army commonly complained that the militia ballot sapped their pool of recruits and that its system of paying 'substitutes' pushed up the cost of bounties. More pervasively, the creation of two identical hierarchies with identical ranks, but where officers qualified in different ways and were unsure about questions of precedence, complicated everyday encounters between the branches of the service. As we have seen, the army and militia had contrasting identities that were defined against one another, which could lead to mutual distrust and even contempt. It is certainly possible to detect a defensiveness on the part of militia officers regarding their military status and expertise, and on the part of the army regarding their political status and social standing.

When studying the values and manners of officers, it is important to consider the extent of overlap between the military and civilian spheres. The court martial charge of 'conduct unbecoming' shows how the standards expected of an officer were inseparable from those of a gentleman. But it is possible that officers from the regulars and the militia – who necessarily had different relationships with mainstream society – inflected social codes in subtly different ways. The regular army's commitment to a very formal model of polite masculinity, and the militia's readiness to embrace the new civilian vogue for male feeling, suggest that the antagonism between them could often be a comedy of manners. From the point of view of military history, inter-service rivalry is worth studying in its own right; but the case of the militia and the regular army in the mid-Georgian period also promises to shed light on the relationship between the military and society.

I would like to thank all the chapter authors and Rosi Carr for their help with this chapter. This research was funded by the AHRC.

---

68 As argued by Hannah Smith, 'The Army, Provincial Urban Communities and Loyalist Cultures in England, c. 1714–50', *Journal of Early Modern History*, 15 (2011), pp. 139–58.

Part 3

Discipline

5

'The Soldiers Murmured Much on Account of this Usage'

Military Justice and Negotiated Authority in the Eighteenth-Century British Army

William P. Tatum III

Authority in the eighteenth-century British Army was far from absolute. Instead, the practical bounds of military authority were the result of give-and-take interactions between officers and enlisted men. For example, amongst the many complaints of ill-treatment levelled against Lieutenant William Catherwood of the 66th, was that he had shortened the men's rations unfairly, to which the men of his company 'murmured much on account of this usage'. In response, Major William Coates, who commanded the regiment at the time, swiftly removed Catherwood from his post and installed a replacement, who restored the company's rations, ending the murmuring in the ranks. As this episode demonstrates, officers were sensitive to the thoughts and actions of their subordinates and responded to them, although they did not always do so in such a positive manner.[1]

This chapter will examine the spectrum of tactics employed by soldiers to exert influence upon their officers in the execution of military justice. These approaches ranged from outright protest to fulsome co-operation, with various forms of negotiation accounting for the majority of interactions which ended in mutually beneficial solutions to problems. The records generated by the military justice process provide an unparalleled source to explore these disputes and interactions between officers and men. While a growing number of soldiers' accounts have come to light over recent decades, few of these provide any penetrating commentary on their authors' relations with their officers.[2]

---

1 TNA, WO71/53, fols 67, 85, 119.
2 For example, Thomas Sullivan's narrative provides a visceral account of his feelings

Officers' diaries and correspondence tend to be similarly silent on the issue.[3] In contrast, the records generated by the military justice process preserve significant details of the complicated interactions through which soldiers and officers negotiated the bounds of military authority. Previous commentators have interpreted enlisted men as the hapless victims of brutal officers. In contrast, this chapter will analyse common soldiers as active agents in a system whose structure shaped their options in ways that differed significantly from their civilian labourer counterparts.[4]

PROTESTING MILITARY INJUSTICE

EXISTING SCHOLARSHIP on common soldiers' protests has focused narrowly on instances of mutiny and desertion, but taking a broader view to include forms that hitherto have been overlooked provides a more detailed understanding of how these pointed acts of resistance could lead to

---

towards military authority, but other accounts from individuals including Roger Lamb, William Todd, and John Robert Shaw remain largely silent on the issue. See: William Todd, *The Journal of Corporal William Todd 1745–1762*, ed. A. Cormack and A. Jones (Stroud: Sutton, 2001); John Robert Shaw, *An Autobiography of Thirty Years, 1777–1807*, ed. by O. Teagarden and J. L. Crabtree (Athens, OH: Ohio University Press, 1993); Roger Lamb, *A British Soldier's Story: Roger Lamb's Narrative of the American Revolution*, ed. D. N. Hagist (Baraboo, WI: Ballindalloch Press, 2004); Thomas Sullivan, *From Redcoat to Rebel: The Thomas Sullivan Journal*, ed. J. L. Boyle (Bowie, MD: Heritage Books, 1997).

3 Examples include John Peebles, *John Peebles American War: The Diary of a Scottish Grenadier, 1776–1782*, ed. I. D. Gruber (Mechanicsburg, PA: Stackpole, 1998); BL, ADD MSS 36592, Col. C. Whiteford Correspondence, 1738–1752; BL, ADD MSS 50260, Horsbrugh Papers, Vol. V, letter book of Major Horsbrugh.

4 Frey, Gilbert, and Steppler have essentially interpreted soldiers as hapless victims while Way has suggested that soldiers were equivalent to civilian labourers. Arthur N. Gilbert, 'Why Men Deserted from the Eighteenth-Century British Army', *Armed Forces & Society*, 6.4 (1980), pp. 553–67; Arthur N. Gilbert, 'The Regimental Courts Martial in the Eighteenth Century British Army', *Albion*, 8.1 (1976), pp. 50–66; G. A. Steppler, 'British Military Law, Discipline, and the Conduct of Regimental Courts Martial in the Later Eighteenth Century', *English Historical Review*, 102.405 (1987), pp. 859–86; Sylvia R. Frey, 'Courts and Cats: British Military Justice in the Eighteenth Century', *Military Affairs*, 43.1 (1979), pp. 5–11; Sylvia Frey, *The British Soldier in America: A Social History of Military Life in the Revolutionary Period* (Austin, TX: University of Texas Press, 1981); G. A. Steppler, 'The Common Soldier in the Reign of George III, 1763–1792', PhD dissertation (Oxford University, 1984); Peter Way, 'Rebellion of the Regulars: Working Soldiers and the Mutiny of 1763–1764', *The William and Mary Quarterly*, 3rd Series 57.4 (2000), pp. 761–92.

negotiation.[5] The concentration previously displayed in the historiography is understandable in light of its writers' use of the records of the highest military tribunals, the general courts martial, which are the most accessible. Military crimes were not very precisely defined during the period, and charges of mutiny and desertion were open to interpretation and uneven application by officers.[6] Officers applied criminal labels increasingly inconsistently at the system's lower levels. There is a need, therefore, for a more nuanced approach to explore protest from within the army's ranks.

As Colonel Lawrence J. Morris has observed, military justice systems exist to enforce discipline and maintain an army as 'an effective fighting force'.[7] This overall aim of maintaining social control meant that officers approached enlisted men's actions from the perspective of what was best for the army, largely failing to take offenders' intent into account. As a result, criminal labels recorded in primary sources cannot be taken at face value, since not all of the actions that officers viewed as resistance could be classed as protest (the latter requiring some degree of intent). For example, Arthur Gilbert has observed that out of 455 general courts martial desertion cases, approximately only a quarter gave any indication of the offender having planned his escape. The remaining three hundred cases were either unintentional desertions (men wandering off while drunk) or did not include an explanation.[8] Thus cases involving acts of resistance must be examined for signs that the perpetrator intended his infraction as some form of protest. For this reason, protest is not easily quantified.

Adding to the problem of perspective is the issue of precision. For most of the century, military crimes were not defined outright by any specific set of regulations or guides. The Articles of War made reference to the 'Custom of War', which one may presume was an oral tradition handed down by generations of officers that may have provided some guidance. Since officers

---

5 John Prebble, *Mutiny: Highland Regiments in Revolt, 1743–1804* (London: Secker and Warburg, 1975); Paul E. Kopperman, 'The Stoppages Mutiny of 1763', *The Western Pennsylvania Historical Magazine*, 69.3 (July 1986), pp. 241–54; Peter Way, 'Rebellion of the Regulars'; Arthur N. Gilbert, 'Why Men Deserted'; Sylvia Frey, *The British Soldier in America*; G. A. Steppler, 'The Common Soldier'.

6 For examples, see: *An Act for Punishing Mutiny and Desertion, and for the better Payment of the Army, and their Quarters* (London: John Baskett, 1718) and *Rules and Articles for the Better Government of Our Horse and Foot-Guards, and all other Our Land-Forces in Our Kingdoms of Great Britain and Ireland, and Dominions beyond the Seas* (London: John Baskett, 1718). See also Steppler, 'The Common Soldier', pp. 184–7 for a discussion of how officers applied criminal labels.

7 Col. Lawrence J. Morris, *Military Justice: A Guide to the Issues* (Oxford: Praeger, 2010), p. 3.

8 Gilbert, 'Why Men Deserted', pp. 561–3.

were left with the power of levying charges, the definition of any given crime lay with the prosecutor. Glenn Steppler has shown how officers' judgement played a crucial role in defining desertion in the First Regiment of Foot Guards, with some men being declared as deserters after a day's absence and others listed as merely absent without leave after being gone for months.[9] In the case of ten men of General Wolfe's regiment of Marines charged with mutiny in 1742, the officers sitting in judgement disagreed with the perspective of the lieutenant levying the charges. The court found the men innocent of mutiny, but convicted them of disobedience of orders, a lesser charge often tried by regimental courts martial or dealt with through summary justice.[10] Table 5.1 demonstrates the issue of the complexities of defining crimes, taken from orders for summary justice given by the military governors of Gibraltar between 1727 and 1745.[11] In each case, the governor stated the actual infraction then threatened any offenders with punishment for disobedience of orders. The variety of offences captured under this heading demonstrates the challenges of using sources that record the charge but do not provide clear details of the actual criminal act.

The structural complexities of the military justice process compounded the problems created by contemporary military criminal nomenclature. Like the civilian criminal justice system, martial law consisted of several stages of adjudication, which can be reduced to three principal levels: summary justice, regimental courts martial and general courts martial. These divisions were intended to reflect the seriousness of the infraction, summary justice being used to deal with minor, everyday offences, while general courts martial were reserved for capital crimes.[12] The extent of personal interpretation regarding charges meant that the same offender could be tried at any of the three levels for one act, depending on how an officer levying charges perceived the infraction, as seen in the example of the First Regiment of Foot Guards noted above. This issue is complicated by the fact that each of the three levels generated very different styles of data. General courts martial proceedings provide the most detailed accounts of enlisted men's actions (albeit through the lens of the officers' perspective) and also survive in the greatest amount.[13] Regimental courts martial proceedings have not been preserved to the

---

9 Steppler, 'The Common Soldier', pp. 184–7.

10 TNA, WO71/37, fols 66–9.

11 NAS, GD21/1/625, Orderly Book of Archibald Cunninghame, General Orders Gibraltar. Cunninghame's orderly book preserves 216 disciplinary orders in total, though they do not all pertain to summary justice.

12 For more information on the military justice process and the court system, see: Steppler, 'British Military Law' and Gilbert, 'The Regimental Court Martial'.

13 Trial proceedings including witness testimony survive in TNA WO71.

Table 5.1   Varieties of actions covered by disobedience of orders charges at Gibraltar, 1727–45

Offending Action	Frequency
Sentries not relaying 'All is Well'	1
Corporals reminding sentries of their orders	2
Corporals not relieving sentries at sentry boxes and allowing boxes to be dirty	1
Soldiers switching guard shifts with each other	1
Stealing eggs from partridge nests and meddling with young partridges	4
Cutting grass on the hill	1
Renting quarters to soldiers and camp followers of Colonel Hought's regiment	1
Not returning before the Southport Gate was shut	1
Sentries refusing to obey orders from non-commissioned officers of the guard	1
Serving as porters	5
Assaulting the executioner	2
NCOs not confining men whom they witnessed assaulting the executioner	2
Firing muskets without permission	1
Disobeying orders of the hospital director	1
Striking and insulting engineers	1
Not killing dogs	2
Swimming in the sea at places other than Ragged Staff	1
Sailors and soldiers of General Kirk's regiment being in town at night without passes	1
Soldiers visiting and conversing with sick sailors	1
Visiting the Spanish church	1
Harassing witness from trial of General Fuller's servant	1
Working without permission	1
Leaving stones in sentry boxes	1
Corporals not confining soldiers who left stones in sentry boxes	1
Corporals not relieving sentries every two hours	1
Total	36

Source: NAS GD21/1/625, Orderly Book of Archibald Cunninghame, General Orders Gibraltar.

same degree, nor do they reflect an amount of detail comparable to their higher counterparts.[14] The best sources on summary justice are orders issued by commanding officers and recorded in orderly books. These directives, however, do not tell us how often soldiers committed offences or why. As a result, quantifying protest can only be impressionist.

Despite these challenges, several important points can be asserted. First and foremost, soldiers' acts of protest fell along a continuum ranging from relatively innocuous complaints to massive riotous mutinies. Second, these tactics demonstrate patterns distinguishing acts seemingly designed to directly confront military authority from others intended as an indirect or passive means of engaging with officers. Finally, protests demonstrate a division on the issue of ultimate goals, with some soldiers intending to bring their officers to the negotiating table while others sought an immediate solution to their problems. This multiplicity of strategies and goals demonstrates that, in the minds of some common soldiers, military authority was far from total.

Protest from the ranks took varying forms in the eighteenth-century British Army and, in some cases, followed a clear arc of escalation when officers failed to address a grievance. The case of the ten men of General Wolfe's regiment of Marines mentioned above provides an instructive example. The marines stood accused of mutiny for refusing to do duty in the fleet until their sea pay, which was two years in arrears, was given to them. In their lengthy defence, the purported mutineers offered a detailed account of the courses they had pursued to gain redress beginning with a verbal airing of their concerns to Captain Robert Shafto, the regiment's paymaster, who promised to pay them. The soldiers then sent written petitions requesting relief to their colonel and to the Secretary at War, neither of which were answered. Some of the marines engaged in additional acts of resistance at the time of their arrest. Private Thomas Clarke 'flung down his hat in an insolent manner' when refusing to go on board the transport, while Private Thomas Priggs threatened to write to the Secretary at War to have one

---

14 For a typical example, see 'Court martial July 17th 1744', BL, ADD MSS 36592, Col. C. Whiteford Correspondence, 1738–1752. This chapter draws on abstracts of trials held in regiments on the Irish Establishment from 1774 to 1778. Records survive for the 1st, 2nd, 3rd and 4th Regiments of Horse; the 8th, 12th, 13th and 18th Regiments of Light Dragoons; the 9th Regiment of Dragoons, and the 3rd, 11th, 36th, 67th and 68th Regiments of Foot. These abstracts only include the date of the trial, the defendant's name, his rank, his crime, the sentence handed down by the court, and information on whether the sentence was executed, mitigated, or pardoned. No trial testimony has been preserved. See: House of Lords Record Office, HL/PO/JO/10/7/544.

officer cashiered, and behaved in a 'very insolent' manner.[15] Thus soldiers tended to begin with peaceful appeals and escalated to violence.

While unusual in the degree of detail that it reveals on the progression of protest, the case of Wolfe's marines is indicative of the variety of approaches soldiers used when confronting their officers. For example, fourteen men of Wills' regiment approached Lieutenant-Colonel Alexander Rose on 27 July 1724 to request their arrears of pay.[16] When faced with illegal deductions from their pay in 1768, soldiers of the Royal Irish Regiment elected a representative, Matross David Blakeney, to present their grievance to the officers.[17] When verbal action failed or was inappropriate due to distance, enlisted men turned to the written word to express their concerns and demands. A general court martial tried Private Daniel O'Neal of the Coldstream Guards for 'Delivering a petition to Lieut[nt]. general Cadogan highly Reflecting on Coll[o] Caesar' in 1715 – an example of protest that fell on deaf ears.[18] In 1737, John Railton sent petitions to the Secretary at War citing various infringements by his officers.[19] While we may never be able to account for the frequency of these styles of complaint, it is clear that enlisted men made attempts to seek redress in person or by letter as a first step in the protest process.

When verbal and written complaints failed, soldiers turned to more severe forms of remonstrance. These included disobedience of orders, insolence, and varying forms of violence. Table 5.2 shows that soldiers on the Irish Establishment between 1774 and 1778 embraced these strategies fairly frequently. As noted above, disobedience of orders was a catch-all charge, and several of these instances of insolence and violence were coupled with drunkenness. While general courts martial records shed more light on soldiers' motivations, highlighting instances of soldiers disobeying orders as a form of protest, they also emphasise the complicated role of alcohol. Corporal William Lees of the Royal Artillery was charged with disobedience of orders in 1753 after refusing to mount guard because his officer would not allow him to serve as a sergeant, an important step for corporals seeking promotion.[20] In November 1758, Sergeant Solomon Bush of the Maryland Provincial

---

15 TNA, WO71/37, fols 67–9. Priggs and Clarke were singled out for additional punishment due to their outbursts.

16 TNA, WO71/35, fol. 39.

17 Charles Lucas, *A Mirror for Courts-Martial: In which the Complaints, Trial, Sentence, and Punishment of David Blakeney, are represented and Examined with Candour* (London: D. Steele, 1768), pp. 14–17.

18 TNA, WO71/14, fol. 54.

19 Railton, *The Army's Regulator, or the British Monitor*, 2nd edn (London: E. Davis, 1738), p. 22.

20 TNA, WO71/41, fols 45–8.

Forces refused orders to be mustered, having not been paid for the previous ten months.[21] When refused release from the guard house at Albany, New York, in 1759, Private Peter McMartin cursed his colonel and was charged with mutiny. In his defence, he claimed to have been drunk at the time.[22] In July of the same year, after being beaten by his sergeant, Private Thomas Reid of the 17th hit the man, took his cane, and beat him with it until the cane broke. When brought up on mutiny charges, Reid claimed to have been under the influence of alcohol. Incidents like these marked the most extreme forms of protest.

Table 5.2   Incidence of disobedience of orders, insolence, and violence charges from Irish Regimental Courts Martial, 1774–8

Charge	Frequency
Disobedience of orders	59
Insolence	52
Abusing/Assaulting/Fighting/Striking/Quarrelling	41
Rioting	32
Total	184

Source: House of Lords Record Office, HL/PO/JO/10/7/544.

This spectrum of enlisted men's challenges to their officers can be separated into two rough groupings based on form. The strategies employed by Wolfe's marines represent the confrontational variety of protest, which loomed large in the historical record. Contemporary soldiers did not limit themselves to direct action, however, engaging in more indirect and passive forms of protest as well. First among these latter approaches were desertion and other forms of unauthorised absence, through which a soldier could escape an unpleasant situation, either temporarily or permanently. Defendants in a quarter of the general courts martial cases examined by Gilbert claimed to have deserted the army due to some unaddressed grievance. An extreme example comes from the testimony of Private William Costin of the Coldstream Guards, who was tried for desertion in 1716. He admitted to the charge and credited his crime to his captain's threat to flog him to death. The soldier 'therefore rather chose to be Shot' for desertion, a wish the court

---

21 TNA, WO71/67, fols 25–6.
22 Ibid., fols 149–51.

granted him.[23] Drunkenness followed a close second. As Paul Kopperman has discussed, alcohol abuse nearly reached pandemic levels in the ranks. Some of these men were certainly driven to drink as a means of coping with the stress of military life. As Gilbert has noted, over a quarter of the men tried for desertion during this period pleaded intoxication as their defence. Whether this was the truth or a convenient fiction behind which to conceal motives that were less likely to meet with sympathy from military judges is difficult to discern. Regardless of the reliability issues inherent in defendant testimony, such indirect protests were less likely to bring down the full force of the military justice system than the more extreme confrontational approaches discussed above.

Soldiers' protests also divided between those actions that were intended as a precursor to negotiation and those approaches designed to provide instant relief. Most of the strategies discussed above were aimed at the former, and often provided soldiers with a higher likelihood of having their demands met. Verbal complaints, petitions, and even disobedience of orders served little purpose other than to bring officers to the negotiating table, although not all approaches were so peaceful. The men of the 17th Regiment of Foot sent two letters to their lieutenant-colonel in the 1750s, threatening the officers of the corps with death if certain grievances were not resolved.[24] While these threatening dispatches contained overtures of violence, most attempts at opening dialogues with officers did not involve the use of force. Since the Articles of War and the Mutiny Act left no doubt that assaulting a superior officer was a capital crime, one can only conclude that those soldiers who engaged in such behaviour were seeking immediate relief of their grievance, having been pushed past the point of negotiation. Likewise, those men who deserted with no intention to ever return were electing to opt out of the negotiation cycle. While deserters stood a respectable chance of being forgiven, as will be seen below, running away from the army was still a risky business and opened a soldier to the same variety of severe consequences that accompanied an assault upon a superior. The disruptions caused by these more extreme forms of direct and indirect protest on the daily life of the army, as well as the stiff punishments meted out by officers through the military justice system, naturally channelled soldiers' actions towards negotiation as a primary means of resolving grievances.

---

23 TNA, WO 71/14, fols 111–13.
24 TNA, WO71/67, fols 164–5. The letter quoted in this trial is similar to civilian letters discussed in E. P. Thompson, 'The Crime of Anonymity' in *Albion's Fatal Tree: Crime and Society in Eighteenth-Century England*, ed. by D. Hay (New York: Pantheon, 1975), pp. 255–308.

Co-operating with the System

Just as some soldiers chose to challenge military authority in order to resolve their grievances, others chose to ally themselves with their officers. Co-operation generated dividends for both enlisted men and officers. Soldiers could ingratiate themselves with their commanders, which might result in preferential treatment, advancement in rank, and forgiveness for disciplinary infractions. In so doing, enlisted men made themselves complicit in the decisions and policies of the military authorities, increasing their investment in the status quo. Co-operation could also differentiate types of soldiers. For example, those men who viewed soldiering as their career could be relied upon to execute their duty with vigour and efficiency to further distinguish themselves.[25] Those soldiers who co-operated less could be singled out as apathetic or as individuals who sought to use the system for their own advantage.

The military justice system created numerous opportunities for enlisted men to aid their officers and gain favour. The justice process itself was long and involved, requiring significant amounts of time, energy and manpower that often fell on the shoulders of the rank and file. Three of the most basic and essential duties assigned to common soldiers were serving as escorts to the provost marshal or his deputies, policing and apprehending their misbehaving comrades, and serving as witnesses at trials. Examining these duties provides a means of charting positive engagement in military justice by soldiers and the impact they could have on their superiors' operations.

Provost marshals and their deputies constituted the only police forces in the eighteenth-century British Army, though they seldom appeared anywhere in force. For example, Gibraltar mustered a single provost marshal and a garrison that numbered in the thousands.[26] To offset these ratios, commanding officers frequently assigned detachments of soldiers to aid provost marshals in patrolling military posts and the perimeters of armies in the field, and in operating the handful of military prisons. At Gibraltar in 1726, the governor directed the officer of the guard to provide an escort of soldiers to assist the provost whenever a prisoner was confined or brought out for trial.[27] The Governor of Louisbourg issued similar orders in 1746.[28]

---

25 Stephen Brumwell, *Redcoats: The British Soldier and War in the Americas, 1755–1763* (Cambridge: Cambridge University Press, 2002), pp. 81–2.

26 The provost marshal is only mentioned in single quantities in the Cunninghame Orderly Book, which provides a record of the number of regiments stationed at Gibraltar. For regimental strengths, see John Houlding, *Fit for Service: The Training of the British Army 1715–1795* (Oxford: Clarendon Press, 1981), pp. 415–22.

27 Cunninghame Orderly Book, G.O. Gibraltar, 14 October 1727, p. 39.

28 Ibid., General Orders Louisbourg, 26 July 1746, p. 226.

In May 1743, George II directed the provost marshal to patrol the camp with a corporal and six men,[29] and General Sir William Howe and Charles Cornwallis authorised similarly sized escorts in 1777 and 1781.[30] The soldiers assisting the provost marshal could also be called upon to aid in the execution of summary justice. Corporal William Todd recorded an episode of a provost marshal's party hanging a man for attempted rape in 1758.[31] Without the aid of such detachments, the provost marshal might have been totally ineffective.

Despite these escorts, the challenge of suppressing disorder extended far beyond the provost marshal's means. In order to bridge the resulting gap, officers frequently dispatched small detachments of soldiers, usually under the command of a non-commissioned officer, to patrol military zones independently. In 1735, Major Jean Paul Mascarene, Commander-in-Chief in Nova Scotia, ordered the officer of the guard to send a file of men to suppress any disturbances occurring at sutlers' houses, while also regularly dispatching patrols to insure that soldiers were inside their barracks after tattoo (the time when off-duty soldiers were required to retire for the night).[32] The governors of Gibraltar routinely ordered detachments from the daily guard mounts to patrol the town throughout the night, arresting anyone who could not produce an appropriate pass or was drunk.[33] Such work was not confined to fortresses: during the American Revolution, Howe assigned segments of Boston, Halifax, and New York to specific regiments, tasking their commanders with patrolling those districts and taking 'into Custody all Suspicious and Disorderly Persons found in the Streets at Improper hours'.[34] As these operations were largely unsupervised, frequently at night, and away from the eyes of superior officers, soldiers could expect greater rewards for their behaviour.

The trial process offered additional opportunities for soldiers to aid their officers in the operation of military justice. Beginning in late 1715, the king required general courts martial proceedings to record greater amounts of

29 NAS GD224/626 Orderly Book of the British Army at Dettingen with Orders of George II, 1743; Orders 16 May 1743, Orders at Spieres 28 September 1743.

30 'General orders by Major General the Honourable William Howe', *Kemble Papers, Vol. I, 1773–1789* (New York: New York Historical Society, 1883), p. 481; A. R. Newsome (ed.), 'A British Orderly Book, 1780–1781', *North Carolina Historical Review*, 9 (1932), p. 180.

31 Todd, *Journal*, pp. 46–7.

32 BL, ADD MSS 19069, 'Orders and Paroles of Major Paul Mascarene at Canso, 1735–6', 3 September 1735. Sutlers often served alcohol to soldiers in addition to selling food and other items, making their houses and stalls a focus of disorderly behaviour.

33 Cunninghame OB, G.O. Gibraltar, pp. 29, 34, 53, 71, 88–90, 93, 97, 104–6, 122, 128, 132–3, 146, 156, 158.

34 Howe Orderly Book, pp. 270, 285, 315, 323, 348, 435–6.

evidence, increasing the number of witnesses necessary for the judges' verdict and sentence to be confirmed.[35] General courts martial proceedings began to include testimony from enlisted men from early 1716. Their statements, particularly those of the sergeants and corporals who provided most of the day-to-day supervision of common soldiers, often provided the majority of the evidence upon which the court martial judges convicted defendants. For example, Sergeant Samuel Burnett's testimony that he had personally read the Articles of War to deserter William Bovet and seen him do duty in the King's Regiment was central to the latter's conviction in 1734.[36] This pattern repeated in most cases involving the rank and file throughout the century. Soldiers also played a vital role in confirming evidence offered by officers. When Lieutenant Arkman of the Royal Scotch Fusiliers brought Drummer John Bourne of Colonel Guise's regiment before a court martial on charges of desertion from Gibraltar in 1759, he called on two sergeants to confirm his testimony.[37] Without soldiers' support, the court martial judges would have been hard-pressed to meet the king's evidentiary requirements.

Not all enlisted men embraced these opportunities for co-operation with equal enthusiasm. Orders issued at Gibraltar in the second quarter of the century provide examples of soldiers ignoring various types of offences. In February 1728, Governor Jasper Clayton threatened any sergeant or corporal with immediate demotion if they did not report soldiers gambling.[38] Governor Joseph Sabine issued similar orders in January 1732, targeting non-commissioned officers who failed to arrest all men found drunk and outside of their barracks after tattoo.[39] Clayton also targeted enlisted men in December 1728, directing any sentry who witnessed a theft or embezzlement and did not stop the perpetrator to be fined the full value of the goods taken.[40]

---

35 TNA, WO71/14, fol. 67: In a letter to Judge Advocate General Edward Hughes on 13 December 1715, Secretary at War William Pulteney noted that the king expected all future court martial proceedings to clearly state why the judges came to their verdict; TNA, WO71/14, fol. 88: On 28 February 1716 Deputy Secretary at War J. Merrill wrote to Hughes stating that the king would no longer confirm any death sentences unless the court martial proceedings proved that the defendant had heard the Articles of War.

36 TNA, WO71/36, fol. 298. For another example, see the trial of Private John Allison of the 51st Regiment of Foot from 1759 in TNA, WO71/67, fol. 67.

37 TNA, WO71/67, fols 64–5.

38 This order was repeated in September 1728 and in March and November 1730. See: Cunninghame OB, G.O. Gibraltar, pp. 44, 51, 58, 63.

39 This order was repeated in August 1735, July 1739 and August 1741. See: Cunninghame OB, G.O. Gibraltar, pp. 71, 93, 105–6, 122, 135.

40 Cunninghame OB, G.O. Gibraltar, p. 51.

In contrast to these indications of reluctant assistance, some soldiers zealously embraced opportunities to aid the military authorities in maintaining social control. In July 1759 Private Hugh Frasier of the Royal Highland Regiment caught Private Thomas Dadley of the 17th Regiment rummaging through another man's knapsack and turned him in, though Frasier appeared to have no personal stake in the crime.[41] Instances of soldiers apprehending deserters provide particularly clear examples of co-operation. While pursuing another deserter in November 1724, Corporal John Painter of General Kirk's regiment encountered Privates Baptist Millar and Mathew Dickson of the same corps in a pub in Falladam. When they failed to produce furloughs, he arrested them and brought them back to the regiment as deserters.[42] In June 1723, Sergeant William Fuller of Groves's Regiment encountered Private Edward Wright of the same corps, 'disguis'd like a Native of the Country'. Recognising him as a comrade, the sergeant, though not on duty, arrested Wright and brought him back to the regiment.[43] On 6 September 1734, Corporal Thomas Street of Howard's Regiment went a step further in pursuing deserter Edward Horshoer. Having tracked the latter down to the town of Redminster, Street called on Private Jeremiah Reynolds of the same regiment, who was on furlough there. Together with men from the town watch, Street and Reynolds cornered Horshoer and arrested him.[44] Neither Wright, Painter, nor Reynolds were required by regulations to go to these lengths to bring in soldiers, nor is there any indication that they received the bounty offered by the Mutiny Act for capturing deserters. While Street had been ordered to capture Horshoer, he went above the call of duty in enlisting local watchmen and calling in a furloughed soldier to aid him.

Enlisted men who used the military justice system for their own ends offer a third form of co-operation, which fell somewhere between the extremes of indifference and vigour noted above. Clear examples of this practice appear in the form of soldiers who turned in their comrades in order to settle personal scores or escape punishment. In July 1759 outside the lines of Fort Ticonderoga in New York, Private John Stevenson of the 17th Regiment of Foot reported his comrade Thomas Bayley for robbing

---

41 TNA, WO71/67, fols 244–5. Dadley's captain testified that he knew the prisoner was convicted of theft on two prior occasions. The court sentenced Dadley to 1,500 lashes.

42 TNA, WO71/35, fols 57–9. Both men were tried for desertion and sentenced to receive lashes, though they claimed they 'had no design to desert and beg'd for Mercy'.

43 TNA, WO71/35, fols 22–3. In his defence, Wright claimed that a 'countryman' had seduced him to desert and provided him with civilian clothes. The private further added that a corporal had abused him and threatened to beat his brains out on the drill field, though he had no witnesses to substantiate this claim.

44 TNA, WO71/16, fols 31–4.

him of his pocket book (containing three half guineas and four dollars) and his handkerchief.[45] Privates Alexander Rowan and Alexander Brodie of the Earl of Hume's Regiment were convicted of encouraging men to desert and desertion (respectively) by comrades who had participated in a plan to abscond from the army but turned king's evidence to save themselves.[46] In these cases the self-interest of enlisted men seems to have triumphed over any abiding concern for the welfare of the army.

In co-operating with the military authorities, enlisted men responded to a range of rewards that extended well beyond avoiding punishments. Contemporary guide books for officers recommended that 'deserving soldiers' be granted 'every reasonable indulgence' that could contribute to their 'happiness and content'.[47] Co-operating with the military authorities in maintaining social order in the ranks constituted one measure of this 'deserving' status, and could be rewarded with furloughs home to see friends and entry into a regimental order of merit.[48] Authorities also offered cash rewards to encourage soldiers to turn in criminals. The Governor of Gibraltar offered bounties to men who reported soldiers who had not followed orders to kill their dogs, were spreading 'scandalous papers' through the garrison, or who threw dirt over the rampart at inappropriate spots.[49]

Co-operation also offered significant career advantages. Advancement in rank depended upon officers' recommendations, which were most readily given to co-operative soldiers.[50] Co-operation also created a safety net for soldiers if they ever fell afoul of martial law. Numerous general court martial trials feature defendants calling upon their officers to serve as character witnesses. Men who could establish a good record through this testimony could receive reduced sentences, recommendations for mercy, or pardons.[51]

---

45 Ibid., fols 198–9. The officers confined Bayley to the quarter guard until he confessed his guilt. At his trial, several witnesses came forward who implicated him in other crimes and testified that Bayley had been tried at least twice before by general courts martial and bore an infamous character in the regiment. He was sentenced to death.

46 TNA, WO71/67, fols 53–8.

47 Bennet Cuthbertson, *System for the Complete Interior Management and Oeconomy of a Battalion of Infantry* (Bristol: Rouths and Nelson, 1776), pp. 138–9.

48 Ibid., pp. 128–9, 139.

49 Cunninghame OB, G.O. Gibraltar, pp. 77, 122, 197–8.

50 On 24 November 1740, Colonel Fuller of the 29th Regiment ordered his officers to send in lists of corporals whom they would recommend for promotion to sergeant. On 11 April 1741, Fuller ordered his officers to report any misbehaviour among these candidates so that the offenders could be struck off the list. See: Cunninghame OB, Regimental Orders Gibraltar, pp. 2, 4.

51 For example, character witnesses saved Privates Joseph Waters and Samuel Holton from punishment for sleeping on their post in 1759, while the favourable testimony of

Through these rewards, officers tempered their authority in order to cultivate co-operative attitudes in their men and offer soldiers a guarantee, insofar as was possible, of decent treatment without having to resort to protest.

Negotiated Authorities

B ETWEEN THE EXTREMES of outright resistance to military authority and co-operation with it lay a shifting zone of negotiation, which presented officers and men with a range of options for resolving conflicts. Neither the Mutiny Act nor the Articles of War sanctioned compromise in any form: both armed officers with extreme powers, including capital punishment, for the suppression of any challenge to their authority. As contemporary writers noted, however, courts martial were expensive undertakings, to be avoided whenever possible.[52] While summary justice provided a quick solution, it was far from a guaranteed means of cowing enlisted men. Prior to being relieved of duty, Lieutenant Catherwood, mentioned at the start of this chapter, used multiple forms of summary justice, all of which failed to stop the murmuring in the ranks of his company.[53] From the enlisted perspective, protest was a very dangerous strategy to employ in dealing with officers, while co-operation did not always guarantee good treatment, especially in the face of overbearing commanders. Thus, for both parties, negotiation provided a means of resolving disputes with minimal effort.

Despite the lack of overt approval from the martial law codes, in practice negotiation was a popular option for both officers and men. For example, most instances of large-scale mutinies during the eighteenth century were resolved through negotiation. As John Prebble has noted, these uprisings began as reactions to perceived violations of contracts and generally ended, after some minor violence, when the authorities resolved the soldiers' grievances.[54] A case in point is the mutiny of the 83rd Regiment of Foot at Portsmouth in 1783, which was sparked by rumours that the regiment would soon be sent to India after boarding transports. Lord George Lennox, Governor of Portsmouth, personally assured the men that they would not be sent to India, while the regimental officers attempted to bribe their men with three guineas bounty apiece to stay on board and sail for India,

---

two captains saved Private James Mcwhan from a capital sentence for desertion in the same year. See: TNA, WO71/67 fols 61–3, 80–2.

52 Cuthbertson, *System*, pp. 121–2.

53 TNA, WO71/53, fols 66–9.

54 Prebble, *Mutiny*.

which every soldier refused. After the mutineers landed at Portsmouth, officers harangued them, paraded the regiment while calling the men to their colours, and made numerous other appeals that fell upon deaf ears. In the end, the authorities acceded to the soldiers' demands to be discharged, as per the conditions of their enlistment.[55] This scene repeated with other Scottish regiments during the course of the American Revolution, as well as with English troops at Louisbourg in 1747 and throughout North America in 1765.[56] In these earlier cases, much as in that of the 83rd, the only successful means for ending mutiny was to give the private men what they wanted. The two instances in which the military authorities used force to suppress mutinies (that of the Highland Regiment of Foot in 1743 and recruits of the 42nd and 71st regiments at Edinburgh in 1779) resulted in bloodshed and additional grievances among the rank and file.

Negotiated conclusions to mutinies were not, however, always a case of soldiers dictating terms to their officers. On 3 December 1729, Major General George Wade arrived in Nottingham to handle a mutiny in progress in a troop of dragoons that was in the process of disbanding. In his report, Wade observed that the dragoons were insisting on 'Terms Inconsistant with His Majesty's Orders of Reduction' and behaved insolently towards their officers. The officers of the squadron had already read the official disbandment orders to the men, taken their arms back into stores, and sold all of their horses, which raised the question of whether these men were still subject to martial law. The soldiers resolved the situation on 6 December, when they submitted to Wade's authority and begged for his forgiveness. Not having found the men 'guilty of any outragious Acts of Mutiny, tho' very Seditious and Insolent to their Officers', Wade promptly forgave and dismissed them.[57] While not an example of the most formal style of negotiation, the practice of soldiers submitting after protesting was not uncommon during this period. In July 1716, Private Samuel Squire of the First Regiment of Foot Guards refused to do duty and persuaded two other men to follow him into mutiny. Their captain confined all three to the guardhouse, pardoning the other two the next morning when they submitted, acknowledged their fault, and pleaded ignorance of the consequences

55 NAS, GD26/9/520/14, Marshal to Balgonie, Portsmouth, 12 February 1783 Wednesday; NAS, GD26/9/520/15, Marshal to Balgonie, Hilsea Barracks, 12–13 March 1783.

56 Like the more famous mutiny of 1765, the uprising at Louisbourg was caused by stoppages placed on soldiers' pay for rations they had previously received free of charge. See: NAS, GD110/919/12 Suttie to Hew Dalrymple Louisbourg 30 June 1747; Way, 'Rebellion', Kopperman, 'Stoppages Mutiny'.

57 TNA, SP36/16/28, George Wade to unknown, Nottingham, 3 December 1729; George Wade to unknown, Clifton, 6 December 1729.

of their actions due to their youth. Squire would not relent and was punished as a result.[58]

In contrast to mutinies, episodes of desertion provide examples of more flexible exchanges between officers and men, which included an element of forgiveness that allowed soldiers to return to the service without fear of punishment, while officers were able to restore the manpower and discipline of their units. Prior to the 1750s, most deserters for whom records survive appear to have stayed within the larger confines of the army, moving from regiment to regiment in their travels. The military authorities issued regular amnesty proclamations, allowing any deserters who identified themselves as such to stay with their current unit without undergoing punishment. The incidence of these amnesties dropped off significantly after mid-century, recurring occasionally during times of intense warfare, as officers engaged in a newer approach to negotiating with military runaways.[59] Regiments began placing detailed advertisements in local newspapers describing deserters and offering additional bounties beyond that authorised by the Mutiny Act for their capture. In some of these instances, officers offered pardons if deserters returned of their own volition within a set period of time.[60] These conditional pardons were not directed at any specific type of deserter; they seem to reflect the choices of individual officers rather than a more general trend.

A final area of negotiation for resolving disciplinary issues lay in the mitigation or outright pardoning of court martial sentences. As with civilian courts, these measures were probably a result of conscious manipulation of the court system by authorities to play on the emotions of common soldiers.[61] This practice was clearly at work in the trial of Private John Sutherland of the 64th Regiment in July 1779. Tried for deserting from British forces outside of New York City, Sutherland was sentenced to death, in the words of Captain John Peebles, 'by a mode of procedure in Court that I never saw or hear'd of before, & cannot reconcile to justice & humanity'. After

---

58 TNA WO71/14, fol. 138.
59 For examples of amnesty declarations, see: TNA, WO26/20, fols 8, 107, 236. Ad for John Martin, *Felix Farley's Bristol Journal*, Vol. XXVI, No. 1362, Saturday, 29 March 1777; Ad for Alexander Macalister, *Caledonian Mercury*, Wednesday, 9 February 1780.
60 Ad for deserters from the 94th Regiment, *Exeter Flying Post*, Vol. XVI, No. 833, Friday, 4 February 1780; Ad for John Martin, *Felix Farley's Bristol Journal*, Vol. XXVI, No. 1362, Saturday, 29 March 1777; Ad for Richard Farr, *The Bath Journal*, Vol. XXXIX, No. 2031, Monday, 16 December 1782.
61 D. Hay, 'Property, Authority and the Criminal Law' in *Albion's Fatal Tree: Crime and Society in Eighteenth-Century England*, ed. by D. Hay (New York: Pantheon, 1975), pp. 17–64.

making various representations on Sutherland's behalf, Peebles learnt that Sutherland would be pardoned at the gallows.[62] Such last-minute pardons, designed for shock value, were highly favoured during the reigns of Queen Anne and King George I. When multiple men were sentenced to death by the same court martial, these monarchs often directed that the convicts cast lots to decide who of their number would live or die.[63] Mitigations and pardons of sentences more generally could reflect power struggles within regiments as much as they did concern with manipulating the dynamics of officer–enlisted relations, but nevertheless acted as a means for skirting the extremes of protest and co-operation while offering a practical solution to soldiers' grievances.

Conclusion

ALTHOUGH, officially, the Mutiny Act, the Articles of War, and the wording of officers' commissions left little room for compromise, enlisted men had a variety of strategies at their disposal through which they could exert their agency and shape their fates. Manifesting as a broad spectrum of behaviours, the ways in which soldiers interacted with their officers were bounded on the extremes by protest and co-operation, with a broad middle ground of negotiation. Protest has been the most studied form of these strategies, yet far from being confined to acts that officers interpreted as mutiny or desertion, protest could manifest in behaviour as simple as verbal complaints in the ranks and often seems to have followed a sliding scale of escalation depending on officers' responses. The majority of approaches in this category were non-violent in nature, including making verbal complaints, writing petitions, and refusing to obey orders. In extreme cases, disgruntled soldiers engaged in violent action, both physically and verbally, for which they often received extreme punishment that eliminated any hopes of having their grievances heard. While consisting of both confrontational and escapist elements, strategies focusing on protests ultimately did not yield significant dividends for enlisted men.

While largely ignored by modern scholars, co-operation provided many soldiers with their best means of exercising some control over their lives and influencing the operation of military justice. There were numerous opportunities for soldiers to aid the military authorities in the course of the military justice process. While many soldiers chose to ally themselves with

---

62 Peebles, *Diary*, p. 279.
63 Examples from TNA, WO 71/14, fols 82, 87, 93; WO71/34, fol. 95.

their superiors, co-operation was neither uniform in its quality nor entirely reliable. As indicated by contemporary orders, some enlisted men turned a blind eye to their comrades' misbehaviour when not under the direct supervision of authority figures. Other individuals, particularly non-commissioned officers, went above the call of duty in apprehending offenders. Some soldiers appeared to have co-operated with their officers only so far as it served their own purposes, such as by reporting comrades who had wronged them or by turning king's evidence. In general, officers encouraged soldiers to co-operate by offering them rewards ranging from preferential treatment (such as furloughs) to promotion and character witness testimony that could swing court martial judges in a merciful direction. The combination of extreme punishments for protest and rewards offered for co-operation made the latter option an obvious, and probably popular, choice for enlisted men.

Negotiation provided a means for skirting between protest and co-operation, avoiding the long and involved elements of the military justice process, and offering satisfaction for both officers and men. Most eighteenth-century mutinies were resolved through negotiation, either by officers meeting enlisted men's grievances or soldiers submitting to the military authorities and begging forgiveness. In the form of general amnesties and offers of individual pardons through deserter advertisements, officers presented military runaways with a means of returning to their posts that avoided severe punishment, though it did not offer a dialogue. Through a selective practice of mitigating or pardoning sentences that mirrored civilian legal practices of the period, officers could also provide enlisted men with a means of relief that nevertheless did not prevent misbehaving soldiers from serving as an example to their comrades.

This examination of the ways in which enlisted men interacted with their officers reveals that no single perspective dominated the rank and file's view of the nature of military authority. Those who protested against their officers likely did not believe in the sort of absolute monolithic social hierarchy that the Mutiny Act and the Articles of War sought to create, while the soldiers who chose to co-operate may well have accepted this view of their reality. Examples of negotiation indicate that there was a significant degree of flexibility within the army's social dynamic and that officers were willing to put their own limits onto the exercise of their discretionary powers. As such, it is clear that soldiers took an active role in determining their own fortunes. In so doing, they left their mark on the eighteenth-century British Army by providing limitations that shaped the ultimate form of military authority.

6

Discipline and Control in Eighteenth-Century Gibraltar

Ilya Berkovich

O NE OF THE MORE COLOURFUL PORTRAYALS of the power of discipline in old-regime armies comes from the pen of Sir Michael Howard:

> It might be suggested that it was not the least achievement of European civilization to have reduced the wolf packs which had preyed on the defenceless peoples of Europe for so many centuries to the condition of trained and obedient gun dogs – almost, in some cases, performing poodles.[1]

The significance of such views, presenting the eighteenth-century soldiery as a closely controlled and obedient lot, extends beyond the remit of old-regime military history. Social and cultural historians often see early-modern armies not only as disciplined but also disciplining forces which played a major role in bringing the European population under the closer and closer control of their respective states. This was a broad process which operated on a number of levels, but at its root lay the growing standardisation of social institutions and mores replacing tradition with regulation, informalities with formalities, compromise and negotiations with direct power and hierarchical dictates. Regular armies were not only the product of this development but also among its major promoters. However, the role of the military went beyond the coercion of those whose traditional lifestyle had fallen prey to the reforming zeal of the authorities. It has been argued that the disciplining of the soldiery enabled the social disciplining of the population at large. Their

---

1 Michael Howard, *War in European History*, rev. edn (Oxford: Oxford University Press, 2009), p. 76.

position as the most tightly controlled social institution in old-regime Europe allowed armies to become a testing ground for policies of social management and surveillance before they befell the rest of society, from the introduction of elementary education to a more regularised penal system.

Recent studies have usually taken a more nuanced view of social disciplining and growing state control, at least as far as civil society is concerned. Rather than being entirely coercive and imposed from above, it was largely based on negotiation and consent, often relying on intermediaries accepted by both the authorities and their subjects. The move towards greater uniformity was also a gradual one. To cite one example, contrary to the argument raised by Michel Foucault in his classic *Discipline and Punish*,[2] the regularisation of the legal system in old-regime France was a slow and measured process, rather than the product of the relatively abrupt upheaval which took place in the end of the eighteenth century. As shown by scholars working in French legal history, the move towards a more procedural, less arbitrary penal system began a century before the revolution.[3]

Nor did the traditional view of armies as the most disciplined (read 'civilised') part of society remain unchallenged. Peter H. Wilson, for instance, has turned Otto Büsch's classical thesis on its head, arguing that rather than militarising eighteenth-century German society it was the constant interaction with the civil sphere that actually civilised German armies. A number of recent studies covering the conditions of common soldiers arrived at similar conclusions. Stephen Brumwell, who studied the British Army in North America during the Seven Years War, refutes the traditional view of the eighteenth-century redcoat as a meek brutalised automaton. Instead, members of the rank and file had a firm perception of their worth and of the rights which they considered due to them. Failure of the military authorities to meet the expectations of their subordinates often provoked varied forms of resistance including petitions, threats and public displays of resentment.

---

2 Michel Foucault, *Discipline and Punish: The Birth of the Prison*, trans. by Alan Sheridan (London: Allen Lane, 1977).

3 Richard M. Andrews, *Law, Magistracy, and Crime in Old Regime Paris, 1735–1789* (Cambridge: Cambridge University Press, 1994); Julius R. Ruff, *Crime, Justice and Public Order in Old Regime France: The Sénéchaussées of Libourne and Bazas, 1696–1789* (London: Croom Helm, 1984); Lisa Silverman, *Tortured Subjects: Pain, Truth, and the Body in Early Modern France* (Chicago, MI: University of Chicago Press, 2001). For similar developments taking place in other parts of continental Europe, see: Petrus Cornelis Spierenburg, *The Spectacle of Suffering. Executions and the Evolution of Repression: From a Preindustrial Metropolis to the European Experience* (Cambridge: Cambridge University Press, 1984); Richard J. Evans, *Rituals of Retribution: Capital Punishment in Germany, 1600–1987* (Oxford: Oxford University Press, 1996), pp. 41–50, 109–21.

Individual soldiers who felt injured by their officers often deserted, while similar slighting to the whole body of the troops could result in equally radical collective action, as happened in the mass mutinies of 1763–4, when almost every major garrison in North America rose up after the introduction of excessive peacetime stoppages for food and equipment.[4]

Brumwell's findings on the British soldiery were paralleled by Jörg Muth in his important but, unfortunately, overlooked monograph on late-Frederickan Postdam. Despite its reputation for disciplinary brutality, Muth shows that the punishments employed in the Prussian military were no worse than in other old-regime armies, and that desertion rates from its ranks were often lower than elsewhere in Europe. Most importantly, Muth points to the contractual nature of old-regime military service. The conclusions of Brumwell and Muth, who see enlisted men as assertive actors rather than as passive subjects dominated by their officers, hark back to André Corvisier's magisterial study of the eighteenth-century French common soldier. According to Corvisier, soldiers saw themselves as part of reciprocal relationship with their superiors. In exchange for their obedience, soldiers expected to be treated fairly and paid regularly; when this did not happen, they perceived the bond to be invalidated.[5]

Nonetheless, despite the growing recognition of the limits of old-regime military discipline, it is still commonly characterised as 'brutal'. Moreover, while mutiny and desertion demonstrate the occasional failures of the eighteenth-century disciplinary system, those were radical forms of resistance that often resulted from extreme conditions and involved only a minority of the soldiers. The majority of the rank and file, however, did not mutiny and did not desert. Was it, perhaps, a sign of the overall success of the disciplinary project to control the daily lives of the majority of soldiers most of the time? This chapter attempts to answer this question by considering an

4 Peter H. Wilson, 'Social Militarization in Eighteenth-Century Germany', *German History*, 18 (2000), pp. 1–39; Otto Büsch, *Military System and Social Life in Old Regime Prussia 1713–1807: The Beginnings of the Social Militarization of Prusso-German Society* [1962], trans. by John G. Gagliardo (Atlantic Highlands, NJ: Humanities Press, 1997); Stephan Brumwell, *Redcoats: The British Soldier and War in the Americas, 1755–1763* (Cambridge: Cambridge University Press, 2002), pp. 126–37. On the mutinies at the end of the Seven Years War, see: Paul E. Kopperman, 'The Stoppages Mutiny of 1763', *Western Pennsylvania Historical Magazine*, 69 (1986), pp. 241–54; Peter Way, 'Rebellion of the Regulars: Working Soldiers and the Mutiny of 1763–1764', *William and Mary Quarterly*, 3rd Series, 57 (2000), pp. 761–92.

5 Jörg Muth, *Flucht aus dem militärischen Alltag: Ursachen und individuelle Ausprägung der Desertion in der Armee Friedrichs des Großen* (Freiburg-im-Breisgau: Rombach, 2003); André Corvisier, *L'Armée française de la fin du XVIIe siècle au ministère de Choiseul: Le soldat*, 2 vols (Paris: Presses universitaires de France, 1964).

extreme test case. By looking at the garrison of Gibraltar, a particular site in which, one could argue, the potential for direct control and surveillance was at its highest, it is hoped to determine the actual power wielded by old-regime authorities not only over their militaries but also over civil society at large.

Captured by a combined Dutch-British force in the name of Archduke Charles, the Austrian claimant during the War of the Spanish Succession, Gibraltar was formally ceded to Great Britain by the Treaty of Utrecht. Although British politicians were willing at first to relinquish this conquest in exchange for political concessions elsewhere, these attempts were blocked by parliament, usually enthused by public outcry, as well as by Spanish unwillingness to compromise.[6] In 1727, citing breaches in the conditions under which Gibraltar was handed over to the British, Spain attempted to retake it by force, but the four-month siege ended in a costly failure. Although the possibility of its return to Spain was mentioned a few more times, Gibraltar evolved from a potential bargaining chip into to a major British garrison. Usually held by about five regiments, the fortress also functioned as a naval base holding a small squadron but was also capable of hosting much larger fleets, as happened during the Seven Years War, when the main British Mediterranean station in Minorca was temporarily lost. During the 1760s and early 70s its fortifications were thoroughly strengthened just in time to withstand another Spanish effort to regain the territory.[7] Commonly referred to as the Great Siege, the successful three-year defence provided Britain with a major morale boost in what was otherwise a failed war. The position of Gibraltar, not only as an important imperial outpost, but as a symbol of British military might, was now secure.

Unlike much of the published material devoted to Gibraltar,[8] this paper is not concerned with the operational accounts of its sieges. True, the

---

6 The best general history of Gibraltar currently available is William Jackson, *The Rock of the Gibraltarians: a History of Gibraltar*, 2nd edn (Grendon: Gibraltar Books, 1990). See also: Stetson Conn, *Gibraltar in British Diplomacy in the Eighteenth-Century* (New Haven, CT: Yale University Press, 1942).

7 For the naval history of Gibraltar, see: Tito Benady, *The Royal Navy at Gibraltar* (Liskeard: Martime, 1992). On its fortifications, see: Darren Fa and Clive Finlayson, *The Fortification of Gibraltar, 1068–1945* (Oxford: Osprey, 2006); Ken Anthony, 'William Green: The Men who Saved Gibraltar', *Gibraltar Heritage Journal*, 4 (1997), pp. 32–40.

8 Ernle Bradford, *Gibraltar: The History of a Fortress* (London: Hart-Davis, 1971); Maurice Harvey, *Gibraltar* (Staplehurst: Spellmount, 1996); Marc Alexander, *Gibraltar: Conquered by No Enemy* (Stroud: The History Press, 2008). The best account of its military history, based on much original research, is George Hills, *Rock of Contention: A History of Gibraltar* (London: Hale, 1974).

investment of 1779–83 stands out as one of the longest sieges on record, but neither this nor the siege of 1727 were unique in the annals of fortress warfare in terms of their conditions, siege methods or equipment. What made Gibraltar exceptional among a myriad of eighteenth-century fortress towns was its situation as a sealed territorial enclave. The tenth article of the Treaty of Utrecht forbade direct land communications with Spain. Following the 1729 Treaty of Seville, which reconfirmed the 1713 agreements, Spain put this wording into practice by building a fortified line across the isthmus essentially shutting Gibraltar off from the mainland.[9] This was part of a consistent strategy to make conditions in the city 'as uncongenial as possible', as was the introduction of quarantine for all ships arriving from Gibraltar at Spanish ports. This is not to say that Gibraltar was sealed hermetically. Sea communications were maintained with North Africa from where came most of its supplies, and there was also a flourishing smuggling business as well as more formal postal exchange with Spain proper.[10] Nonetheless, as far as the garrison was concerned, its life was limited to the fortress and its adjacent rock, a territory of some six square kilometres.

In addition to the isolation of Gibraltar from the outside world, the conditions inside the fortress, although formally no different from those prevailing in other garrison towns, reached an unprecedented extreme. The stronghold was under the authority of a governor, a royal appointment officially answerable directly to the monarch, but reporting in reality either to the Secretary of State for the Southern Department or to the Minister for the Colonies. However, instructions from London would take at least a fortnight to arrive, leaving the governor with substantial independence in his actions. This included not only his status as military commander-in-chief, but also as the highest temporal authority as far as the civilian population was concerned. In 1749, Governor Bland issued twelve articles regulating the rights and responsibilities of the populace. Bland is usually seen as a humane governor who wanted to safeguard the rights of Gibraltar's cosmopolitan non-military community. Nevertheless, considering that the articles were granted by a military man who required no approval from any equivalent civil

---

9 Jose Manuel Algarbani Rodríguez, 'Las Fronteras de Gibraltar en el Siglo XVIII: Las Luchas Diplomáticas', *Almoraima: Revista de Estudios Campogibraltareños*, 34 (2007), pp. 13–14; Jackson, *Rock*, pp. 139–40.

10 Jackson, *Rock*, p. 139; H. W. Howes, *The Gibraltarian: The Origin and Development of the Population of Gibraltar from 1704* [1951], 3rd edn (Gibraltar: MedSUN, 1993), pp. 7–11; Stephen Constantine, *Community and Identity: The Making of Modern Gibraltar since 1704* (Manchester: Manchester University Press, 2009), pp. 41–3, 53; Richard J. M. Garcia and Edward B. Proud, *The Postal History of Gibraltar 1704–1971* (Heathfield: Postal History Publications, 1998), pp. 53–9.

authority, their case demonstrates well where the actual power in Gibraltar lay. Civilians were neither allowed to enter nor leave the garrison without permission. Settling, doing business and acquiring property also required leave from the governor, who also had it in his power to expel anyone out of the town.[11]

Gibraltar and its populace were thus subject to one hierarchy – the military one. Civil administration was non-existent and the daily running of the place was the responsibility of the town major, usually a middle-ranking officer. Criminal cases remained under the jurisdiction of courts martial until 1752 and the establishment of justices of the peace that year did not result in a radical transformation. Two of the three justices were the military judge-advocate and the governor, who also retained his position as chief justice before whom all appeals were heard. This arrangement remained in force until the end of the Napoleonic Wars, when the first independent civilian courts were finally established. The lesser legal status of the civilians was clearly underscored when in 1726 Lieutenant-Governor Kane announced that any civilian hit by a soldier should complain, but any civilian striking a soldier would be whipped and banished from the garrison.[12] The precedence of military administration and law in Gibraltar was also linked to the makeup of the population. The censuses taken in 1751 and 1753, considered as representative for the eighteenth-century as a whole, show that half of the inhabitants, some 3,000 men, were soldiers of the garrison. Another quarter was soldiers' families who, as such, were subject to military discipline as their husbands and fathers were. Altogether, the civilians, who included a few English, but were mostly Jews, Genoese and Spaniards, made only a quarter of the population.[13] As demonstrated by William Tatum in the previous chapter, soldiers often

---

11 On the governor and his powers, see: E. G. Archer, *Gibraltar, Identity and Empire* (London: Routledge, 2006), pp. 74 and 76; Constantine, *Community*, pp. 70 and 90–1; Jackson, *Rock*, pp. 142–3; Thomas Finlayson, 'The Gibraltarian since 1704', *Gibraltar Heritage Journal*, 8 (2001), pp. 30–1. See also the comments by eighteenth-century visitors in: Robert Poole, *The Beneficent Bee, or Traveller's Companion: a Voyage from London to Gibraltar, Barbados, Antigua etc.* (London: E. Duncomb, 1753), pp. 59 and 136; Richard Twiss, *Travels through Portugal and Spain, in 1772–1773* (London: G. Robinson, 1775), p. 273.

12 British subjects were exempted from this order, see TNA, WO 284/1, 29 March 1726; on the legal situation in the enclave, see: Archer, *Gibraltar*, p. 77; Constantine, *Community*, pp. 12, 17–19, 76–81; Tito Benady, 'The Complaint of the Chief Justice of Gibraltar', *Gibraltar Heritage Journal*, 4 (1997), pp. 18–23.

13 On the size and composition of the population of eighteenth-century Gibraltar and its garrison, see: Howes, *Gibraltarian*, pp. 1–40; Hills, *Rock*, pp. 229, 293, 360; Constantine, *Community*, pp. 16 n. 11, 20–9, 39, 72–3, which includes much additional bibliography.

co-operated with the military authorities. That rendered half of Gibraltar's population potential informants and enforcers.

This said, it should be remembered that those were the soldiers who were the most closely-controlled members of the populace. Their descriptions recorded upon enlistment and then kept centrally by their regiments and the War Office, made what was probably the closest eighteenth-century equivalent of a modern identity database. Their physical whereabouts were confirmed at two daily roll calls. Their provisions, often supplied by hired contractors in other garrisons, were even more dependent on central distribution, as Gibraltar lacked an agricultural hinterland and all of its foodstuffs had to be imported. Their uniform, at least part of which was to be worn when off duty, clearly marked them as members of a distinct and separate social group, although, in Gibraltar, they were a majority. Their time was more regimented than that of any other eighteenth-century social group other than, perhaps, convicts and monks. The reveille and tattoo, played every morning and every evening, clearly defined the boundaries of the military day, while exercise and fatigue duties – public works for the benefit of the service – took much of the time in between. During the period of initial drill, major stress was put upon instilling men with a proper air, looks and behaviour, aiming to create not only a military professional but an amended human being. And these are only external attributes to which one should add the social norms prevailing inside the military, which could differ greatly from society at large.

In addition to legal and disciplinary management, the soldiery in Gibraltar was also subject to extreme physical controls. To the north of the town were a number of consecutive lines of moats and ramparts beyond which lay a few hundred yards of exposed killing ground. To the east was the rock, whose relatively moderate western slope was followed by an almost sheer drop on its eastern side.[14] There was also the possibility of jumping over the sea wall and trying one's luck swimming away, but most would probably find it to be a particularly precarious escape option in a period when even most sailors did not know how to swim. Another point that makes the place stand out from most other eighteenth-century British garrisons is that the troops were largely housed in barracks, mostly converted convents. By contrast, troops stationed in Britain were largely billeted on the civil population well into the 1790s.[15]

---

14 See Edward P. F. Rose, 'Geology and the Fortress of Gibraltar', in *Geology and Warfare: Examples of the Influence of Terrain and Geologists on Military Operations* ed. by Edward P. F. Rose and C. Paul Nathanail (Bath: Geological Society, 2000), pp. 236–9.

15 Clive Emsley, 'The Military and Popular Disorder in England 1790–1801', *Journal of the Society for Army Historical Research*, 61 (1983–4), pp. 17–21.

In terms of the potential for internal surveillance, Gibraltar must come close, at least by old-regime standards, to Bentham's panopticon – the imaginary building whose population can be scrutinised by a small group of centrally placed overseers. It was this concept that Foucault later developed as a metaphor for modern disciplinary society.[16] The question, however, is whether Gibraltar's unique situation also produced equivalent results and whether the troops garrisoning its fortress were more disciplined than their eighteenth-century counterparts. The remaining parts of this chapter will attempt to gauge the actual effectiveness of control mechanisms operating in the enclave by isolating two parameters: the fights against drunken soldiers, and free-roaming dogs.

The evidence we used is largely drawn from the order books of the Gibraltar garrison, which are preserved almost in full, as part of the War Office papers in the National Archives in Kew. Another product of the general trend towards greater regularity and better administration which prevailed in almost every late seventeenth-century European army, the order book is essentially the diary of a unit. A daily entry would usually begin with the parole and the countersign issued to the detachment doing guard duty, followed by other relevant information and orders which were often read verbatim to the troops assembled for one of their roll calls. Orders would usually proliferate on their way down the military hierarchy. Those of the senior commander-in-chief were read first, followed by specific orders issued by brigade, regimental and battalion commanders and concluding with orders concerning individual companies. In the current chapter, we will concern ourselves with garrison orders only. In 1720, the first year covered by the extant Gibraltar order books, this practice was well established, and the basic format of the books, as described in the next paragraphs, remained unaltered until the end of the century.

The issue of the parole would often be followed with information pertaining to daily routine, such as naming the officer of the day, and the allocation of men to guard detachments and work parties. Order books would commonly mention promotions so that men would know whom to salute. In Gibraltar, men were also informed of regular events of garrison routine, such as change of quarters, church parades, public observances of the king's birthday and other festivities. Sometimes, on top of their role as a daily advertiser, the books functioned as notice boards in the most direct sense of the term, advertising for lost property. Items lost by members of the garrison, mostly officers, but occasionally also sergeants, included

---

16 Jeremy Bentham, *Panopticon or the Inspection House* (London: T. Payne, 1791); Foucault, *Discipline and Punish*, pp. 195–228.

books, jewellery, clothing items, watches and purses.[17] The public reading of the orders was also intended to enforce discipline, and sentences of general courts martial, the court responsible for capital offences, were often included in the books. Forthcoming executions were mentioned for the same reason.

On this later point, it is important to note that the public reading was not just a passive means of conveying mundane information. It is clear that the orders were intended not only to inform but also to shape, as they were often accompanied by explanatory texts clearly intended to mould their perception in a way desired by the authorities. For instance, when, on 27 May 1787, the garrison was notified of a coming execution of four deserters, Governor Elliot added that he has given 'this awful but necessary order with the outmost reluctance but justice demands it, the recent instances of His Majesty's Clemency on similar occasion having made not impression on the minds of these unfortunate men'. The aim of this and similar messages was not only to dissuade further men from deserting, but also to present the governor as being both merciful and stern.[18] The concern of the authorities for the common soldiery was underscored while warning that men should not presume to abuse the humanity of their superiors. When informing the garrison of a court of enquiry which inspected a case of an ensign wounding a soldier after, apparently, losing his temper during a drill session, General O'Hara assured 'the soldiers they should always experience from him the strictest attention to justice. At the same time that he highly disapproves of all *factious Malicious* and *ill-grounded* complaints'.[19] In a way, order books should be understood as one side of an ongoing dialogue between the military authorities and their subordinates. Men would provide their answer either by obeying as desired, or not.

What makes this source particularly interesting, however, is that orders were often issued as direct responses to particular events. Sometimes this is stated clearly, as with the prohibition from 1725 to soldiers from entering the Catholic church during mass, which also instructed their officers to avoid causing any offence 'as has lately been done'. However, even when no reference to any particular incident is made, many orders are too specific to

---

17 See examples of orders regarding promotions: TNA, WO 284/2, 7 February 1747; 284/3 1 June 1754; 284/4, 22 May 1769; 284/5, 20 July 1775. And lost property: WO 284/1, 6 October 1727; 284/2, 23 December 1741, 1 June 1747; WO 284/4, 25 January 1766.

18 WO 284/7, 27 May 1787. Compare to similar announcements, this time, advertising pardons: WO 284/4, 18 December 1762; WO 284/5, 17 December 1768; WO 284/6, 22 July 1779.

19 TNA, WO 284/7, 16 June 1787, terms in italics are underlined in the manuscript original; compare with WO 284/1, 25 May 1736 and 284/4, 6 July 1762.

be issued at random. For instance, when on 30 January 1736 it was declared that '[w]hoever pelts the Jews as they go along the streets shall be severely punished,'[20] it is clear that such an outrage has recently taken place. Thus, the books tell us much about what was actually happening in the garrison, cutting through the otherwise dry language of army regulations. While both these sources are a product of the official viewpoint and tilt heavily towards disciplinary infringements, the latter present a static picture of disciplinary policy. The order books, on the other hand, actually allow an assessment of the extent to which it was implemented in practice. Moreover, when order books are considered for a substantial time period, this allows the building of a more consistent picture than the anecdotal evidence coming from a handful of memoirs or other first-hand recollections. The usefulness of unit order books as a source for daily life and discipline of the soldiery is well acknowledged by modern scholars.[21] In the case of Gibraltar, the garrison books also offer much information on the population at large, as many of the orders pertain directly to civilians.

Drinking was clearly a problem in the garrison in mid-1720, when the first extant garrison order book was produced. The remaining months of that year alone include five orders against selling wine at unregulated hours, as well as an additional order against drinking and gambling and another against drunkenness on duty. Furthermore, NCOs were directed not to place intoxicated men on guard and warned that soldiers confined for drunkenness were to have nothing but bread and water.[22] Assuming that these orders reflected ongoing reality, the situation described that year is not unrepresentative for the rest of the century. Although not every calendar year has as many entries, and a few have none, orders against drunkenness were usually issued every few months. Particular stress was put on drunkenness on duty and, specifically, on guard. Rather than merely stating the prohibition, a typical order also threatened the transgressors, the precise wording being 'with severe' or even 'severest punishment'. Nevertheless, despite the first impression that it was rigorously persecuted, the campaign against drunkenness in the garrison largely failed. The number of the repetitious

---

20 TNA, WO 284/1, 7 November 1725, 30 January 1736; for other similar examples see: 284/2, 19 February 1742; 284/5, 13 March 1773; 284/7, 1 February 1784.

21 Order books were mined intensively for evidence by studies such as Sylvia Frey, *The British Soldier in America: A Social History of Military Life in the Revolutionary Period* (Austin, TX: University of Texas Press, 1981); Glenn Steppler, 'The Common Soldier in the Reign of George III, 1760–1793' (Unpublished DPhil thesis, University of Oxford, 1984); Brumwell, *Redcoats*.

22 TNA, WO 284/1, 25 July, 11 August, 22 October, 26 October, 31 October, 7 November, 16 November, 28 November, 10 December 1720.

orders already provides an indication that drunken soldiers remained a constant problem, further suggesting that the punishments against these men failed to deter them. The actual penalties that were meted out, which are occasionally mentioned in the orders, explain why.

The orders of 25 April 1721 declared that sentinels found drunk on their posts were to be relieved and sent to a day at the king's works and then to remount their guard the day afterwards. Apparently, this prospect of a day's labour at the fortifications or road-building held little terror as eight days later the orders stated that 'if any soldier is found drunk on his guard he shall be punished severely v[iz] work two days at the king's works for nothing'. Two months afterwards, on 3 July, the punishment was amended further and men arriving drunk to the mounting of the guard were to forfeit a day's pay and do duty the following day. Over the next few years, the orders continued in similar vein. In 1722, drunken soldiers arrested on the street were to be sent for a night in the black hole followed by an additional guard shift the next day. Skilled soldiers who were earning as craftsmen were warned that if found drunk they would be forbidden to hire themselves to the inhabitants; drunk NCOs were threatened with demotion and further advised that they would never to be promoted again. In 1723, officers were instructed to punish drunken soldiers by extraordinary duty or by ordering them to be tied neck to wheel, an uncomfortable posture, but still short of flogging. In 1732, such men were to be put on bread and water for a week and their pay was to be divided between the provost and the soldier who replaced them on duty. In 1743, the equivalent penalty was four days at the king's works, part of the offender's pay going towards the compensation of the replacement and the rest to the hospital.[23] The severity of the measures against drunken troops should thus be seen in perspective. Drunkenness, even on duty, did not necessary result in corporal punishment, which is typically perceived as the usual way of dealing with disciplinary infractions of this kind.

It is not that drunken soldiers in eighteenth-century Gibraltar would necessarily escape the lash. In 1727, summary punishment of fifty lashes was allowed on top of extra duty, and similar orders were repeated in 1739 and 1741. In 1743, drunken guards were to be tried before a garrison court martial, a tier above the regimental courts, and to spend seven days at the provost's. Three years later, they were threatened with 200 lashes and a month under arrest. Finally, in September 1752, it was declared that drunkenness on duty would result in general court martial, which, as the men were reminded,

---

23 Ibid., 25 April, 3 May and 3 July 1721; 22 May, 13 June and 3 August 1722; 15 July 1723; 9 January 1732; WO 284/2, 8 January 1743.

could adjudicate capital punishment.[24] Nevertheless, the apparent trend towards heavier penalties is not as obvious as it might appear. In the case of the last measure, it was clearly an empty threat, as confirmed by the order books themselves. In October a drunken soldier who attempted to wound a sergeant was sentenced to 300 lashes, while general courts martial for 1753 included instances of desertion, mutiny, rape, murder and theft, but not a single case against a soldier found drunk on guard. In 1754, the order books began mentioning cases coming before garrison courts martial and it is clear that drunken sentries remained clearly within their remit. The penalties they received are not mentioned, but the total number of their cases is telling. In that year, drunkenness on duty produced fewer than ten cases. It is unlikely, therefore, that more than a small minority of all drunken guards actually ended before such courts.

Moreover, while the entry for 1 July 1754 again threatened men found drunk on duty with a general court martial and all other drunks with a regimental one, further orders suggest these measures were not implemented. On 4 September, after a preamble which acknowledged that whipping had failed to provide a deterrent, flogging sentences at regimental courts martial were essentially called off. Instead, officers were ordered to replace punishments numbering between fifty and 100 lashes with one day at the king's works; any additional 100 lashes were to be exchanged likewise. Furthermore, this order essentially nullified a much more severe threat issued earlier in May to punish soldiers overstaying in wine houses with three weeks' arrest on bread and water.[25] Thus, throughout that year, the men were receiving conflicting messages about what punishment they could expect for the same offence, a situation not unlike that which prevailed in previous decades, when summary lashings, arrests, fines and extra duty were all invoked interchangeably. The number of these threats is not only suggestive of their failure to prevent alcohol abuse among the troops, but also their inconsistency. In June 1772, for instance, after pardoning all soldiers confined for drunkenness on guard, Governor Cornwallis declared such leniency would never be exercised again. Less than three months later, a man sentenced for 300 lashes for that very offence was pardoned 'on the application of some gentlemen'.[26]

Moreover, the retraction of previous disciplinary measures is not the only example of what was, essentially, a double message. In 1724, pickets were

---

24 TNA, WO 284/1, 12 February 1727; 284/2, 9 December 1739; 27 March 1741; 25 December 1743; 23 February 1744; 17 November 1747; 284/3, 25 September 1752.

25 TNA, WO 284/3, 10 May, 1 July, 4 September 1754. Substitution of flogging with extra duty for most drunken offences was repeated again in 1762 and 1764. See: WO 284/4, 13 March and 14 July respectively.

26 TNA, WO 284/5, 16 June, 11 September 1772.

ordered not to take more than a pint of wine on guard. Ironically, a year later, officers were to inspect their guards every two hours to make sure they remained sober. In 1779, during the Great Siege, men were not allowed to take wine on duty unless permitted to do so by their officers. Moreover, the governor occasionally intervened to limit the cost of wine. For instance, in 1748, after communications with Spain were partially reopened, sutlers were issued with maximal prices and threatened with expulsion if they charged more. As shown by Paul Kopperman, who examined drunkenness in the eighteenth-century British army, the attitude of the military authorities towards alcohol consumption was ambivalent. While drunkenness was obviously seen as a major disciplinary problem, alcohol was often considered beneficial for the men's health. It was also a great morale booster.[27] Consequently, officers directed their punitive actions not against drinking but against drunkenness. Another facet of the half-hearted policy was the treatment of sutlers. While drunken soldiers were often punished, few commanding officers genuinely tried to limit the activities of the vendors who provided the men with alcohol in the first place. The policy in Gibraltar fits well into this general pattern.

At first glance, trade in alcohol in the garrison was strictly regulated, as there was hardly a year during which an order pertaining to sutlers and wine-house owners was not issued. Business hours were subject to restrictions, as were, occasionally, the type of drink to be sold as well as the persons who were allowed to trade. As in the case of drunken soldiers, the entries were largely a set of prohibitions which, with few exceptions, exhibit no genuine resolve to cut alcohol consumption. In the early 1720s, no drinks were to be sold between the mounting of the morning guard and the evening tattoo. In 1725, the opening hour was moved back to midday and, the following year, sutlers were to close their doors as early as four in the afternoon, a situation which remained in force during the siege the next year. In 1730, however, the next occasion when official trading times are mentioned, these lasted from eleven in the forenoon to nine in the evening, and, in 1741, soldiers could buy alcohol as early as nine in the morning.[28] Nor were the occasional attempts to ban the sale of spirits pursued without any greater consistency. In 1722, soldiers were banned from buying liquor, but this apparently made little impression, as in December 1726 all sutlers were ordered to report their stocks

---

27 TNA, WO 284/1, 1 January 1724; 4 March 1725; WO 284/6, 30 October 1779. For examples of orders limiting the prices of wine, see: WO 284/2, 29 November 1748, WO 284/5, 18 January 1882; Paul E. Kopperman, "'The Cheapest Pay': Alcohol Abuse in Eighteenth-Century British Army', *Journal of Military History*, 60 (1996), pp. 445–70.

28 TNA, WO 284/1, 22 October 1720; 21 June 1721; 1 December 1725; 29 April, 6 June 1726; 16 February, 4 May 1727; 29 July, 29 August 1730; 27 January 1735; WO 284/2, 19 September 1741.

of brandy to the town major. After the start of the siege, shortly afterwards, all spirits were ordered to be collected, while wine could be sold in exchange for ration tickets not exceeding one pint per day. Although the garrison books contain no reference to the countermanding of these orders, it is clear that spirits were again available in 1730 as the year contained entries regulating the licensing system under which they could be sold. Liquor was supposedly collected again in June 1754, but the efficiency of this measure is doubtful as the prohibition against soldiers and their wives selling brandy had to be repeated in subsequent years. Regulation of its importation from 1758 also signifies that spirits could again be lawfully brought into town.[29]

Similar inconsistency prevails in the punishments threatened against retailers breaking the regulations. The most common penalty invoked in the order books was summary expulsion from the garrison, which was occasionally inflicted.[30] Nevertheless, sequences of contradictory orders make one doubt whether such punishments were actually implemented with any frequency. In December 1725, any sutler who opened his business at forbidden hours was to be expelled, but less than three months later the punishment was to be a fine of half a dollar. Similarly, in January 1735 alone, a threat to revoke the selling license was followed by an entry which specified a fine of ten dollars for the very same offence. Transgressing sutlers were to be turned out of the town in September 1741, but next year they were only to forfeit their licenses and their stocks of liquor.[31] Cases when lenient punishments followed on the heels of much sterner measures were unlikely to add towards the deterrent effect of the former, even if the earlier severe commands were never formally countermanded.

As noted by Kopperman, in their business the sutlers depended on the goodwill of the military authorities. This would be particularly true in Gibraltar, not only because the issue of vending permits was a prerogative of the governor, but because the supply of wine and spirits depended entirely on import, as they could not be produced within the enclave. Moreover, Gibraltar's sutlers were even more vulnerable to direct action by the authorities as there was no civil jurisprudence to rely upon. Yet, despite the fact that the potential to limit their sales within Gibraltar was higher than elsewhere, alcoholic drinks remained easily available within the garrison. Moreover, it is

---

29 Ibid., 3 May 1722; 17 May 1724; 24 December 1726; 25 February, 10 May, 5 June, 11 June 1727; 25 June, 2 July 1730; WO 284/3, 13 June 1754, 8 January 1758, 18 February 1758, 8 June 1759, 13 November 1765. See also: Tito Benady, 'The Governors of Gibraltar II (1730–1749), *Gibraltar Heritage Journal*, 10 (2003), p. 46.

30 TNA, WO 284/3, 27 August 1754.

31 TNA, WO 284/1, 1 December 1725; 26 February, 29 April, 6 June 1726; 1 and 27 January 1735; WO 284/2, 19 September 1741, 8 May 1742.

possible that Gibraltar's unique situation actually undermined the resolve to act determinedly against the sutlers as the governor was a major beneficiary of their trade. In the late 1740s, for instance, it was argued that duties on wine and spirits made up about 20,000 dollars, or well over a third of his income. As Constantine has pointed out, some governors were not above playing a double game, smuggling in defiance of both the treaty of Utrecht and formal instructions from London. The same may very well have applied in connection with the sale of spirits, since the closure of wine houses or a general ban on all imports would have affected profits from what was well known to be a very lucrative post.[32] What is more important to our case, though, is that soldiers' civilian accomplices were sometimes just as difficult to discipline as the soldiers themselves. The limits of control exercised over either group are also made clear in our second test case.

The authorities in Gibraltar led a ceaseless struggle against dogs. Its motive, as stated in the order books, was the protection of the flocks grazing on the hill and the prevention of rabies, although another reason may have been general hygiene, as two entries from the early 1740s specify that a portion of the fine levied from dog owners was to go to the street cleaners.[33] The policy alternated between banning dogs from parts of the garrison, such as the grand parade and the hill, to the general extermination of all dogs in town. For most of the century, however, inhabitants were allowed to keep dogs as long as they were tied indoors, but this indulgence did not extend to the soldiery. A typical culling order directed soldiers to kill their own dogs as well as all others they encountered on the streets. Guards were instructed to dispatch dogs that passed near their post. NCOs were to ensure that no dogs were kept by their men in barracks. The first order authorising the killing of all loose dogs dates to 1727, and it was renewed twelve times in the next twenty years alone. Civilians whose dog was killed on the street were to be punished, as were soldiers discovered to be keeping a dog in spite of the prohibition.[34] Yet, despite these regulations, it appears that the campaign against dogs largely failed.

As with the measures against drunkenness, the orders against dogs often sent a conflicting message. In August 1740, not only the soldiers but also the civilian inhabitants were ordered to kill all their dogs or have their houses

---

32 Kopperman, 'Cheapest Pay', pp. 469–70; Constantine, *Community*, pp. 46–7; see also Tito Benady, 'The Governors of Gibraltar I (1704–1730)', *Gibraltar Heritage Journal*, 9 (2002), pp. 48–9.

33 TNA, WO 284/2, 17 September 1740; 19 May 1741.

34 A selection of such orders from across the century includes: TNA, WO 284/1, 24 April 1724, 13 October 1727, 17 July 1736; 284/2, 1 October 1744; 284/3, 8 February 1752; 284/4, 9 November 1762; 284/5, 4 November 1774; 284/6, 23 May 1782; 284/7, 20 April 1786.

pulled down. Next month, as numerous dogs were still seen on the streets 'and even the parade', the order was repeated but the punishment threatened for civilians was a fine of ten dollars. In 1753, inhabitants who failed to secure their dogs indoors were to be prosecuted before the newly established civilian courts as maintainers of public nuisance. Next year, however, it was clear that dogs were allowed to roam freely in town, as orders forbade them to appear on the hill only.[35] Another important point is that the culling had an element of privatisation, as owners who did not tie their dogs were required to pay the person who killed it on the street. Although obviously intended to provide encouragement for private individuals to help in its execution,[36] this order also meant that its enforcement was actively delegated to the subject population under the positive assumption that the inhabitants would be obliging enough to control and discipline themselves. Rather than providing testimony for the success of direct controls in the garrison, this measure could well be indicative of their inadequacy. The latter option becomes likelier when one considers the practicalities under which the actual culling was to be carried out.

Although their owners were to keep them tied in the immediate aftermath of a culling order, officers' dogs were not necessarily condemned to a life indoors. For instance, in 1733, a strongly worded order commanding all soldiers and NCOs to kill their dogs was followed by another instruction which allowed dogs to go outside again. This indicates that once stray animals and soldiers' dogs were eliminated, those belonging to their superiors could roam the streets as before. Moreover, order books sometimes mention individual animals exempted from the killings. The orders of 1740 specified three such dogs, and in 1742 the list mentioned fourteen animals, not including those whose descriptions were posted separately in the regimental barracks. Although commonly mentioning attributes such as colour and size, the descriptions were not very detailed. A typical exemption was granted to 'a small black dog with a yellow collar about his neck' or 'a motted dog with a red collar Ensign Mageough['s name] wrote on it'.[37] Since the primary identi-fication was often provided by the name or initials of the owner, a sentinel wishing to adhere to the culling order, but also to avoid the risk of harming an officer's pet, had to catch the animal and read whatever was engraved on its collar. Moreover, the exemption orders assume that soldiers in Gibraltar were not only endowed with excellent memory but were also literate. These

---

35 TNA, WO 284/2, 21 August, 17 September 1740, 18 July 1753, 21 June, 28 June 1754.

36 For references to rewards due to dog killers, see: TNA, WO 284/1, 2 May 1731, 28 June 1735; 284/2, 30 May 1743; 284/3, 20 July 1754.

37 TNA, WO 284/1, 7 May and 15 May 1733; 284/2, 23 May 1741; 20 October 1742.

were unrealistic expectations of the men which undermined the success of the campaign against dogs. In 1746, following an outbreak of rabies, officers stationed at the gates were instructed to order the killing of all dogs passing through their posts. This, however, was followed with a warning to try any officer who would hinder their guards from executing this command. The order against officers interfering in the killing of dogs was repeated the following year, implying that, not unlike the failure to curb irregular wine sales, not only the soldiers but also their superiors could act against the very orders they were meant to implement.[38]

According to Wilson, 'as with other areas of legislation in early modern Europe, the very volume of official decrees indicates how poorly they were enforced'.[39] The inconsistency of the penal measures, combined with the issue of stern orders which were often countermanded almost as quickly as they were drafted, was unlikely to inspire much awe and compliance. As shown by evidence drawn from their own order books, the authorities in eighteenth-century Gibraltar were largely unsuccessful in preventing soldiers from getting drunk, or civilians from providing them with liquor. Nor could these two groups be forced to destroy their dogs, despite attempts to encourage the population to partake in the pursuit. Despite its territorial isolation, its subjugation to military law and the unprecedented number of would-be enforcers within its tiny area, the situation in the garrison corresponded to what Lars Behrisch fittingly defined as the paradox of overregulation and under-government.[40] Despite the unique conditions prevailing within the enclave, the actual power of the authorities in Gibraltar was limited, even on relatively trivial matters. As we have argued, Gibraltar stood out in terms of the potential for monitoring and direct control over both its civil and military populace. What does this tell us, therefore, about the chances of successfully disciplining soldiers and civilians in more characteristic parts of eighteenth-century Europe?

---

38 TNA, WO 284/2, 16 December 1746; 28 September 1747.

39 Peter H. Wilson, *War, State and Society in Württemberg, 1677–1793* (Cambridge: Cambridge University Press, 1995), p. 82.

40 Lars Behrisch, 'Social Discipline in Early Modern Russian, Seventeenth to Nineteenth Centuries', in *Institutionen, Instrumente und Alteure sozialer Kontrolle und Disziplinierung im frühneuzeitlichen Europa* ed. by Heinz Schilling and Lars Behrisch (Frankfurt am Main: Klostermann, 1996), p. 332.

Part 4

Gender

7

Conflicts of Conduct
British Masculinity and Military Painting
in the Wake of the Siege of Gibraltar

Cicely Robinson

B RITISH VICTORY at the Siege of Gibraltar (1779–83) was achieved in the midst of overwhelming British defeat in the American Revolutionary War. This victory was subsequently represented in several large-scale pictures, painted by leading contemporary artists. John Trumbull's *The Sortie of the Garrison at Gibraltar* (painted 1789, Fig. 1) depicts a successful British attack upon the invading Spanish forces at the Rock on 26–27 November 1781. John Singleton Copley's *The Defeat of the Spanish Batteries at Gibraltar* (painted 1783–91, Fig. 2) recounts a later British victory over the Franco-Spanish allied attack which took place on 13–14 September 1782. Both works were publicly exhibited in London in the decade that followed British defeat in America. Trumbull exhibited *The Sortie* in a one-work show in the Ansell Auction Rooms at Spring Gardens in April 1789. Two years later, in 1791, Copley exhibited *The Defeat of the Spanish Batteries* in a one-work show in a temporary pavilion at Green Park. The public exhibition of these martial narratives invites us to consider how contemporary military action, and the men who participated in this conflict, were presented to, and received by, the late eighteenth-century British public.

Trumbull's depiction of *The Sortie of the Garrison at Gibraltar* recounts the events when the British garrison set a surprise attack upon an invasive Spanish encampment.[1] Captain John Drinkwater recorded the progression of

---

1 In his *Autobiography*, Trumbull recounts walking down Oxford Street in May 1787 with Antonio Poggi, who told him 'the story of the sortie from Gibraltar'. See: John Trumbull, *Autobiography, Reminiscences and Letters of John Trumbull from 1756 to 1841* (New York and London: Wiley Putnam, 1841), p. 148.

Figure 1   John Trumbull, *The Sortie of the Garrison at Gibraltar, 26th–27th November 1781* (1789): oil on canvas (180.3 × 271.8 cm).

Purchase, Pauline V. Fullerton Bequest; Mr and Mrs James Walter Carter and Mr and Mrs Raymond J. Horowitz Gifts; Erving Wolf Foundation and Vain and Harry Fish Foundation Inc. Gifts; Gift of Hanson K. Corning, by exchange; and Maria DeWitt Jesup and M. Acc.n.: 1976.332. Photo: Geoffrey Clements © 2012. Image copyright The Metropolitan Museum of Art/Art Resource/Scala, Florence.

events in the *History of the Late Siege of Gibraltar*, first published in 1785.[2] On the night of 26 November 1781, the British garrison marched upon a Spanish camp. Before dawn, the British forces had demolished it in a particularly brutal act of martial aggression. Trumbull depicts the encounter in its later stages as dawn is breaking. While Spanish troops are depicted fleeing to the upper left of the painting, British soldiers continue with the onslaught in the middle distance; a wielded pick and axe are clearly visible against the clouded sky. In the centre of the composition, the British general George Eliott offers aid to the fallen Spanish officer, Captain Don José de Barboza. When British officers offered to remove him to a place of safety, Barboza refused, wishing instead to die upon the ruins of his post. In his autobiography, Trumbull explains his reasoning for isolating this moment in the narrative:

2 John Drinkwater, *A History of the Late Siege of Gibraltar* [1785] 2nd edn (London, 1786), pp. 196–203.

Figure 2   John Singleton Copley, *The Defeat of the Spanish Batteries at Gibraltar, 13th –14th September 1782* (1783–91): oil on canvas (302 × 762 cm).

Guildhall Art Gallery, London.

'I was pleased with the subject, as offering, in the gallant conduct and death of the Spanish commander, a scene of deep interest to the feelings.'[3] Trumbull painted three versions of *The Sortie*.[4] This account of British martial magnanimity and enemy valour was the subject of each work. The third and final version of *The Sortie*, painted in 1789 and exhibited at Spring Gardens, will be the subject of this enquiry.

Copley's *Defeat of the Spanish Batteries* depicts a later and culminating victory at Gibraltar against the allied Franco-Spanish attack.[5] Drinkwater's

---

3 Trumbull, *Autobiography*, p. 148.

4 The first version of *The Sortie*, measuring 36 × 53 cm, was finished in 1787. It was given to Benjamin West, but is now lost. The second version, measuring 50.8 × 76.2 cm, was finished in 1788. This version is now in the Cincinnati Art Museum, Ohio. The third version was painted in 1789 (measuring 180.3 × 271.8 cm) and is now in the New York Metropolitan Museum of Art. Trumbull subsequently painted two replicas of *The Sortie* between 1840 and 1843. For a discussion of these works and the relevant preliminary drawings, see: Jean Lambert Brockway, 'Trumbull's Sortie', *The Art Bulletin*, 16.1 (1934), pp. 4–13.

5 For a detailed description of this painting, see: Jules Prown, *John Singleton Copley*, 2 vols (Cambridge, MA: Harvard University Press, 1966), esp. 2, pp. 330–6.

History of the Late Siege outlines the progression of events.[6] On the morning of the 13 September 1782, the Spanish anchored their battering ships in the bay at a range of 900 to 1,200 yards from the British bastion. These 'batteries' were old men-of-war that had been cut down and reinforced with metre-wide timbers and packed with wet sand. They were thought to be unsinkable. Able to fire at close quarters with fatal accuracy, they were a grave threat to the British garrison stationed at the Rock.[7] In retaliation, under the command of General George Eliott, the British fired heated shot into the Spanish ships. As Drinkwater describes, 'for some hours, the attack and defence were so equally well supported, as scarcely to admit [...] superiority [...] on either side'.[8] In the afternoon, however, smoke began to appear from the Spanish ships and by one o'clock the following morning the closest battering ship burst into flames. This lit up the harbour, allowing the British gunners to fire with increased accuracy throughout the night.[9] Copley depicts the Bay of Gibraltar on the morning of 14 September 1782.[10] Rather than dramatising the attack itself, this work shows the subsequent rescue attempt in which the British endeavoured to save their Spanish adversaries from the wreckage of the burning battering ships. The garrison officers observe the progression of events from the British bastion. Within the seascape, two British gunboats under the command of Sir Roger Curtis and Captain Bradshaw Smith progress towards the burning Spanish battering ships. The written explanation of this narrative, published in the Green Park exhibition catalogue, describes how 'a detachment of British seamen [...] at the hazard of their own lives, are rescuing their vanquished enemies'.[11] In *The Defeat of*

---

6 Drinkwater, *History of the Late Siege*, p. 291.

7 For an examination of events leading up to and including the siege, see: T. H. McGuffie, *The Siege of Gibraltar 1779–1783* (London: B. T. Batsford Ltd, 1965), esp. pp. 13–22 and 35–7.

8 Drinkwater, *History of the Late Siege*, p. 291.

9 Copley worked closely with Drinkwater during the production of *The Defeat of the Spanish Batteries*. As a mark of gratitude, Copley made a late compositional addition including Drinkwater's portrait on the far right of the officer group. This addition is thought to have been made after 1788. See: Prown, *John Singleton Copley*, p. 330. A written annotation in Drinkwater's personal copy of the *History of the Late Siege* (end note) records that this addition was a 'spontaneous proposal of Mr Copley in compliment, as he also was pleased to observe to the Historian of the Siege, & also as a return to Col. D. for the many hours He devoted to affording Mr C. Information'. National Maritime Museum library as cited by Prown, *John Singleton Copley*, p. 330.

10 A description of the scene across the bay at daybreak was published in *The Annual Register*, 1782, p. 238.

11 British Museum, 1908,0717.1, *Proposal for publishing by Subscription, An Engraving from the historical Picture of the Siege and Relief of Gibraltar, painted by J. S. Copley, R.A., Now*

the Spanish Batteries, Copley presents a narrative of martial compassion amid the ongoing devastation of British military dominance.[12]

This enquiry will consider how the construction of martial action and the representation of military men within these paintings conveyed differing facets of male identity to the eighteenth-century British public.[13] We must examine the types of martial masculinities that are exhibited within these two all-male narratives and consider the presentation of a multifaceted gender formation.[14] In the century of 'polite' society, this investigation will consider the potential tensions that arise when the desire to align martial identity with a hegemonic masculine position – as something crucially different from woman, the homosexual man, the effeminate fop and the French – is simultaneously reliant upon the socialising impact of these influences.[15] The public exhibition of these works invites us to explore how the display of military painting within British society provided a means to mediate the potential tensions between the civic and martial spheres. In an examination of these two paintings, this enquiry will consider how the potential tensions that arise between man as soldier and gentleman are combated by an idealised representation of martial behaviour upon the battlefield. In the wake of British defeat in the American Revolutionary War, we are presented with an episode of heightened national anxiety. The public exhibition of these martial paintings invites us to consider the national significance of British victory at Gibraltar. We must examine how representations of this victorious action were employed as a means to reassert public confidence and national status in the wake of an overwhelming defeat across the Atlantic.

---

exhibiting in a Pavilion erected by the gracious Permission of the King, for that purpose, in the Green Park (Subscription Notice, 1791), p. 2.

12 The London Metropolitan Archives, London (LMA), General Records Office, Common Council, Journal 68, fol. 298, *Common Council Committee Minutes*. The commission for this painting came from the Corporation of the City of London. The committee minutes show that in February 1783, the Corporation first articulated a desire to express its 'respect and attention' for those who had successfully defended the Rock against the Franco-Spanish alliance, specifying that they wanted to acknowledge 'the illustrious General Eliott, Lord Howe and the Officers of His Majesty's army and navy'. Both Copley and Benjamin West applied, but Copley secured the commission by proposing to complete the work for a lower fee.

13 For a discussion of multiple masculinities, see: R. W. Connell, *Masculinities* (Cambridge: Polity Press, 2005), esp. pp. 76–7; Paul Higate, *Military Masculinities: Identity and the State* (Westport, CT: Praeger Publishers, 2003).

14 Connell, *Masculinities*, p. 77; R. W. Connell and James W. Messerschmidt, 'Hegemonic Masculinity: Rethinking the Concept', *Gender and Society*, 19.6 (2005), pp. 829–59.

15 Tim Hitchcock and Michèle Cohen (eds), *English Masculinities 1660–1800* (London: Longman, 1999), pp. 1–22.

THE OFFICER-GENTLEMAN:
EXERCISING CIVILITY UPON THE BATTLEFIELD

As WE SAW in chapter 4, British men in the eighteenth century were urged to reform their rough manners and to become 'polite'. This civilising of the gentleman remained reliant upon a significant female influence.[16] This is evident in a vast amount of contemporary conduct literature. For example, James Forester's *The Polite Philosopher* was one of the many widely published treatises on the education of the gentleman; first published in 1734, the eighth edition was reprinted in 1776. Within this treatise, Forester advised that 'It is to the Fair Sex we owe our most shining qualities [...] Men of true taste feel a natural complaisance for women when they converse with them, and fall, without knowing it, upon every art of pleasing [...] that habit is the very essence of politeness.'[17] Forester proposed that 'It is the conversation of women that gives a proper bias to our inclinations and, by abating the ferocity of our passions, engages us to that gentleness of deportment which we style *humanity*.' Where the social conduct and the training of a gentleman remained reliant upon the civilising influences of female company, the all-male martial environment presented a direct challenge to this mode of gender formation. Upon the foreign battlefield, in the absence of a civilising female presence, how could the intrinsic 'ferocity' of male nature be tempered and controlled?[18] This anxiety was surely heightened by the act of war itself, which facilitated and essentially remained reliant upon acts of violence. In a review of *The Sortie* published on Thursday 7 May 1789, *The World* remarked upon 'the distinction which the Painter has so judiciously observed, between the Soldiery – the executive part of an Army, and the Officers, who are the soul of the machine'.[19] Where the all-male violent battlefield was a potential site for social and civil anxiety, I want to explore how this concern was alleviated through the mythic construction of the British officer-gentleman.

---

16 Robert Shoemaker, *Gender in English Society 1650–1850: The Emergence of Separate Spheres* (London: Longman, 1998), pp. 21–36; Michèle Cohen, 'Manliness, Effeminacy and the French: Gender and the Construction of National Character in Eighteenth-Century England' in Hitchcock and Cohen (eds), *English Masculinities*, pp. 44–62; Lawrence Klein, 'Politeness and the Interpretation of the British Eighteenth Century', *The Historical Journal*, 45.4 (2002), pp. 869–98.

17 James Forester, *The Polite Philosopher or An Essay on that Art which makes a man happy in himself, and agreeable to others* [1734] 8th edn (Edinburgh: printed for Alexander Donaldson, 1776), pp. 62–3.

18 Forester, *The Polite Philosopher*, pp. 65–6.

19 *The World*, 733, Thursday 7 May 1789.

In both *The Sortie* and *The Defeat of the Spanish Batteries*, attempts have been made to distinguish and isolate the main officer party from the continuing action. In *The Sortie*, the majority of the officers are positioned in a group towards the right of the painting. They are compositionally separated from the British action on the left by the central episode between the British General Eliott and his fallen Spanish adversary, Don José de Barboza. In Copley's *Defeat of the Spanish Batteries*, this compositional isolation is exaggerated further. The officer party is positioned at the far right of the painting upon the British bastion. From this point of compositional detachment they observe the rescue attempt underway in the water below. In both paintings, the officer party observe but, crucially, do not participate in the action that surrounds them. The immaculate condition of their uniforms further proclaims a physical detachment from any acts of actual aggression or violence that would otherwise jeopardise their status as gentlemen. All the while, military attributes provide a prosthetic reassertion of their command. In *The Sortie*, a discarded musket lies upon the floor in the right foreground and in *The Defeat of the Spanish Batteries* a cannon is present upon the bastion. However, both weapons remain crucially unfired. This is emphasised within *The Defeat of the Spanish Batteries* by Major Vallotton, who uses the cannon as a support for his telescope. The inactivity of these weapons reinforces the physical detachment of the officer party from any acts of actual violence that would risk their civility. Simultaneously, these martial prosthetics present us with a latent threat which is subsequently realised through the actions of their subordinates.

The garrison officers are collectively set against a backdrop of the ongoing events. In both works, clouds of smoke from the enduring British destruction billow up into their compositional space and a narrative of the unfolding events is underway behind them. Much like a contemporary martial portrait, the circumstances of their triumph are employed as a background against which their personal status and position can be solidified pictorially. In *The Sortie*, General Eliott is shown with the Star of Bath clearly exhibited upon his chest. Following victory in Gibraltar, Eliott was awarded a peerage on 6 July 1787, becoming 1st Baron Heathfield. In the following year, on 19 May 1788, the general was formally installed as a Knight of the Bath.[20] This newly acquired social elevation was a direct result of his military success. The inclusion of the order within Trumbull's narrative pictorially solidifies this

---

20 Dorinda Evans, *Mather Brown: Early American Artist in England* (Middletown, CT: Wesleyan University Press, 1982), p. 81; G. E. Cokayne, *The Complete Peerage of England, Scotland, Ireland, Great Britain, and the United Kingdom*, 8 vols (London: G. Bell & Sons, 1887–98); *The Gentleman's Magazine*, 60 (1790), p. 671.

Figure 3   John Singleton Copley, *Study of General Eliott on Horseback, Mounted on Rearing Horse to Left, Preliminary Drawing for the 'Defeat of the Spanish Batteries'* (c. 1780s): black and white chalk on blue paper (36.8 × 33.5 cm).

British Museum, London. © Trustees of the British Museum.

accession in both civic and martial status. However, Trumbull's inclusion of the order, an award issued in the wake of the victory, disrupts the illusion of an historic narrative. A preliminary sketch for *Defeat of the Spanish Batteries* suggests that Copley experimented with positioning General Eliott in profile upon a rearing horse (Fig. 3). In the final painting, however, the equestrian portrait is firmly stationed upon the bastion and depicted from the front. This revised position of the equestrian arrangement successfully covers the right breast. Eliott is neither shown with or without the order and the illusion of narrative may be sustained without unfavourably presenting the general without this mark of status.

The pictorial construction of the idealised gentleman-officer can be seen to culminate with the presentation of General Eliott. In *The Sortie*, the general is positioned at the centre of the painting. A review of *The Sortie* published in *The World* described how 'the figure of Lord Heathfield stands as it ought, nobly conspicuous in that mild and amiable dignity which should characterize a victorious Hero'.[21] In the midst of the battle, Eliott and Captain Alexander Mackenzie of the 71st Regiment have paused to offer their hands to the wounded Don José de Barboza. Much like a duel, Eliott adheres to the rules of a fair fight and has ceased his aggression now his opponent has fallen.[22] General Eliott's raised arm references the Apollo Belvedere, which further monumentalises the magnanimity and heroic restraint of his actions. Eliott's hand is held out, not in a gesture of command or aggression, but as an expression of aid towards his wounded adversary. In this central narrative, Eliott exhibits a rationalised and manly sentiment. His hand, along with those of Barboza and Mackenzie, provides a fulcrum around which the rest of the composition unfolds. The entire narrative is hinged around this central exhibition of British restraint and compassion made in the midst of the ongoing battle.

When we consider Copley's *Defeat of the Spanish Batteries*, the written account published in the Green Park exhibition catalogue describes the upper right section of the painting as exhibiting 'the Victory of the Garrison, and in the moment of their triumph, a display of humanity, that highly exalts the British character'.[23] In a preliminary drawing, it seems that Copley entertained the idea of depicting the entire officer party celebrating the 'Victory of the Garrison', cheering and waving their hats in the air (Fig. 4: see the drawing of the 'cheering group' in the upper right). In the final version, the officers no longer revel in their success. Instead, following the commanding gesture of the mounted General Eliott, they attentively observe the rescue attempt with gentlemanly reserve and concern. The single bicorne that lies upon the floor at the lower right of the bastion provides perhaps the slightest suggestion that such behaviour has already taken place.

The equestrian portrait situates General Eliott at the summit of a hierarchical pyramid. Positioned to the left of Eliott, Major Green, the founder of

---

21 *The World*, Thursday 7 May 1789.
22 Robert Shoemaker, 'Male Honour and the Decline of Public Violence in Eighteenth-Century London', *Social History*, 26.2 (May, 2001), pp. 190–208, esp. p. 198; V. G. Kiernan, *The Duel in European History* (Oxford: Oxford University Press, 1988).
23 *Proposal for Publishing by Subscription*, p. 2.

Figure 4   John Singleton Copley, *Study for 'The Siege of Gibraltar': Figure Reaching; Sprawling Figures; Cheering Group; Dying Sailors* (1785–6): black chalk and white chalk heightening on light blue laid paper (37.1 × 58.4 cm).

The Metropolitan Museum of Art, Harris Brisbane Dick Fund, 1960 (60.44.15). © 2012. Image copyright The Metropolitan Museum of Art/Art Resource/ Scala, Florence.

the Royal Engineers, looks directly up at his commander, firmly reinforcing this system of rank. The equestrian portrait positions Eliott within an iconographic lineage of martial command. This compositional reference to the statue of Marcus Aurelius (The Capitoline Museum, Rome) further imbues the general with a classicising gravitas. In the preliminary drawing of the equestrian portrait, Eliott was positioned upon a rearing horse gesturing as if leading a charge (Fig. 3). In the final work, Copley firmly stations the horse upon the bastion. Eliott's gesture towards the enemy is transformed from a sign of aggression to one of aid. Here, the general's outstretched arm commands the British relief effort. Within the battlescape, Sir Roger Curtis mirrors Eliott's stance; a pictorial motif which conveys this communication of orders across the canvas.

Within these depictions of British martial victory, the officer-gentleman is shown to be a crucially rational and magnanimous figure. General Eliott's actions provide an idealised model for both martial and gentlemanly conduct. Within Trumbull's *Sortie*, General Eliott's offer of aid is the ultimate assertion of civilised British self-discipline. Copley's *Defeat of the Spanish Batteries* presents us with the innate magnanimity of the British officer in the face of victory. When exhibited to the British public, the presentation of these acts of physical restraint and martial magnanimity would combat the anxieties that the homosocial martial battlefield produced. This idealised presentation of the officer reaffirms the civility of gentlemen when upon the battlefield. In the absence of a civilising female influence, these men do not intrinsically fall into acts of uncivilised brutality. Through this construction of a rational and manly sentiment, martial painting can perhaps be seen to directly challenge society's standardised mode of gentlemanly training, identity formation and the need for a significant female influence. Through this pictorial confirmation of inherent male civility, these works can perhaps be seen to reassert the autonomy of male civility and conduct.

Active Soldiers

Since aggression and violence posed a challenge to civility, we should explore the presentation of martial action within these idealising battlescapes. One would have thought that a narrative of violence would have directly challenged the behavioural codes of civil conduct and confirmed concerns regarding brutality upon the battlefield. Where gentlemanly civility encouraged restraint, I want to explore how representations of military action, isolated from British soil and society upon the foreign battlefield, provided an environment where an explicitly *active* masculinity could be exhibited. We should consider the ways in which an active masculinity could reassert a male position that was arguably under threat within society. In the 1757–8 publication *The Estimate of the Manners and Principles of the Times*, John Brown identified a destabilisation in gender divisions within the heterosocial public sphere:

> The Sexes now have little other apparent Distinction beyond that of Person and Dress: Their peculiar and characteristic Manners are confounded and lost: the one Sex having advanced into *Boldness*, as the other have sunk into *Effeminacy*.[24]

Where gentlemen had 'sunk into effeminacy', a culture of politeness, essential in the fashioning and refining of the gentleman, can be seen to challenge a previously distinct and dominant male position.[25] Heterosocial interaction

---

24 John Brown, *Estimate of the Manners and Principles of the Times* (London: printed for L. Davis and C. Reymer, 1757), p. 51.

25 For a discussion of violence and masculinity, see: John Archer (ed.), *Male Violence* (London: Routledge Press, 1994); Jeff Hearn, *The Violences of Men* (London: Sage,

within polite society can be seen as a problematic challenge to a man's patriotic loyalties. As much recent scholarship has discussed, this culture was laced with French influences: the food, wine, language, costume and even this civilising fashion for female conversation were all modelled upon seventeenth-century French salon culture.[26] This Francophilia, evident predominantly among the British aristocracy, would directly conflict with a man's patriotism once relocated to the continental battlefield. The public display of British victory upon the continental battlefield invites a consideration of how military painting was able to recover a specifically British and dominant form of martial masculinity.

We should explore how the actions of the ordinary soldier provided an outlet for eighteenth-century male anger and aggression which was otherwise repressed within society. The *Sortie* exhibits various states of active and aggressive behaviour within the dramatisation of the ongoing British assault. Spanish troops can be seen fleeing off to the upper left while the British continue with the onslaught in the middle distance. Soldiers pass weaponry and tools towards the front; an axe is passed forward to aid with the destruction of the Spanish works. This representation of the soldiers charging towards the enemy conveys the dynamism and strength of the British forces. In the left foreground, a group of British soldiers is depicted in the throes of warfare, and involved in a particularly violent scene of military aggression towards their kneeling adversary. They wield a pick and an axe, workmen's tools rather than conventional weaponry, which stand out against the smoke filled background. Workmen's tools were present at the sortie for the purpose of dismantling the Spanish works.[27] However, within Trumbull's dramatisation the soldiers used all available arms, in an unorthodox and fundamentally brutal manner, in order to secure victory.

This overt display of British aggression is in dramatic juxtaposition to the chivalrous reserve exhibited by the officer party. Where anger and aggression were considered to be specifically masculine traits, they needed to be disciplined. As John Fawcett advised in the 1787 *Essay on Anger*, 'we are

---

1998); Stephen Whitehead, *Men and Masculinities: Key Themes and New Directions* (Cambridge: Polity Press, 2002). For further discussion of 'effeminacy' in eighteenth-century society, see: Philip Cater, 'An "Effeminate" or "Efficient" Nation?', *Textual Practice*, 11.3 (1997): 429–43; Matthew McCormack, 'Dance and Drill', *Cultural & Social History*, 8.3 (2011), p. 318.

26 Cohen, 'Manliness, Effeminacy and the French', in Hitchcock and Cohen, (eds.) *English Masculinities*, p. 44; Linda Colley, *Britons: Forging the Nation 1707–1837* (New Haven, CT: Yale University Press, 1992), p. 88; Philip Mansel, 'Monarchy, Uniform and the Rise of the Frac 1760–1830', *Past & Present*, 96 (1982), pp. 10–16.

27 Drinkwater, *History of the Late Siege*, p. 197.

not to submit to anger as our master but to govern it as our servant'.[28] We should acknowledge the presence of several officers within the action who, amid the violence on the left of *The Sortie*, can be seen to lead the attack. Captain Cuppidge of the Royal Artillery can be seen passing an axe up to one of the troops while Captain Hay is positioned at the summit of the violence. Holding an axe intended for the dismantling of the Spanish encampment, Captain Hay turns to observe the progression of the attack. With his cocked hat raised in the air, he is shown leading the troops towards victory. The presence of the officer within this scene of military attack legitimises and mediates the violence acted out by the ordinary soldier. The officer's presence implies a sense of order and rational necessity to these acts of barbarism. It is pictorially made clear that the violent actions of the ordinary troops are conducted for a purpose, that of national defence. This depiction of conflict and legitimised aggression upon the foreign battlefield allowed the nation to assert and externalise a hyper-masculine position that was otherwise denied and repressed within civilised society.

In Copley's *Defeat of the Spanish Batteries*, the representation of the British rescue attempt successfully evades the depiction of actual violence on behalf of the British troops. Several soldiers in the left of the seascape have climbed aboard one of the battering ships, where they proceed to strike out against the Spanish ensign. The soon to be destroyed Spanish colours are positioned in dramatic juxtaposition against the British ensign, which billows from the stern of Captain Smith's gunboat in a symbolic display of dominance. In contrast to the immaculate presentation of the officer party, many of the ordinary troops have been stripped of their uniforms. The physical strength exhibited by the British soldiers as they haul bodies from the water, emphasised by their exposed and straining muscular bodies, indirectly symbolises the power of the British military force.

While actual physical violence is absent from Copley's narrative, the depiction of the rescue attempt is in itself a proclamation of British victory and an admission of prior aggression. However, as Captain Drinkwater emphasised in the *History of the Late Siege*, this concluding attack on Gibraltar was initiated in the first instance when the Spanish anchored their battering ships in the bay on the 13 September 1782.[29] In *The Defeat of the Spanish Batteries*, the British rescue attempt is conducted by Sir Roger Curtis and Captain Smith. Again, the presence of British officers legitimises the actions of the ordinary soldiers. Their commanding presence confirms that the ordinary troops are acting in the nation's interests. The British action at

---

28 John Fawcett, *An Essay on Anger* (Leeds: Thomas Wright, 1787), p. 11.
29 Drinkwater, *History of the Late Siege*, p. 291.

Gibraltar was projected to the public as an act of defence. Acting in the defence of Britannia, martial violence is realigned with the language of conduct literature. Upon the battlefield, the potentially uncivilised, brutish soldier becomes civilised precisely through his supervised acts of violence, which were enacted in the chivalric defence of a vulnerable and, crucially, feminised home.

THE MARTIAL MARTYR

WE MUST ACKNOWLEDGE the centralised position within both paintings which is allotted to the figure of the defeated fallen soldier. In *The Sortie*, the fatally wounded Spanish captain is positioned propped up upon the deceased body of an anonymous British soldier. Positioned in the distance, seen beneath Barboza's raised left arm, the declining Baron Von Helmstadt of the Walloon Guards is depicted as fatally wounded; he died soon after the battle in the British garrison.[30] In *The Defeat of the Spanish Batteries*, amid the wreckage of the burning Spanish battering ships, countless bodies are depicted in varying states of consciousness. Upon the battlefield, within this multifaceted hierarchy of masculine identities, the wounded or fallen soldier occupies a potentially subordinate role. In a consideration of these pictorial examples, we can begin to explore how these dramatisations of martial action convey and memorialise physical loss upon the battlefield through the construction of a secular sacrificial language.

The fatally wounded Barboza is positioned at the edge of the picture plan, his head bent downward in the stance of *The Dying Gladiator* (The Capitoline Museum, Rome).[31] As the colour drains from his face, the Spaniard's averted gaze directs the viewer towards an anonymous fallen British soldier who lies upon the ground underneath him. This gesture deliberately disrupts the flow of movement across the canvas, which forces the viewer to rest upon this pairing. As Barboza gazes upon the body of the anonymous fallen soldier he acknowledges and resigns himself to his fate. In this decidedly modern memorialisation of military heroism, Trumbull relies upon the contemporary setting and accurate depiction of uniforms to convey the actuality and immediacy of their mutual sacrifice.[32] The martial hero is exhibited

---

30 *References to the Print of the Sortie of Gibraltar, Engraved by William Sharp, from the Original Picture painted by J. Trumbull esq.* (London: A. C. de Poggi, 1799).

31 Trumbull, *Autobiography, Reminiscences and Letters*, p. 148.

32 This grand-manner approach, employing accurate uniforms and a contemporary setting, was first introduced by Benjamin West in his painting of *The Death of General*

in both pre- and post-death states. The ghostly pallor of the fallen British warrior is in dramatic contrast to the red coats and flushed faces of the active soldiers. The collapsed position of this anonymous soldier, arms outstretched towards the picture plane and body limp upon the floor, echoes imagery of the Deposition of Christ. This use of Christian iconography pictorially sanctifies the actions of the anonymous man and ultimately constructs a heroic type which could be memorialised as a martial martyr.[33] Barboza is presented as critically injured but crucially alive, suspended in this pre-death sacrificial state.[34] This central juxtaposition of the fatally wounded Barboza propped up upon the body of a fallen British soldier forces the viewer to confront a universal sacrificial position. With his arm raised in a gesture of refusal towards the assisting British officers, Barboza's stance recalls the *Noli me Tangere*.[35] While the viewer remained geographically removed from the actual site of the battle, this Christian reference emphasises the secularised faith that the public must maintain in the real bodily sacrifice of the soldier.

In Copley's *Defeat of the Spanish Batteries*, the construction of a transnational martial martyr can be identified in the figure of an anonymous, upturned man in the centre of the seascape. Positioned with his arms outstretched, in a crucifix stance, he stares directly out towards the viewer. Again Christian sacrificial iconography is employed to heighten the display of martial martyrdom. Significantly, this man is the only figure within the entire composition to look directly out of the picture plane. His gaze engages the viewer at the point of greatest immediacy. It is only when stood directly in front of the painting that one is confronted by a pair of hands positioned

Wolfe. See: Ann Uhry Abrams, *The Valiant Hero: Benjamin West and the Grand Style History Painting* (Washington DC: Smithsonian Institution Press, 1985).

33 Compositionally, this position pictorially quotes a fallen soldier on the right of J. S. Copley's earlier painting, *The Death of Major Peirson*, which was exhibited in 1784.

34 See Holger Hoock's discussion of 'continual suffering' in *Empires of the Imagination: Politics, War and the Arts in the British World, 1750–1850* (London: Profile Books, 2010), p. 162.

35 John 20:17: 'Jesus saith unto her, Touch me not; for I am not yet ascended to my Father: but go to my brethren, and say unto them, I ascend unto my Father, and your Father; and *to* my God, and your God.' See: *King James Bible* (Oxford: Oxford University Press 'Authorized Version', 2010). Within Christian representations of this narrative, Mary Magdalene is often depicted with her arm outstretched towards, but crucially separated from, the resurrected body of Christ. Rather than touch the body of Christ in order to affirm her belief, she is asked to have faith in the actuality of the resurrected body. Within the context of Trumbull's martial narrative, this visual reference to the *Noli me Tangere* encourages the viewing public to maintain a secularised faith in the real bodily sacrifice of the soldier when isolated from society, upon the foreign battlefield.

just above the water line which grip tightly to this upturned man's right arm. These hands belong to a fully submerged, invisible but crucially alive figure. From across the water, British soldiers within Curtis's gunboat gesture directly towards this group of Spanish soldiers. Within this micro narrative, the immediacy and humanity of the unfolding British rescue attempt is realised. Copley allots this central sacrificial role to an unknown, unidentifiable man. In a preliminary sketch of the central upturned figure, it seems that this man was initially presented clothed in a Spanish uniform (Fig. 4: see the drawing of the 'dying sailor' in the lower right). In the final version, however, he is stripped of both his jacket and shirt. With these symbols of martial allegiance removed, we are presented with the bare torso of an anonymous man. This Christ-like soldier is suspended at the edge of physical expiry, compositionally trapped in an act of perpetual sacrifice. Where Trumbull juxtaposed the physical loss of the two forces, Copley presents a single anonymous martial martyr as an acknowledgement of physical loss. Much like a Deposition altarpiece, the body of this universal martial martyr is pictorially sanctified as it is lowered towards the viewer.[36]

In both paintings, the role of the pre-death martial martyr has been allotted to a Spanish adversary. Both artists have positioned the defeated opposition in a position of wounded physical subordination. Within this all-male hierarchy of masculinities the enemy is effectively diminished. Against the image of the emasculated enemy, British martial masculinity may be strengthened and British officers may exhibit their magnanimity and compassion from a position of overt dominance. In earlier grand-manner battlescapes, this central sacrificial position was more commonly occupied by the fatally wounded British protagonist, such as General Wolfe or Major Peirson.[37] Depicted expiring in the moment of their victory, any anxiety surrounding the presentation of these commanding leaders in a position of physical subordination was supplanted by the memorialisation of their heroism and national victory. However, in the wake of the American Revolutionary War, at a time of heightened national anxiety, perhaps an overt display of British physical loss would only have reinforced an overwhelming sense of defeat. Within these representations of British victory at Gibraltar, both Trumbull and Copley offer an indirect memorial to British martial sacrifice through the construction of a universal code of martial martyrdom.

---

36 See William L. Pressly's discussion of the 'secular altarpiece celebrating Britain's benevolent Empire' in E. B. Neff, *John Singleton Copley in England* (London: Merrell Holberton, 1996), p. 41.

37 Benjamin West, *The Death of General Wolfe* (1770) measuring 151 × 213 cm, National Gallery of Canada, Ottawa; J. S. Copley, *The Death of Major Peirson, 6 January 1781* (1783) measuring 251.5 × 365.8 cm, Tate Gallery, London.

Public Spectacle and the One-Work Exhibition

IN April 1789, an exhibition of Trumbull's *Sortie* opened to the public in the Great Room in Ansell's Auction House at Spring Gardens. The visitor was charged a one shilling admittance fee, which included a descriptive catalogue.[38] For a further three guineas, the visitor could subscribe to an engraving of the painting which was produced by William Sharp.[39] The Spring Gardens at Vauxhall were a significant attraction in London society. An advertisement in the *Bath Chronicle* in April 1789 advertised Spring Gardens as 'now open for the season' with 'Subscriptions for Ladies and Gentlemen walking in the Gardens at 3s each for the season'.[40] We should take note of the heterosocial group to which this advertisement was appealing. In June 1791, John Singleton Copley exhibited *The Defeat of the Spanish Batteries at Gibraltar* within a temporary pavilion installed in London's Green Park.[41] This exhibition followed a similar structure with a one shilling admittance fee, which also included an explanatory catalogue. Again, the visitor could subscribe to an engraved copy of the painting for a further fee. The public exhibition of these two dramatisations of martial victory invites us to consider how the representation of warfare, and the presentation of the men themselves, was received by the British public.

The one-work exhibition provided London with a social spectacle. A review of Copley's Green Park pavilion published in *The Oracle* on 10 June 1791 provides us with a description of the interior: 'the grand picture is 25 feet wide by 22 ½ feet high; it is placed at the extremity of the Tent, fronting the entry, surrounded by a crimson valance, and laterally decorated by two Ionic Columns, in a very chaste and corresponding style'.[42] A predella panel depicting the *Final Relief of Gibraltar*, painted by Dominic Serres, was hung below the main painting. Two medallion portraits of the commanding naval officers, Admiral of the Fleet Richard Howe, 1st Baron Howe (1726–99) and Admiral Samuel Barrington (1729–1800), were hung at either end.[43] The Green Park exhibition received a royal visit prior to the public opening of the show. As reported in the *Diary or Woodfall's Register* on Friday 10 June

---

38 *The World*, 725, 28 April 1789.

39 *Diary or Woodfall's Register*, 24, Saturday 25 April 1789.

40 *Bath Chronicle*, 1483, Thursday 30 April 1789.

41 See John Bonehill, 'Exhibiting War: John Singleton Copley's The Siege of Gibraltar and the Staging of History', in *Conflicting Visions: War and Visual Culture in Britain and France c. 1700–1830*, ed. by John Bonehill and Geoff Quilley (Aldershot: Ashgate Publishing Ltd, 2005), pp. 139–67.

42 *The Oracle*, 635, Friday 10 June 1791.

43 Prown, *John Singleton Copley*, pp. 335–6.

1791, 'On Tuesday morning last their Majesties did Mr Copley the honour to visit his grand Pavilion, erected in Green Park.'[44] As *The World* observed on Saturday 11 June 1791, 'An artist sanctioned by such a Sovereign, cannot fail of receiving the support of a generous public.'[45] This widely published royal approval would have significantly raised the prominence of the exhibition within society; many would have wished to follow this royal precedent.[46]

An engraving by Francesco Bartolozzi provides us with an artistic impression of the social spectacle that Copley constructed at Green Park (Fig. 5). Groups of both male and female spectators are gathered around within the pavilion. A collection of figures stands directly in front of the centre of the picture, gathered before the wide-eyed upturned martial martyr. From Bartolozzi's engraving, we can see that from the height at which the painting was hung within the pavilion, the outward gaze of this figure was positioned directly upon the viewer's eyeline.[47] Set further away from the painting on the left, a man is in discussion with two women. Appearing to be in quasi-military dress, this figure perhaps represents the many military men who, on returning from war, reassume their position as gentlemen within society. Gesturing dramatically towards the officer group positioned upon the bastion, he is perhaps recalling personal experiences from that or other battles. On the far left of Bartolozzi's engraving, a man and woman are shown deep in conversation paying little to no attention to the painting itself. These one-work exhibitions of military painting were consumed as part of a prosperous urban renaissance that was active in late eighteenth-century Britain. Along with many other cultural activities, including the theatre, public gardens and concerts, the art exhibition provided a means to facilitate society and encourage necessarily civilising conversation in the process.[48]

---

44 *Diary or Woodfall's Register*, 691, Friday 10 June 1791.

45 *World*, 1387, Saturday 11 June 1791.

46 Trumbull mentions in his *Autobiography* the onset of the king's 'distressing illness', presumably as an attempt to legitimise the absence of a royal presence at his exhibition two years earlier, pp. 148–9.

47 LMA, GRO, CC, J. 68, F. 298, *Common Council Committee Minutes*. As Copley offered to complete the work for a smaller fee, he secured the commission. He stated that he hoped 'the advantages of an exhibition of the picture and the publication of a print from it will compensate him for the time and study requisite from completing so large a work'. It is significant to note that even at the outset of the project Copley was planning the composition of the work with an exhibition in mind. Once the work was relocated to the Common Council Chamber, it was in a position high above the viewer. From this height, the seascape would become a mass of bodies and fire and the human impact of Copley's narrative would be greatly diminished.

48 See Shoemaker's discussion of the development of an eighteenth-century 'Urban Renaissance' in *Gender in English Society 1650–1850*, pp. 269–304; see also: Peter

FAC-SIMILE OF TICKET OF ADMISSION TO COPLEY'S "SIEGE OF GIBRALTAR."   (FROM ENGRAVING BY BARTOLOZZI.)

Figure 5   Francesco Bartolozzi, *Mr Copley's Picture of the Siege of Gibraltar as Exhibited in the Green Park near St James's Palace* (1791): engraving (9.9 × 12.8 cm).

British Museum, London. © Trustees of the British Museum.

On entering either exhibition, the viewer was issued with an explanatory catalogue. In the Green Park pavilion, this printed pamphlet primarily functioned as an advertisement for the engraving that could be ordered at the exhibition. Including both a written description of the painting and an illustrative key, it also functioned as an exhibition catalogue (Fig. 6). The illustrative key identifies the British and Hanoverian officers standing upon the British bastion and Sir Roger Curtis and Captain Smith within the seascape. The whereabouts of the catalogue for Trumbull's Spring Gardens exhibition is currently unknown, but it is likely that it followed a similar pattern. The key to the engraving of *The Sortie* by William Sharp

---

Borsay, *The English Urban Renaissance: Culture and Society in the Provincial Town, 1660–1760* (Oxford: Oxford University Press, 1989).

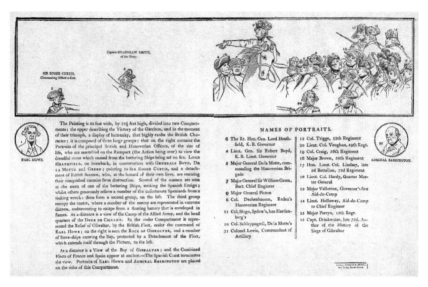

Figure 6   *Proposal for publishing by Subscription, An Engraving from the Historical Picture of the Siege and Relief of Gibraltar, Painted by J. S. Copley, R.A. Now Exhibiting in a Pavilion, Erected by the Gracious Permission of the King, for that Purpose, in the Green Park* (1791): subscription notice (27.5 × 43.1 cm).

British Museum, London. © Trustees of the British Museum.

provides an example of the type of illustrative key that would have been provided in the exhibition (Fig. 7). Again, it identifies all the officers present within the painting. Both illustrative keys present the officers numbered and listed by both their name and military rank. The inclusion of identifiable portraits within these martial paintings allowed the viewer to engage with the work, either through direct recognition of the sitters or a familiarity with the contemporary reports of the event. As a portrait group, these paintings positioned the officers involved at the very heart of civilised society. The exclusion of the ordinary soldiers from the illustrative keys reinforces martial hierarchy and the acknowledged position of officers within society. This exclusion emphasises the anonymity of the ordinary troops and perhaps implies society's neglect of their martial significance. The inclusion of martial action within these works can, on one level, be understood as a dramatisation of officerial control pictorially employed to legitimise their subsequent martial and civic awards. On the other hand, the anonymity of the troops allowed for the display of particularly aggressive hyper-masculine violence to be exhibited without jeopardising the civility of any individual.

Figure 7   Print made by William Sharp, published by Antonio Cesare Poggi after John Trumbull, *References to the Print of The Sortie made by the Garrison of Gibraltar* (1810): engraving (24 × 35.5 cm).

British Museum, London. © Trustees of the British Museum.

Through public exhibition, the all-male martial environment is situated at the heart of civilised heterosocial engagement. Where British society has been seen to potentially repress and inhibit the display of certain facets of male identity, the martial battlescape offered a forum for the exhibition of diverse modes of masculine behaviour. These martial paintings visually resolve the potentially conflicting position of civic and martial masculinity through the multifaceted depiction of troops in varying stages of military engagement. Warfare offered a scenario where socially induced anxieties about effeminacy, foppishness and Frenchification could be combated through various virile, aggressive and dominant types of masculine behaviour executed and legitimised in the name of national defence.[49] Through public exhibition, this was repeatedly employed as a means to reaffirm both the ability of the British military and the status of the nation. Where masculinity is essentially performative, it remains in a perpetual state of flux.[50] At a time of national

49 The term 'Frenchification' is used by Hitchcock and Cohen in the 'Introduction' to *English Masculinities*, p. 20.

50 Connell, *Masculinities*, p. 76; Rachel Woodward, 'Locating Military Masculinities:

anxiety in the wake of defeat in America, there was arguably a demand for the construction of a dominant hyper-masculine martial ideal. Once victory in the Revolutionary and the Napoleonic Wars was achieved, British national standing was arguably reaffirmed and the previous presentation of the British hero as the sacrificial protagonist, particularly in representations of Admiral Horatio Nelson, can be seen to resume. Encompassing a full spectrum of masculine behaviour, these dramatisations of the all-male battlefield presented a hegemonic and specifically British code of masculinity to the late eighteenth-century public.[51]

Space, Place and the Formation of Gender Identity in the British Army' in Higate (ed.), *Military Masculinities*, pp. 43–55.

51 Connell, *Masculinities*, p. 77; R. W. Connell, and James W. Messerschmidt, 'Hegemonic Masculinity: Rethinking the Concept', *Gender and Society*, 19.6 (2005), pp. 829–59; Graham Dawson, *Soldier Heroes: British Adventure, Empire and the Imaging of Masculinities* (London: Routledge, 1994), p. 2.

8

Scarlet Fever
Female Enthusiasm
for Men in Uniform, 1780–1815

Louise Carter

I N 1804 *Sporting Magazine* carried a letter to the editor alerting readers to a 'dangerous disorder prevalent in wartime', principally afflicting women. The main symptoms of the malady were listed as an excessive regard for clothing of a deep red hue, a remarkable attachment to military music, sighing, listlessness and an inattention to all topics and company unconnected with the military. The author cautioned that particular attention needed to be paid to sufferers when the disease was at its crisis because they became 'uncommonly desirous of a jaunt in a post chaise, a passage through the back door or window, or a trip up or down a ladder'.[1] The name of the condition, according to this wit, was scarlet fever. Unlike its pathological namesake, this variety of scarlet fever did not result in a rash, sore throat or raised temperature. Nevertheless, it was to be regarded as potentially just as dangerous since it caused women to swoon and throw caution to the wind at the sight of a military man turned out in his regimental finery. The contagion was also reported to be highly infectious and already spreading rampantly through boarding schools and families with young daughters. Indeed, since military men themselves seemed only too keen to encourage a full-blown epidemic to blossom, the author feared that evermore British women might soon succumb to the passions and follies aroused by scarlet fever.

---

1 *Sporting Magazine*, Vol. 24, June 1804, pp. 142–3. The purported author of the letter was Fanny M. of Hull but, although much of the magazine's content did come from readers' letters, in this case it seems highly likely it was a pseudonym for one of the journalists.

This chapter turns to the military man as a focus of female admiration and considers what the discourse surrounding scarlet fever might reveal about Georgian society and the position of the soldier within it. On one hand, we might dismiss women's attraction to men in uniform as simply 'natural' and ahistorical – an attraction between the sexes being a constant across time and it therefore being unsurprising that a portion of it was directed towards military men, particularly since the warrior has repeatedly been valorised by various societies as the apotheosis of masculinity. Yet, as this chapter will explore, a study of the precise form that this association took and the attitudes and assumptions it exposed can provide us with a glimpse into several key contemporary debates and concerns. Scarlet fever was deliberately fostered and encouraged and offered a variety of benefits, yet it also remained unpredictable and could hold concealed dangers for men and women alike. As such, the discourse surrounding scarlet fever reveals a dichotomy at the heart of attitudes towards women's relationship with military men. Whilst some discussions of scarlet fever suggest that contemporaries found it exciting, titillating and often humorous (as the wag writing in *Sporting Magazine* evidently did), it is equally apparent that at other times the discourse surrounding the phenomenon reflected and revealed some of society's deepest fears and anxieties.

I

USAGE OF THE TERM scarlet fever to describe female enthusiasm for military men appears to have been fairly common by the turn of the century. A military dictionary of 1810 defined it as a term in familiar use in England to describe an 'overweening fondness for the outward appendages of a soldier'.[2] Female characters in an 1808 novel discussed the 'scarlet fever' that had induced them all to marry military men and commented on their distaste for men in 'plain clothes'.[3] The term seems to have been in circulation until at least the mid-nineteenth century, Henry Mayhew commenting that nurse maids were particularly susceptible to it and that 'a red coat is all powerful with this class, who prefer a soldier to a servant, or any other description of man they come into contact with'.[4] Though not everyone used the term

---

2 Major Charles James, *A New and Enlarged Military Dictionary in English and French*, 2 vols, 3rd edn (London: T. Egerton, 1810), 1, MIL.
3 *Sketches of Character, or Specimens of Real Life. A Novel. In Three Volumes* (London: Longman, Hurt, Rees and Orme, 1808), 1, pp. 251–3.
4 Henry Mayhew, *London Labour and London Poor: A Cyclopedia of the Condition and*

Figure 8   Thomas Rowlandson, *The Wonderfull Charms of
a Red Coat and Cockade* (*c.* 1785–90).

© Birmingham Museums and Art Gallery.

itself, and it does not appear to have been widely used prior to the early
nineteenth century, the idea that women were peculiarly attracted to military
men and were apt to act rashly as a consequence of the desires aroused by the
sight of a scarlet coat was well established from at least the 1780s onwards.
Numerous prints, novels, plays, poems and ballads all echoed this theme.
An early example, *The Wonderfull Charms of a Red Coat and Cockade* (Fig.
8), is typical in implying that even a well-dressed, respectable and attractive
young woman could be sufficiently fascinated by a red coat to overlook the
less-than-youthful or beguiling specimen of manhood actually wearing it. As
such, the allure of the red coat was portrayed as possessing an almost magical
power to bewitch women.

Earnings of Those That Will Work, Those that Cannot Work and Those that Will Not Work,
4 vols (first pub. 1861–2; reprinted New York: Cosimo Books, 2009), 4, p. 235.

It is easy to understand why some women were so dazzled by the sight of men in scarlet. Myerly makes the point that brilliant spectacle was an intentional and defining feature of the British Army, to the extent that it was privileged even where it was known to impede practicality and efficacy.[5] Spectacle aided the prestige, order, recruitment and mystique of the service. The precise style and colour of uniforms varied, with infantry regiments and engineers traditionally wearing scarlet, cavalry regiments wearing scarlet or dark blue, artillery regiments favouring dark blue and rifle units tending towards dark green. Officers' coats were made of finer cloth and were elaborately decorated with the facings, braid and lace associated with individual regiments. Buckles, buttons, headgear and hairstyles similarly varied, but each element was fashioned to enhance the splendour of the individual's appearance and the aura of the service he represented. Appearance also influenced recruitment and promotion to a surprising degree in some regiments, with the tallest, finest-looking men receiving favour from some commanders simply because their fetching looks and smart attire increased the prestige of the unit.[6] To some extent, therefore, whilst the splendour of military dress was intended to induce awe and admiration and to assert pre-eminence and power within a homosocial environment, it was hardly surprising that such a display also turned female heads. Military men were amongst the best dressed and most smartly turned out in Georgian society and, whether in scarlet, blue or green jackets, women certainly noticed them.

Whilst the brilliance of regimental uniforms may not have been designed to elicit female attention, scarlet fever itself was actively and deliberately encouraged. Arthur Young was far from alone in the fevered wartime climate of the 1790s in arguing that the 'influence of the sex' should be exerted in the national interest by women foregoing the company of men who were unwilling to fight and encouraging the company of those who were.[7] A more jocular pamphlet similarly depicted single women slighting potential suitors who were 'lukewarm' in defence of king and country and refusing to accompany them in dancing or conversation.[8] Meanwhile, a contributor to the *Bath Herald and Register* reasoned that the presence of women at military training sessions and trials would prove 'the greatest inducement' that young

5 Scott Hughes Myerly, *British Military Spectacle from the Napoleonic Wars through the Crimea* (Cambridge, MA: Harvard University Press, 1996), pp. 23–7.

6 Myerly, *British Military Spectacle*, p. 19.

7 Arthur Young, *National Danger and the Means of Safety* (London: W. Richardson, 1797), p. 29. Young was the father of three daughters so doubtless had some first-hand experience of female youthful enthusiasms.

8 Anon., *The Female Association for Preserving Liberty and Property* (London: J. Asperne, 1803).

Figure 9   Charles Williams, *The Consequence of Invasion or the Hero's Reward* (1803).

BM Satires 10047. © Trustees of the British Museum.

men could receive towards participating in such activities.[9] Even dissenting ministers, who were usually far from prominent enthusiasts of the war effort, urged women to foster masculine martial ambition 'by exciting everywhere a spirit of heroism'.[10] At the furthest extreme, women were even urged to use their scorn to 'drive the COWARD from society' on the basis that a man's death should be seen as preferable to suffering the stigma of cowardice and since 'the BRAVE alone should bask in the smile of Beauty'.[11]

The Consequence of Invasion, or, The Hero's Reward (Fig. 9) further illustrated the amatory repercussions of men's martial or civilian choices. In this print

---

9 *Bath Herald and Register*, 17 January 1795.

10 Rev. David Rivers, *A Discourse on Patriotism, on the Love of Our Country* (London: T. Plummer, 1803), p. 19. See also: *A Memorial for the Present Age and Information to Posterity* (Bristol: W. Matthews, 1797), p. 35.

11 *Alfred's Address to the Ladies* (London: J. Ginger, 1803). Such extreme sentiments were rare. I have come across only one other source which took such a hard line approach towards men – the poem 'The Spanish Mother' by a Lady in *The Gentleman's Magazine* (May 1809, p. 453) similarly exhorted 'Return a hero or return no more', but these examples are unusual in their lack of acknowledgement of female and motherly concern for the risks taken by men during war.

Figure 10   Cruikshank, *Female Opinions on Military Tactics* (1798).
BM Satires 9314. © Trustees of the British Museum.

a soldier was depicted hoisting aloft the severed heads of French invaders like trophies, whilst he was lavished with female praise and attention. Meanwhile, a fey civilian in the corner jealously observed the scene and sighed, 'I wish I had been a soldier too, then the girls would have run after me, but I never could bear the smell of gunpowder.' The strap line that 'none but the brave deserve the fair' made plain the implied potential ramifications for men who failed to take up arms. Similarly, the print *Female Opinions on Military Tactics* (Fig. 10) played on the idea that women were sexually attracted to soldiers and that their amorous interest and admiration could be secured through a masculine military appearance. In a series of tableaux various couples were depicted discussing weaponry, tactics, performance and frequency of action in terms loaded with suggestive sexual double entendres, for example, concerning the cock and swell of a musket. All of the scenes echoed the association between masculine military participation and the subsequent promotion of female desire.

The association of female attention with military service was a recurrent and deliberate theme in wartime discourse and propaganda, and for obvious reasons. The prospect of female admiration was dangled as an enticing reward awaiting those men who stepped forward to defend their nation. Amidst the fierce political and philosophical debates that accompanied the early revolutionary phase of the 1793–1815 wars in particular – the rights and wrongs of the French Revolution; the merits or failings of the current British political system; and the benefits or otherwise of loyalism – the assertion that a man's primary duty was to defend women arguably had a far more universal and immediate appeal than reference to country, party or king. Moreover, it promised an altogether more tangible and alluring reward in return.

Goldstein has argued that military service is neither an innate nor rewarding element of masculinity and that 'all evidence indicates that war is something societies impose on men, who most often need to be dragged kicking and screaming into it, constantly brainwashed and disciplined once there, and rewarded and honoured afterwards'.[12] The association of masculinity with the protection of damsels in distress and the receipt of their amorous gratitude following victory has thus been repeatedly fostered in wartime to encourage masculine service. Calls to defend not only sweethearts and wives, but also daughters, sisters and mothers, were arguably a more potent propaganda tool during the Revolutionary and Napoleonic wars than calls to more abstract and contestable notions of patriotism, politics or religion, and as such featured prominently throughout propaganda and wartime discourse.

The portrayal of the soldier as a figure of admiration and even of lust was also part of the wider cultural rehabilitation and re-imagining of the figure of the soldier necessitated by the Revolutionary and Napoleonic wars that Colley has highlighted. Once Britain became more reliant on domestic manpower and recruitment to fight wars, it became necessary to associate the soldier with a more appealing and heroic image in order to boost morale and recruitment. Concerns about the quality of men enlisted into the rank and file were not obliterated by the image of the rakish, well-dressed, heroic lothario, but this imagining of the soldier certainly offered a more attractive alternative to their usual reputation as the dregs of society.[13]

Another positive associated with scarlet fever was the thrill of excitement that it brought into women's lives. Having large numbers of men quartered throughout the nation, who hosted and attended balls in their glittering ball-uniforms, engaged in mock battles, strode about the parade ground or marched through the streets with the boom of the military drum literally reverberating through the bodies of spectators, all brought novelty, diversion, gossip, spectacle and the possibility of a romantic adventure or flirtatious fantasy into women's lives. In an age where many women lived rather quiet,

---

12 Joshua S. Goldstein, *War and Gender: How Gender Shapes the War System and Vice Versa* (Cambridge: Cambridge University Press, 2001), p. 253.

13 Linda Colley, *Britons: Forging the Nation, 1707–1837* (New Haven, CT: Yale University Press, 1992), p. 284.

repetitive and uneventful lives, the entertainment and amusement offered by an influx of soldiers into a neighbourhood could be considerable.

II

DESPITE ALL ITS patriotic and entertaining virtues though, scarlet fever was not without its dangers for either men or women. For women, the most commonly cited danger was elopement, and such episodes were widely reported in newspapers. The *Bath Herald and Register* drew attention to the problem, noting

> Two young women of respectable connexion eloped last week with two soldiers of the guards. These are the fifth who have absconded with the military at the west end of the town within the last month. This gives rise to the report of a dangerous *scarlet fever* raging at present amongst the young ladies of Westminster.[14]

Reports of such occurrences ranged from the daughters of wealthy gentlemen eloping with young officers, to married women absconding with rakish sergeants, and even one report of a 58-year-old widow eloping with a young officer of just 22.[15] Elopements had become a regular occurrence in society following the introduction of the 1753 Marriage Act. Numerous couples sought to circumvent its attempts to limit clandestine and irregular marriages by eloping across the border to Scotland, most famously to Gretna Green, where such restrictions did not exist. Yet it was those intrigues involving military and naval men that most fired the public imagination and became the primary focus of journalists, dramatists, novelists and satirists alike.[16] Elopements featured regularly in the output of satiric artists in this period and almost exclusively with a military or naval man as the male protagonist.

None but the Brave Deserve the Fair (Fig. 11) depicted a rosy view of such elopements with a comely young woman escaping over a wall and

---

14 *Bath Herald and Register*, 7 January 1797.
15 See for example: *Gazetteer and New Daily Advertiser*, 22 April 1791, p. 2; *Morning Post and Daily Advertiser*, 15 February 1785; *Public Advertiser*, 5 November 1787, p. 4; *Bury and Norwich Post*, 3 September 1806, p. 2; *Bury and Norwich Post*, 9 March 1808, p. 1; *The Lancaster Gazette*, 6 February 1813, p. 4; *The Bury and Norwich Post: Or, Suffolk, Norfolk, Essex, Cambridge, and Ely Advertiser*, 26 April 1815, p. 3.
16 G. J. Barker-Benfield, *The Culture of Sensibility* (Chicago, MI: University of Chicago Press, 1992), pp. 326–7, discusses the role of the 1753 Marriage Act and popular culture in developing the practice of elopement.

NONE BUT THE BRAVE DESERVE THE FAIR.

Figure 11   Thomas Rowlandson, *None but the Brave
Deserve the Fair* (1813).

BM Satires 12149. © Trustees of the British Museum.

into the waiting arms of her mounted hussar officer beau. Both protagonists are blushing and have their eyes intently fixed on the other, infusing the scene with a considerable sexual charge. Hussars were often seen as particular womanisers, a charge not helped by prominent scandals such as the elopement of Lord Uxbridge, Henry William Paget, with Wellington's sister-in-law Lady Charlotte Wellesley.[17] This notorious liaison eventually led to pregnancy and brought both parties into divorce proceedings with their previous partners in 1810. Such events only underscored the public perception of the officer as at once both alluring and dangerous.

---

17 *Sporting Magazine*, Vol. 33, March 1809, p. 275. Despite protestations of regret over featuring news of such scandals, the affair was covered in some detail throughout its tortuous course.

Figure 12   Thomas Rowlandson, *The Reconciliation or the Return from Scotland* (1785).

BM Satires 9669. © Trustees of the British Museum.

The Rowlandson print *The Reconciliation or the Return from Scotland* (Fig. 12) depicted a prodigal couple successfully reuniting with one set of parents in the aftermath of an elopement to Gretna Green. It portrays a hesitant and tearful bride, accompanied by a smart groom in regimentals, being received and accepted back into familial society by worried but ultimately forgiving parents. Such a favourable resolution was far from certain and not all elopements ended so well.

Jane Austen memorably portrayed the potential hazards of eloping in *Pride and Prejudice*. In Austen's novel Lydia Bennet narrowly escapes ruin after being dazzled by scarlet and absconding with devious militia officer Captain Wickham. While an elopement itself was bad enough, Austen made clear that an even greater threat was that Wickham might seduce Lydia but fail to follow through with an actual marriage, thereby bringing disgrace on the entire Bennet family. Yet whilst the intelligent Elizabeth is alive to such a risk from an early stage in the novel, her foolish sisters and mother conspicuously fail to appreciate the inherent danger and see little harm in allowing Lydia's continued flirtations with officers. Mrs Bennet even complains to her husband:

My dear Mr. Bennet, you must not expect such girls to have the sense of their father and mother. When they get to our age I dare say they will not think about officers any more than we do. I remember the time when I liked a red-coat myself very well, and indeed so I do still at my heart; and if a smart young colonel, with five or six thousand a year, should want one of my girls, I shall not say nay to him; and I thought Colonel Forster looked very becoming the other night at Sir William's in his regimentals.[18]

Newspapers did their best to alert readers to the threats associated with scarlet fever, though at times the coverage often appeared to revel in the melodrama despite the supposedly disapproving tone of reportage. *The Morning Post and Daily Advertiser* carried a letter purporting to be from a young female reader, in which she thanked the paper for alerting her to the duplicity of men and for providing the warning that she was 'not to give credit for either honour or courage to the outward and visible signs of a red coat and cockade'.[19] A similarly light-hearted tone can be detected in *The Derby Mercury* report that:

The daughter of a lady of fashion on Tuesday last eloped from her mother's house in Isleworth with an officer in the dragoons on a matrimonial expedition to Scotland. The fair fugitive can hardly be excused on the score of juvenile indiscretion as she is on the wrong side of thirty. Her military escort is only nineteen.[20]

Such reports echoed themes found in prints such as *Running Away with an Heiress*, which depicted a naval officer carrying off a rotund young lady who was longing for a blacksmith (i.e. a trip to Gretna Green), whilst the sailor congratulated himself on his weighty prize of £40,000.[21] *Off She Goes* similarly depicted a plump young lady squashing her military beau as she escaped down a ladder whilst jewellery tumbled from her cleavage.[22] Such sources indicate some awareness amongst contemporaries that whilst scarlet fever might incline some women's minds towards fanciful dreams of love and elopement, more mercenary motives might animate some of those who took advantage of such feminine folly.

Such fears informed the more guarded and sober tone with which some contemporary commentators discussed elopement. In contrast to the amusing tone evident in some reportage, other reports were clearly intended to dissuade women from entering into such schemes by stressing the potentially

---

18 Jane Austen, *Pride and Prejudice* (first pub. 1813; London: Penguin, 2003), p. 20.

19 *Morning Post and Daily Advertiser*, 28 March 1775.

20 *The Derby Mercury*, 30 December 1802.

21 Anon., *Running away with an Heiress* (c. 1804), British Museum Satires (hereafter BM Sat.) 10337.

22 Thomas Rowlandson, *Off She Goes*, December 1812, BM Sat. 11974.

perilous rather than comedic consequences that could ensue. *The Sun* warned in 1795:

> The following is given as a caution to young women, against the too frequent custom of their following private soldiers: the daughter of a respectable publican in Leicester was seduced by an Irish recruit quartered in her father's house, and eloped with him to Dublin where he robbed her of her clothes, and left her almost naked and pennyless.

Coverage of the 1808 case involving Elizabeth Banfield and Captain Massey, a married officer in the West Yorkshire Militia quartered in the home of her parents, highlighted the potential dangers of such arrangements and focused on the law case which resulted after she became pregnant and gave birth to an illegitimate child. Council for the Banfields presented Massey as the archetypal military libertine who had seduced and ill-treated the innocent daughter of the house. Meanwhile Massey's council argued that the Banfields had 'afforded every facility to the Defendant to gratify any irregular passions he might have', and in effect that scarlet fever had inclined Elizabeth to forego the chastity and probity expected of women in order to satisfy her desires. A compromise ruling was reached in which Massey was ordered to pay the Banfields £100 compensation for the 'distress of mind and anxiety' occasioned; sufficient to mollify them, but insufficient to make military men too tantalising a prospect for similar lawsuits by aggrieved parents.[23]

Pregnancy was always a considerable risk in such liaisons, most obviously in the period prior to a marriage ceremony actually occurring. Trumbach indicates that army and navy men were the second largest occupational group to have made false promises of marriage to women presenting children to the London Foundling Hospital. His work also suggests that army men were prominent amongst those seducing and abandoning girls who ended up working as prostitutes.[24] Even *Sporting Magazine*, whose jocular take on scarlet fever was discussed in the introduction, quipped that when soldiers moved on they always left something behind them, namely children and debts.[25] Such dangers may have provided some women with pause for thought, yet it is probable that for others the potential risk merely heightened

---

23 *The Examiner*, 14 Aug 1808, cited in Ben Wilson, *Decency and Disorder 1789–1837* (London: Faber and Faber, 2007), pp. 156–7.

24 Randolph Trumbach, *Sex and the Gender Revolution* (Chicago, MI and London: University of Chicago Press, 1992), pp. 279, 249, 164.

25 *Sporting Magazine*, Vol. 24, April 1804, p. 24. The article joked that whilst foreign armies tore children from the arms of their mothers, British soldiers repaired the damage by cultivating the arts of population and providing replacement babes in arms.

the thrill associated with scarlet fever. Despite the risks, elopements continued to occur.

Reports of elopements involving women and military beaux from a wide range of social and military backgrounds arguably became so common that scarlet fever might legitimately be considered to be a feature of a shared military culture. Its influence was evident across the ranks and across the divisions of the regulars, militia and volunteers. Occasionally claims were made that one group or another might be more or less attractive to women. For example, it was argued that the introduction of the militia might provide ladies with a welcome opportunity to 'take an hero to their arms, who can fight for his country, without being sent out of it'.[26] In general though, women's admiration of military men appears to have been a constant across the various strata of society, although shaped by social rank, with ladies swooning over officers and servant girls hankering after men of the rank and file.

Another element to highlight in this scenario is that whilst propaganda encouraged women's admiration of the military, women were not portrayed as mere passive pawns unthinkingly serving the needs of the war machine or the unwitting victims of male seduction. Rather they were seen as active participants deliberately seeking out the objects of their infatuation. The 1797 print *Longings after a Red Coat* (Fig. 13) is typical in this regard in depicting two women relishing the opportunity to watch soldiers practicing their drill in an adjacent parade ground. This print itself is an almost identical replica of another, *The Wishing Females* from 1781, in which the only notable difference is the fashion sported by the women.[27] In both prints the women are portrayed actively enjoying the opportunity to spy on uniformed men and appreciate the spectacle they offered. Clearly, many such images were created and enjoyed by men and fed male fantasies about women, yet evidence suggests that such a portrayal of women's enthusiasms was not a purely discursive construct.

The rash of elopements occasioned by scarlet fever suggests female complicity in such schemes at the very least. Other contemporary evidence also indicates active female admiration for the military in real life. Oldham weaver and diarist William Rowbottom recorded in his diary that when the Lancashire Volunteers marched through town they were 'as usual attended by a large group of females'.[28] Women's letters hint at similar enthusiasms. Lady

---

26 *The Genius*, 13 July 1761.

27 *The Wishing Females*, 1781, BM Sat. undescribed.

28 *The Most Dismal Times: William Rowbottom's Diary Part 1, 1787–1799*, transcribed and annotated by Alan Peat (Oldham: Oldham Education and Leisure Arts Publications,

Figure 13   *Longings after a Red Coat* (1797).

BM Satires undescribed. Registration number: 2010,7081.1252.
© Trustees of the British Museum.

Sarah Spencer confided that whilst she had only intended to watch the arrival of five men-at-war and their sailors in the port of Ryde for a few minutes, she had been so transfixed by the sight she had remained for two hours.[29] Lady Jerningham similarly wrote to her daughter of the impressive spectacle to be seen in London, stating 'I wish you were here, for the brilliant bustle is amazing, and you would enjoy seeing all these Heroes.'[30]

1996), p. 66. See also: A. Hudson, 'Volunteer Soldiers in Sussex during the Revolutionary and Napoleonic Wars 1793–1815', *Sussex Archaeological Collections*, 122 (1984), pp. 165–81.

29 Sarah Spencer to her brother Robert Spencer, 27 August 1809. See also: Mrs Hugh Wyndham (ed.), *The Correspondence of Sarah Lady Lyttlelton, 1787–1870* (London: Murray, 1912), p. 78.

30 *Aristocratic Women: The Social, Political and Cultural History of Rich and Powerful Women*

The outbreak of scarlet fever during wartime, and the discourse which surrounded it, therefore indicates that a more sexualised vision of womanhood in which women might seek amatory gratification (whether overtly or more vicariously) continued to be part of the cultural landscape into at least the early nineteenth century. This tempers the claims of some historians of the body and of medicine that by the mid-eighteenth century women were increasingly viewed as a separate sex, more maternal and more sexually passive than their early modern counterparts and more likely to be 'seduced' than desiring. Perry, for example, asserts that 'the maternal succeeded, supplanted and repressed the sexual definition of woman, who began to be re-imagined as nurturing rather than desiring'.[31] Yet, much like the women depicted in the erotica studied by Harvey, women under the spell of scarlet fever were often represented as active sexualised participants enjoying the pursuit of their military idols rather than as passive ciphers seduced by lustful men.[32] This in turn supports the arguments proposed by Gatrell that a more sexual, more earthy vision of womanhood continued to be enjoyed in satiric prints and other media until the triumph of middle-class evangelical morality in the 1820s snuffed out an appreciation for the bawdy and irreverent.[33]

III

YET whilst women's amorous preference for men in uniform might offer some benefits for them, for individual men and for the nation as a whole, it also carried potential dangers that went beyond an ill-advised elopement. Prints such as *The Wags of Windsor or Love in a Camp* (Fig. 14) offered a humorous but cautionary commentary on the fashionable female pastime of visiting army camps such as Warley or Coxheath and emphasised

---

(Marlborough: Adam Matthew Publications, 1997), Part 2: 7/763, Lady Jerningham to Lady Charlotte Bedingfield, London, 11 June 1814. As members of a Catholic family, it is interesting to note equal enthusiasm for the spectacle of the British Army amongst these female correspondents despite Catholic exclusion from officer ranks.

31 Ruth Perry, 'Colonising the Breast: Sexuality and Maternity in Eighteenth-Century England', in *Forbidden History: The State, Society and the Regulation of Sexuality in Modern Europe*, ed. by John C. Fout (Chicago, MI: University of Chicago Press, 1992), p. 116. See also: Thomas Laqueur, *Making Sex* (Cambridge, MA: Harvard University Press, 1990), pp. 149–50, 199; Tim Hitchcock, *English Sexualities 1700–1800* (Basingstoke: Macmillan, 1997), pp. 99–100.

32 Karen Harvey, *Reading Sex in the Eighteenth Century* (Cambridge: Cambridge University Press, 2004), pp. 105–11 and 221.

33 Vic Gatrell, *City of Laughter: Sex and Satire in Eighteenth-Century London* (London: Atlantic Books, 2006), pp. 351–2, 381–2, 575.

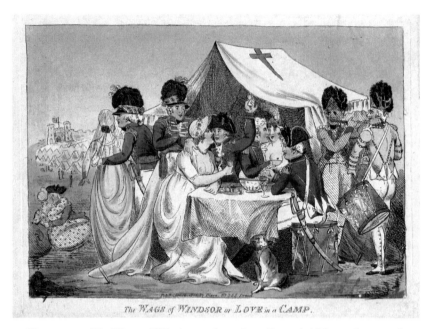

Figure 14   *The Wags of Windsor or Love in a Camp* (16 November 1800).

Lewis Walpole Library 800.11.16.01. Lewis Walpole Library, Connecticut. Courtesy of The Lewis Walpole Library, Yale University.

the potentially corrupting impact of such relaxed and informal interactions between the sexes.[34] The military had always attracted camp followers and prostitutes for obvious reasons, yet in this print the line between such women and respectable female admirers of the military has become blurred amidst the gaiety and informality of the camp. Under such conditions women might abandon decorum and probity and men might become ensnared in liaisons with less-than-desirable husband-hunters or worse. Such risks worried those commentators who viewed women as the natural moral guardians of the nation's character. If even women abandoned modesty, feared one author, then what would be left to 'stem the tide of licentiousness and profligacy?'[35] Unchecked, scarlet fever therefore carried the potential to unstitch the moral

---

34 I am grateful to Professor Vic Gatrell for introducing me to this print.

35 John Bowles, *Remarks on Modern Female Manners as Distinguished by Indifference to Character and Indecency of Dress* (London: F. and C. Rivington, 1802). See also: Henry Handley Norris, *The Influence of the Female Character upon Society, Considered More Especially with Reference to the Present Crisis, in a Sermon* (London: printed for F. and C. Rivington by Thomas Norris, 1801); George Ogg, *Admonition, A Poem on the Fashionable Modes of Female Dress* (London: W. Miller, 1806).

Figure 15   *Military Man-Trap* (1780).

fabric of society and to introduce a deadly moral contagion and malaise just at the time when national unity and virtue was most required in the fight against the French.

In addition to the threat of vice or entrapment, camp followers, hangers-on and prostitutes could also constitute a more immediate threat to soldiers by draining their finances or most worryingly of all, by passing on venereal disease. Several such dangers are implicit in the portrayal of the femme-fatale in *Military Man-Trap* (Fig. 15). The list of expenses in her hand indicates the financial dangers of consorting with her, whilst her crossed legs, low-cut bodice, knowing smile and collection of swords at the back of her tent suggests she is an experienced campaigner who has already achieved several 'victories' plying her charms. The text warns 'She's a Trap to catch Captains; You're lost & undone / If once you attack her – as sure as a Gun.' The dangerous beauty is portrayed in quasi-military costume, aping a patriotic fashion amongst ladies of the bon ton in the 1780s and underlining her own real or affected infection with scarlet fever. Military men were well enough versed in the dangers of consorting with prostitutes to catch the drift of this print. Of course, familiarity with the potential downsides of such dalliances no more prevented all men from running such risks than it did all women. Whilst women who were known to be infected with venereal disease were swiftly drummed out of the camp, there were always plenty more ready to take their place and plenty more customers ready to avail themselves of their services.[36]

Further reservations about scarlet fever were connected to unease about what women might do with their enthusiasms once their military beaux were absent on service. Fears about unrestrained female sexuality seem to have been a recurrent theme in wartime discourse throughout history. In this period, particular fears appear to have clustered around the notion that civilian men might usurp a military man's place in his absence.[37] Men whose civilian occupations gave them intimate access to women, such as male servants, hairdressers, dancing instructors and dressmakers all came to be seen as potential competitors for female affections. Such fears make sense in a deeply patriarchal society and underline the tensions inherent in the attempt to foster female enthusiasm for men in uniform and yet keep such passions under tight control and direction.

Fears were also expressed that female admiration for military men might not last in the event of a man's disfigurement or disability whilst in service. The tale of *Faithless Nelly Gray* told the plaintive story of a disfigured hero returning only to be rebuffed by his sweetheart despite her former promises to remain true to him.[38] The theme of female inconstancy was also explored in a contemporary ballad in which a woman rejected her former beau upon seeing him return from the wars disabled. After losing an arm and an eye in a battle with a French ship, the hero returned to his betrothed only to find:

> But when maim'd and in want I regain'd Plymouth harbour,
> And Nancy beheld my unfortunate plight,
> Next morning she married Tom Frizzle the barber,
> And bade me no more enter into her sight.[39]

---

36 *The Gentleman's Magazine*, Oct. 1793, p. 878.

37 See for example, *The Unexpected Return or Snip in Danger*, 1808, BM Sat. 11116.

38 See Thomas Hood, *Faithless Nelly Gray* (1826) in *The New Oxford Book of Romantic Period Verse*, ed. by Jerome McGann (New York: Oxford University Press, 1993), p. 225. Note, however, that the Thomas Rowlandson print *Platonic Love* (BM Sat. 10926) offers a more ambiguous reading of women's potential relationship to disabled servicemen.

39 Charles Dignum, *The Disabled Seaman* (London: Longman and Broderip, 1798). See

Figure 16   *Military Orders* (1 January 1807).
BM Satires undescribed. Registration number: 1948,0214.725.
© Trustees of the British Museum.

An even more alarming anxiety associated with scarlet fever centred on fears that women might not be sufficiently discriminating in their appreciation of men in uniform and might receive potential French invaders with enthusiasm. The print *Military Orders* (Fig. 16) is typical of this strain of discourse. It depicts two French invaders announcing that they are under orders to violate every female in the parish. Two young ladies kneel before them and make no attempt to plead for their own exemption, but beg the soldiers to spare their aged grandmother, who in turn remarks 'don't talk such nonsense – don't you hear the gentlemen say they are under orders'.[40] Despite the humour of such prints, an underlying twinge of apprehension over the potential ramifications of the fine military appearance of French officers and their reputation for seducing women is also detectable.

---

also: *With Shatter'd Limbs Jack came from Sea, Crippled Jack of Trafalgar* (London: Purday and Button, 1805).

40 Thomas Rowlandson, *Female Politicians*, 1809, BM Sat. 11465, carries the same insinuation that British women might be willingly seduced by French invaders.

Equally, whilst some contemporaries viewed the association between female admiration and military recruitment as one of the foremost merits of scarlet fever when applied to British soldiers, others were critical of it for precisely the same reason. The novel *A Soldier's Tale* told the story of a young carpenter, Llewellyn, who enlisted in the regulars after his betrothed, Fanny, became more and more openly enraptured with the soldiers newly quartered in their town. Whilst Fanny was delighted to see Llewellyn in his uniform, only Llewellyn's parents and his tender-hearted cousin Mary, the daughter of a soldier, fully appreciated the dangers to which his enlistment expose him. Meanwhile, Fanny was depicted as a thoughtless young woman who was oblivious to the true cost of war and saw it as little more than a marvellous opportunity to flirt with officers and attend regimental balls and parades. When Llewellyn eventually returns from war close to death and having missed the demise of his beloved parents, he finds Fanny herself undone by her martial enthusiasms. She has become a drunken camp follower in his absence. Llewellyn is more fortunate and eventually finds happiness as the husband of the faithful Mary, whose heart had always been swayed by his virtues rather than his dashing martial appearance.[41] Such sources suggest at least some level of disquiet over the potential of scarlet fever to lure men into service merely to impress women, without fully appreciating the realities of war.

Despite such fears though, those men who left published accounts of their military adventures tended to stress other motives for enlistment, such as a restless spirit, a desire for adventure, juvenile rebellion, an attempt to escape parental control, a desire to escape a dreary apprenticeship or harsh employer, or simply the hope of diversion and the possibility of bettering their lot.[42] Moreover, the spectacle and allure of the red coat appears to have cast a similarly potent spell on the minds of men themselves, just as it was intended to do. One soldier discussed the thrill of seeing his name appear in the *London Gazette*, whilst another described the factors prompting his decision to enlist, writing:

---

41 J. A. Stewart, *The Young Woman's Companion* (Oxford: Bartlett and Newman, 1814), pp. 104–17.

42 See, for example: *Memoirs of a Sergeant Late in the Forty-Third Light Infantry Regiment, Previously to and during the Peninsular War; Including an Account of his Conversion from Popery to the Protestant Religion* (London: J. Mason, 1835); *The Autobiography of Sergeant William Lawrence, A Hero of the Peninsular and Waterloo Campaigns* (London: Sampson and Low, 1886); J. Donaldson, *Recollections of an Eventful Life Chiefly Passed in the Army* (Glasgow: W. R. McPhun, 1824); John Green, *Vicissitudes of a Soldier's Life* (Louth: J. and J. Jackson, 1827); Edward Costello, *The Adventures of a Soldier; or, Memoirs of Edward Costello* (London: Henry Colburn, 1841).

The roll of the spirit-stirring drum, the glittering file of bayonets, with the pomp and circumstance of military parade, not unmingled perhaps with undefined thoughts of ultimate promotion, passed in review before my imagination, in colours vividly charming: resistance was vain.[43]

Yet, whilst women are largely absent from men's recorded memoirs in terms of influencing their initial decision to enlist, it is clear that many were gratified by the subsequent female attention their uniforms brought them. George Robert Gleig wrote of the pleasure he took in wearing full military ball dress and clearly revelled in the opportunity to flaunt his attire in front of a former flame in the hopes of provoking some jealousy, recalling:

On my arrival at the village where my father resided, I made my appearance in a new character. I wore my regimentals every day, and did not fail, the first Sunday after my arrival, to take a conspicuous seat in our country church, arrayed in 'all the pomp and circumstance of war'. I longed particularly that a lady who had rejected my boyish addresses might see me. 'Now,' said I to myself with youthful vanity, 'I wish her to know that I am not so insignificant, as to worldly means, as she once thought me; I wonder if she would have slighted me had she seen me in this dress before her marriage, but she may now look and die.' However, she did not make her appearance during the service, and the complication of spleen, jealousy, pique, and lurking regard, under which I suffered, were permitted harmlessly to exhaust themselves.[44]

Another veteran confessed that he had basked in the pleasure of finding himself the object of female attention and had taken great satisfaction in his own fine appearance. He wrote 'not a little proud was I on finding myself for the first time dressed out in scarlet and gold,' further noting how surprised and pleased he was to discover 'all the pretty women who unblushingly stared at me'.[45]

But this very attention to the outward spectacle of military appearance was yet another reason why some commentators had misgivings about the influence of scarlet fever. Carried to excess, such vanity could, it was feared, make men superficial, even effeminate, and corrupt their manly character. The essayist and minister Vicesimus Knox warned young recruits to consider

---

43 Jonathan Leach, *Rough Sketches of the Life of an Soldier* (London: Longman, Rees, Orme, Brown and Green, 1831), p. 2; *Memoirs of a Sergeant, Late in the Forty-Third Light Infantry Regiment*, p. 13.

44 George R. Gleig, *The Subaltern's Log Book, Including Anecdotes of Well-Known Military Characters*, 2 vols (London: J. and J. Harper, 1828), i, pp. 18–19, 101.

45 Lt.-Colonel Joseph Anderson, *Recollections of a Peninsular Veteran* (London: Edward Arnold, 1913), p. 3.

that 'an ignorant, rude, and mean mind under a red coat, is no less visible, and more contemptible, than if it appeared under rags, and in the dress of a mechanic'. Knox warned that the soldier was:

> a favourite of the ladies; and really in this his ultimate object he often succeeds; for many of them are as weak as himself, and are ready to run wild at the sight of a red coat. Age and ugliness, disease and rottenness, are all lost in the irresistible charms of a piece of scarlet broad-cloth; and many a young man, who has been repulsed in a common dress, has been arrayed by his taylor for the battle, and gained a complete victory.[46]

Mary Wollstonecraft drew an analogy between the life of subordination, obedience and outward appearances lived by soldiers and the similar experiences of women, arguing that the 'passion for a scarlet coat' exhibited by women was therefore entirely understandable given that society forced both into a position where they had so much in common.[47] William Cobbett carped that many volunteers had 'assumed the sash and gorget merely to excite the idle gaze of thoughtless females at a concert or assembly',[48] a charge that is backed up by Hudson, who suggests that there was at least some truth to the contemporary insinuation that little more than a desire to swagger about in a fine uniform had motivated the establishment of certain volunteer regiments. Yet, despite Lady Holroyd dismissing volunteering as little more than 'a harmless amusement for the Country Gentlemen', it is clear that women still took an active enjoyment in watching volunteers drill, parade and participate in mock battles.[49] As such, scarlet fever does not appear to have discriminated between amateur or professional soldiery, or to have prompted any notable variation in vanity amongst them.

The potential absurdities which an undue interest in uniform could led men into was satirised in the print *Heros in Council* (Fig. 17), which depicts a squabble between four men variously dressed as a medieval knight, Mark Anthony, a hussar and a redcoat. Instead of discussing the relative merits of their apparel in terms of their military practicality or ability to intimidate the enemy, all are solely focused on their ability to captivate women. Only the stout man in his unwieldy suit of armour even mentions safety. The hussar

46 Vicesimus Knox, *Essays Moral and Literary*, 2 vols (London: Charles Dilly, 1782), I, Chapter No. XIX 'Hints to Young Men who are Designed for a Military or Naval Life', p. 92.

47 Mary Wollstonecraft. *A Vindication of the Rights of Woman* (First published 1793; 3rd edn London: J. Johnson, 1796), p. 43.

48 William Cobbett, *Cobbett's Political Register*, Vol. 4.26, Nov 1803, p. 746. The gorget was worn about the neck.

49 A. Hudson, 'Volunteer Soldiers', pp. 168, 175–7.

Figure 17   *Heros in Council – or a Military Squabble about Dress* (1798).

relies on the ability of his whiskers to tickle the fair sex, whilst the Roman trusts in the precedent set by Mark Anthony's capacity to enchant Cleopatra. Finally, the redcoat appeals to the ladies as the final arbiters on the matter and rests his case with the argument that women view him as an Adonis in his uniform, which must prove that it is the best. Such portrayals drove home the message that an excessive interest in inculcating scarlet fever could ultimately detract from military efficacy and make men appear foolish rather than manly.

Fanny Burney satirised the worst excesses of military vanity in her novel *Cecilia*. She described Mr Aresby as a young captain in the militia who:

having frequently heard the words red-coat and gallantry put together, imagined the conjunction not merely customary, but honourable, and therefore, without even pretending to think of the service of his country, he considered a cockade as a badge of politeness, and wore it but to mark his devotion to the ladies, whom he held himself equipped to conquer, and bound to adore.[50]

Whilst a fine military appearance was therefore both desirable and admirable, and could enhance the formation of military masculinity and garner laudable female attention, it had to be accomplished within limits, be underpinned with genuine substance and avoid lapsing into vacuous narcissism. As Cohen has shown, British masculinity was always presented as a more bluff, sincere and character-based affair than French masculinity, which by contrast was portrayed as relying more on outward polish and guile than inner virtue.[51] In order to achieve a vision of manliness that was in keeping with national ideals, British military men were therefore urged to make sure that an imposing outward appearance was backed up by an equally manly, forthright and sincere character within.

IV

S o far, this chapter has argued that far from being ahistorical or simply 'natural' the phenomenon of scarlet fever in the late Georgian period reveals specific insights into the position of the soldier in society, the propaganda needs of wartime, the complexity of contemporary attitudes towards female sexuality and the risks and rewards inherent in scarlet fever for both men and women alike. It has also suggested that the discourse surrounding women's relationship with the military served as a vehicle through which to explore themes as disparate as injury and disability, invasion fears and the moral underpinnings of society. It thus echoes Joan Scott's assertion that gender discourse functions as a key mechanism by which the underlying hopes, fears and anxieties occasioned by war can be expressed.[52]

One final insight into the Georgian experience of scarlet fever might be gained by contrasting it with a similar phenomenon during the First World

---

50 Fanny Burney, *Cecilia, or Memoirs of an Heiress*, 5 vols (London: T. Cadell, 1782), 1, p. 15.

51 Michèle Cohen, 'Manliness, Effeminacy and the French: Gender and the Construction of National Character in Eighteenth-Century England', in *English Masculinities 1660–1800*, ed. by Tim Hitchcock and Michèle Cohen (London: Longman, 1999), p. 60.

52 Joan W. Scott, 'Rewriting History' in *Behind the Lines: Gender and the Two World Wars*, ed. by Margaret Randolph Higonnet, Jane Jenson, Sonya Michel, and Margaret Collins Weitz (London and New Haven, CT: Yale University Press, 1987).

War known as khaki fever (reflecting the changing colour of army jackets but the persistence of women's attraction to men in uniform). Woollacott's research has drawn attention to the wave of concern which accompanied reports in 1914 that numerous young women were hanging around outside army camps, following recruits and engaging in sexual activity with soldiers.[53] Woollacott argues that khaki fever was a particular symptom of the initial stages of the war, when women were excluded from a structured outlet for their patriotic desire to be involved in the national war effort, and so instead achieved a vicarious thrill via liaisons with troops.[54] Once women were able to become involved in war work themselves, she argues, khaki fever quickly subsided. This contrast might therefore provide a final clue into the workings of scarlet fever in the late Georgian era. Whilst Georgian women participated in a number of patriotic and war-related activities, they were not included in any officially sanctioned, formal role in the war effort comparable to that extended to women during the First World War. As such it might be argued that they had far fewer outlets through which to express their patriotic fervour in this era, which might in turn help to explain the more sustained enthusiasm for men in uniform apparent in this period. We might thus see scarlet fever as a symptom of the distinctly gendered way in which Georgian men and women were encouraged to express their patriotism during wartime. Next to the supposed patriotic glory of putting on a red coat yourself, admiring a man wearing one might just have been the next best thing.

---

53 Angela Woollacott, '"Khaki Fever" and its Control: Gender, Class, Age and Sexual Morality on the British Homefront in the First World War', *Journal of Contemporary History*, 29 (1994), pp. 325–47.

54 Ibid., pp. 328, 332.

Part 5

Soldiers in Society

9

Disability, Fraud and Medical Experience at the Royal Hospital of Chelsea in the Long Eighteenth Century

Caroline Louise Nielsen

Tʜᴇ ᴘʀᴏᴍɪsᴇ of a 'Chelsea Pension' for those who became debilitated while serving their king was an attractive prospect for the recruits and soldiers of the later eighteenth-century army and militia.[1] Recruiters and promoters of these services used it to full advantage. It is easy to imagine charismatic recruiting sergeants using 'the Pension' as a prop in their carefully stage-managed performances outside taverns. The promise would have had added resonance as recruiting sergeants were often recently pensioned veterans themselves. However, for many it was only ever a promise. In spite of its prominent position in the many discussions of the benefits of service in the regular, volunteer or militia forces, no serving soldier, however wounded, sick or elderly, was automatically entitled to any of the Chelsea pensions before 1807.[2] Satirical prints such as *The Recruiting Serjeant* (1770) juxtaposed this by picturing crippled veterans watching recruiters perform, contrasting the promised glamour of being treated 'as Gentlemen & provided for accordingly'. The reality was far closer to that of the amputee veteran pictured on the far right of the image: 'Thirty Years have I serv'd and you see what I am come to at last.'[3] By the 1770s, the more common sentimental

---

1 Chelsea was responsible for Marines or Sea Service companies until 1754, when the duty passed to the Admiralty.

2 See, for example: Henry Trenchard, *The Private Soldier's and Militia Man's Friend, Dedicated, by Permission, to Lord Charles Spencer, Representative in Parliament, and Colonel of the Oxfordshire Militia* (London: G. Kearsley, 1786), p. 15.

3 Anon., 'The Recruiting Serjeant' (*Oxford Magazine*, November 1770), British Museum (BM) Satires 4411.

depiction of the veteran soldier was not that of the happy rewarded Chelsea Pensioner, but that of an honourable but decayed elderly man, a victim of both the ineffectual government of army pensions and the insufficient financial gratitude of those above him.

The invalid pensions overseen by the Lords and Commissioners of the Royal Hospital of Chelsea were not automatically granted to all invalid, sick or elderly men, no matter how much the men thought themselves entitled. The records of the hospital testify to its rigid and centralised bureaucracy deeply concerned with its regulations and precedence. The strict admissions requirements effectively excluded large numbers of men from even applying. Pensions could be officially withdrawn without prior notice on the whim of the commissioners or unofficially by Chelsea's inspectors or agents. Many more individuals temporarily lost their pensions through their ignorance of Chelsea's bureaucratic idiosyncrasies. While these issues kept petitioners and successful pensioners in a comparatively weak position, it did not prevent them from actively negotiating with the system in a variety of ways. This chapter examines the procedure of application to Chelsea, and the role of chronic ill health and disability within it. In doing so, it hopes to encourage further investigation into the pensioners of Chelsea and their relationships with this massive nationwide administration.

The Royal Hospitals of Kilmainham, Chelsea and Greenwich were established as part of a wider European movement towards the confinement and regulation of vagrants and other 'problematic' social groups. This ill-defined gradual movement towards confinement and regulation of the poor centred on the combined considerations of charitable relief, public healthcare, morality and political economy.[4] These three institutions regulated their charges through their outdoor pension schemes instead of through large-scale confinement. The rigorous nature of Chelsea's examinations and its annual imposition into the lives of its pensioners were thought to ensure that the state's benevolence was not being wasted on undeserving individuals. Several recent studies have demonstrated this, and have sought to place Chelsea within both wider attitudes towards the confinement of the poor, and the fiscal-military state.[5] However, the provision offered to these military

---

4   See Donna Andrew, *Philanthropy and Police: London Charity in the Eighteenth Century* (Princeton, NJ: Princeton University Press, 1989), chs 1, 2. Temporary confinement of the poor for charitable reasons is a recurrent theme in Ole Grell and Paul Cunningham (eds), *Health Care and Poor Relief in Protestant Europe 1500–1700* (London: Routledge, 1997). On London's comparable institutions, see: Paul Slack's chapter in that volume, 'Hospitals, Workhouses and the Relief of the Poor in Early Modern London', pp. 234–51.

5   There has been a recent upsurge of interest in the hospital in the light of changes in

pensioners has meant that they have previously been marginalised in wider studies of demobilisation and its effects on British society. Contemporaries, and subsequently historians, have focused on the perceived social and economic problems of mass demobilisation during the long eighteenth century, such as crime, vagrancy and unemployment. The emphasis has been on the lack of state provision for the majority of discharged soldiers, and the assumption that local relief provisions were inadequate when compared to the centralised Chelsea or Greenwich pensions.[6] These pensions ensured a fixed income and therefore offered a level of insurance against the worst elements of demobilisation (and of old age), such as unemployment, impoverishment and social alienation. This has meant that the pensioners have been treated as if they were a stable and relatively unproblematic group. While their fixed income did protect the pensioners to some extent, the centralised nature of the pension brought its own difficulties and could exclude pensioners from other forms of charitable relief.

THE ROYAL HOSPITAL OF CHELSEA AND ITS PENSIONS

CHELSEA'S ADMINISTRATION was overseen by the Lords and Commissioners, a select group of some of the most senior government ministers of the time. They could include secretaries of state, the Secretary at War, the Adjutant General, Commanders in Chief, the Paymaster General, the Comptroller of Army Accounts, the Hospital's governor, and the Lieutenant Governor. However, it was rare for all the holders of these offices to attend. The official bureaucratic remit of the commissioners grew rapidly over the first fifteen years of its life.[7] By 1715, they were responsible for

---

the interconnected historiographies of medicine, poverty and warfare. See: Geoffrey Hudson, 'Arguing Disability: Ex-Servicemen's Own Stories in Early Modern England, 1590–1790', in *Medicine, Madness and Social History: Essays in Honour of Roy Porter*, ed. by Roberta Bivins and John Pickstone (Basingstoke: Palgrave Macmillan, 2007); Geoffrey Hudson, 'Internal Influences in the Making of the English Military Hospital: The Early-Eighteenth-Century Greenwich', in *British Military and Naval Medicine 1600–1830* ed. by Geoffrey Hudson (Amsterdam: Rodopi, 2007), pp. 253–72; John Cookson, 'Alexander Tulloch and the Chelsea Out-Pensioners, 1838–43: Centralisation in the Early Victorian State', *English Historical Review*, 125.512 (2010), pp. 60–82. For a recent example of the quantitative studies of local communities in the wake of demobilisation using Chelsea's archive, see: John Cookson, 'Early Nineteenth-Century Scottish Military Pensioners as Homecoming Soldiers', *Historical Journal*, 52.2 (2009), pp. 319–41.

6 Hudson, 'Internal Influences', pp. 256–7.

7 George Hutt, *Papers Illustrative of the Origin and Early History of the Royal Hospital*

the governance of all of the different classes of pensioner, the Invalid Establishment, their independent agents and collectors, and the hospital buildings and offices at Horse Guards and at Chelsea. The Royal Hospital was built on the banks of the Thames, but much of its business took place in Horse Guards and a number of other offices rented by the commissioners. The original buildings at Chelsea, and Chelsea's Irish sister institution of Kilmainhaim, were inspired by the massive *Hôtel Royal des Invalides* in Paris.[8] It offered monarchical display and practical care, with control of publically visible wounded soldiers. Chelsea's open courtyards, high windows, covered walkways and wide staircases and wards were designed to promote the healthy circulation of light and air, which was thought to prevent infectious diseases spreading between inmates and staff.[9] The village of Chelsea was also sufficiently distant from the unclean streets of early eighteenth century London to act as a home for men with 'ruined constitutions'. Infectious fevers were associated with the closed environments of towns, barracks and hospitals, where the 'putrid' air created by the sick was unable to dissipate.[10]

---

at Chelsea (London: Eyre & Spottiswoode, 1872); Charles Dean, *The Royal Hospital Chelsea* (London: Hutchinson, 1950).

8 The most commonly discussed text considered instrumental in the foundation of Kilmainham, Chelsea and Greenwich was *A Pattern of a Well Constituted and Well Governed Hospital, or a Brief Description of the Buildings, and Full Relation of the Establishment, Constitution, Discipline, Oeconomy and Administration of the Government of the Royal Hospital of Invalids near Paris* (London: Richard Baldwin, 1695). French veterans have received more historical attention, see: André Corvisier, *L'Armée française de la fin du XVIIe siècle au ministère de Choiseul: Le Soldat*, 2 vols (Paris: Presses universitaires de France, 1964). For *invalides'* views of life inside the institution, with extensive discussions of the demography of the population from 1780 to 1820, see: Isser Woloch, *The French Veteran from the Revolution to the Restoration* (Chapel Hill, NC: University of North Carolina, 1979); Woloch, '"A Sacred Debt": Veterans and the State in Revolutionary and Napoleonic France', in *Disabled Veterans in History*, ed. by David Gerber (Ann Arbor, MI: University of Michigan, 2000), pp. 145–62. Jean-Pierre Bois complements this, with more emphasis on changing attitudes towards soldiers outside of the institution, in 'Les anciens soldats de 1715 à 1815. Problèmes et méthodes', *Revue Historique* (1981), pp. 81–102; 'Les soldats invalides au XVIIIème siècle: perspectives nouvelles', *Histoire, Économie, et Société*, 1 (1982), pp. 237–58.

9 Christine Stevenson, *Medicine and Magnificence: British Hospital and Asylum Architecture, 1660–1815* (New Haven, CT: Yale University Press, 2000), pp. 56–7.

10 Christine Stevenson, '"From Palace to Hut": The Architecture of Military and Naval Medicine', in Hudson, *British Military and Naval Medicine*, p. 238; *Medicine and Magnificence*, pp. 65–6, 131–3, 137, 152, 160–2. On lay and medical views of infection, see: Roy Porter, 'Laymen, Doctors and Medical Knowledge in the Eighteenth Century: The Evidence of the *Gentleman's Magazine*' in *Patients and Practitioners: Lay Perceptions of Medicine in Pre-Industrial Society*, ed. by Roy Porter (Cambridge: Cambridge University Press, 1985), pp. 283–313.

Weaker individuals, like convalescents, were more susceptible to this type of air and so to subsequent infections and general debility.[11] This was not as much of a problem in more open rural areas. Officers similarly took their invalided men to the outlying parishes of Fulham, Battersea, Chiswick and Putney to wait for their admission to the Chelsea pension lists.[12] The toll of maintaining a standing army, garrisons and active theatres, however, meant that later many sick and wounded men waited outside of London in invalid garrisons and depots.

Chelsea was never envisaged to operate on the same scale as the *Invalides*, and it was hampered by the financial problems of the House of later Stuarts and the House of Orange. The first severely disabled men were admitted to their new home in 1692, and within one month all of the 472 residential places were taken.[13] These were the first 'house' men or 'in-pensioners'. Of these first ninety-nine named entrants, twenty-five were immediately taken into the infirmary.[14] The term 'out-pension' was first used in 1689 to describe an individual waiting for the new hospital to be finished, housed at the government's expense in billets or in invalid garrisons at Windsor, Chester or Hampton Court.[15] The 'out-pension' was formally instituted as the major pension system of Chelsea Hospital in 1703.

Pensions were granted to those considered 'totally unfit' for further service after a series of examinations, initially by their regimental surgeon and finally by the commissioners and the hospital surgeons. Officers had to recommend

---

11 Susannah Ottaway, *The Decline of Life: Old Age in Eighteenth-Century England* (Cambridge: Cambridge University Press, 2004), pp. 29–30. On the generally poor health of the valetudinarians returning from the West Indies and their use of spas, see: Mark Harrison, *Medicine in an Age of Commerce and Empire: Britain and its Tropical Colonies 1660–1830* (Oxford: Oxford University Press, 2010), pp. 205–36. For a contemporary description of the problems facing valetudinarians, see: James Lind, *An essay on diseases incidental to Europeans in hot climates. With the method of preventing their fatal consequences*, 2nd edition (London: 1771), pp. 290–7.

12 The National Archives, London (TNA), WO249/459 (26 May 1716 & 9 July 1716).

13 The selection process of these first applicants is unclear. The earliest hospital board minutes survive only in the form of the edited hospital journal. The Reverend Michael Mann, former chaplain of the hospital and one of its historians, implied that the severity of disability alone was the main reason for the admission of these lucky 472, citing BM Add MSS 3 929, 'A List of Souldiers Disabled by their Wounds now in the Royal Hospital of King Charles ye 2cond', 4 February 1692. At the time of writing, this manuscript was missing. However, the descriptions offered by Rev. Mann do not appear to be significantly different from their out-pension counterparts. The role of patronage is not openly discussed in Mann's narrative. See: Michael Mann, *The Veterans* (Norwich: Michael Russell, 1997), p. 30.

14 Mann, *The Veterans*, p. 30.

15 Dean, *Royal Hospital*, p. 107.

them to the commissioners as deserving cases. Men had to have served over twenty years or have been severely debilitated in the service by wounds or sickness.

In-pensioners received their subsistence, lodgings and clothing from the commissioners in lieu of any pension money. They also received occasional charitable gratuities. The Earl of Ranelagh's legacy financed sentries' coats, and extra provisions for the nurses, although one suspects that the extra small beer provided at the annual 'Restoration Day' celebrations was more popular.[16] Daily life inside the hospital was highly regimented, and men were organised into nine 'companies' under a hierarchy of military staff. The social status of officers was kept, as was the seniority and status of the different regiments of cavalry and infantry. All appointments to the hospital's military posts were based on character recommendations. No member of military staff or in-pensioner was allowed to be absent from the hospital for more than two days without the governor's leave, although it appears that furloughs were routinely granted to all ranks and often extended without issue.

The out-pensioners were the largest group receiving the benefit of Chelsea. From its earliest warrants in 1685, Chelsea always recognised the expectation that the amount of a pension would recognise the status of the applicant's regiment and their personal rank (Table 9.1). These figures were revised again in June 1713 in the wake of a series of embezzlement cases, a recurrent theme in the early hospital. Three pension rates were instituted at 5d, 9d, and 1s per diem until their repeal in late 1806. The 9d and 1s pensions acknowledged *some* individuals' length of service and rank. The 9d pension was limited to the senior Guards Regiments, and emerged out of series of occasional payments to discharged members. Blinded men on 5d could apply for an extra payment of 4d per diem if they submitted to a second examination by the commissioners. This, however, was not automatically or even regularly given, and depended on the nature of the blindness. Men noted in their regimental or Chelsea examination as having 'dim sight' or 'bad sight' did not qualify. The blindness had to be received during active service: those who gradually went blind through age or poor light while doing light duty in Chelsea-ran invalid garrisons similarly did not qualify. They were excused garrison duty and placed onto the 5d basic rate.[17] Barnabus Kelly, however, did qualify 'on account of his great sufferings' on his application in 1783.[18] There are rare instances of men being awarded higher rates or one-off payments in

---

16 Thomas Faulkner, *An Historical and Topographical Description of Chelsea, and its Environs* (London: J. Tilling, 1810), p. 177.

17 For example, TNA, WO250/261, 19 June 1781.

18 TNA, WO250/261, 18 September 1783.

recognition of the severity of their injury or for their bravery. For example, the commissioners ordered that George Bamborough and James Stockden (double amputees) and Peter Rowe, 'who has lost an Arm & who hath constantly been employed in assisting His Comrades in their distress', should be allowed the 1s rate instead of 5d.[19] The unusual nature of these awards is testified by the creation of individual payment warrants for these men.

Table 9.1   Pension rates per diem

Rank	1685	1709	1712
Troopers of guards	1s 6d	1s 6d	1s
Corporals of light horse	1s 6d	1s 6d	1s
Master gunners	1s 6d	1s 6d	excluded
Light horsemen and horse grenadiers	1s	1s	9d
Sergeants	11d	9d	9d
Corporals of dragoons	9d	9d	9d
Corporals of foot and drummers	7d	7d	7d
Gunners	7d	7d	excluded
Dragoons	6d	7d	7d
Privates	5d	5d	5d

This excludes any deductions for hospital fees, regimental stoppages, and debts.
Source: George Hutt (ed.), *Papers Illustrative of the origin and early history of the Royal Hospital at Chelsea* (London: Eyre & Spottiswoode, 1872), pp. 82–4.

'Lettermen' were appointed on the basis of patronage letters solicited from the monarch, aristocracy and senior War Office staff. These letters formed the basis of their admission to the waiting list for the 1s pension. They received 1s per diem. It was one of the few augmentations allowed by the commissioners without a second physical appearance at the board or at the lodgings of the hospital surgeons. Officers' goodwill and patronage were significant factors in all applications to Chelsea, but it was most prominent among the lettermen. This dependence on royal and aristocratic patronage was one of the reasons (as well as the perceived cost) that their numbers were capped at c. 100 in 1718, coinciding with wider concerns about the number of

19 TNA, WO250/260, 6 August 1762.

government pensions. It was raised to around 200 in 1773 and around 400 in 1785. By the late 1720s, however, it had become increasingly the preserve of the senior regiments, especially the Guards.

Between 1713 and 1806, the exact out-pension amount awarded depended on a range of interconnected issues. Several levels of pension operated at different times with different caps. The number of pensioners was highly dependent on the financial and political context of the day. At an individual level, the award depended on, in rough order of importance: the level of recommendations from persons of 'Quality' given on the applicants' behalf;[20] their length of service; the status of their former regiment; their personal social status before and during their life in the army; and finally the specifics of their disability. This order was not enshrined in the Instructions, but can be seen in the different reactions and decision-making processes visible in the near-complete board papers[21] and in the surviving correspondence of the secretaries Kingsmill Eyre and Peregrine Furye.[22] The secretaries were frequently able to predict the outcomes of the invalid cases brought to them by their peers. In some cases, these two men advised how this might be remedied. William Harper was one such example. He had ignored his last summons to the commissioners, and in consequence had lost his pension.[23] Eyre told the gentleman advocating on Harper's behalf that 'I cannot alter [his case] without a letter from ye Secretary at War.' Eyre similarly predicted how the board would handle an errant officer of an invalid garrison. When Lieutenant Lewis Dufour was refused a leave of absence in 1741, he appealed over the head of his garrison commander, Lieutenant-Governor George Gibbons. Eyre assured the insulted Gibbons that it would be remedied 'for the Secretary at War [a commissioner] usually declines it unless the Governor of the place agrees'.[24]

In reality, the sum awarded was often far from what the pensioner

20 A 'person of quality' meant an individual with social status, in practice usually a Justice of the Peace, or an MP.

21 The board papers survive in triplicate in different archival series with varying levels of preservation: TNA, WO250, WO180 and the hospital journal (also WO250). Board papers were housed in the Secretary's Office, and the agent kept a limited number of copies of questionable cases at his office, and by the occasional Inspectors of Invalids employed from the 1760s. Notwithstanding, the frequency of requests for information from the commissioners, agents and inspectors suggest that the only complete series was kept in the Secretary's Office. The hospital journal is a neater bound version of all board rulings kept for reference purposes.

22 TNA, WO246/92–93.

23 TNA, WO246/93, Kingsmill Eyre to Tho. Breuton of Liverpool Esq., Chelsea Hospital, 20 April 1741. The commissioners had refused by 24 April 1741.

24 TNA, WO246/93, Kingsmill Eyre to Rt Hon. Geo Gibbon, 20 April 1741.

received. Out-pensioners had to wait for one year before their payments were authorised, and occasionally longer.[25] This delay created a sellers' market for money-lenders, whose bills of attorney and credit notes became a standard part of Chelsea's finances. Pensioners' other creditors, such as landlords or victuallers, similarly lodged letters of attorney to ensure that they received owed monies. When the pension payment was finally authorised, the money owed was paid directly to them. As the state paid, pensioners would have been an attractive target for money-lenders. This system was so commonplace that some of the clerks lent money. This was certainly the case of John Woodman of Westminster, who had a public dispute with Kingsmill Eyre and Robert Mann when they refused to authorise payment for the 132 pensioners on his books.[26] While Woodman argued his business was legitimate, he acknowledged that the delayed payment system left out-pensioners foul of 'usury and Extortion' often at the hands of 'Clerks &c who [...] pay themselves just what they please'.[27]

In 1754 William Pitt, then Paymaster General, sponsored an Act of Parliament that authorised payments every six months in advance, removing the one year wait.[28] The act voided credit contracts held at the Secretary's Office. An 'Agent of the Out-Pensioners' was appointed. Men within 25 miles of London could still collect their pension at the hospital's office or at the agent's offices in central London. Those who did not live within this area could collect their pensions from one of the local agents appointed by the Agent of the Out-Pensioners. These local agents were usually excise collectors or invalid company officers or agents. None of these measures removed the out-pensioners' risk of destitution. The Pay Office of the hospital, the Secretary of the Hospital and the other clerical staff levied a complex system of officially and unofficially sanctioned fees and pre-requisites, and this continued long after 1754. The standard charge of the Secretary's Office was £3 16s 6d in 1716, and the infirmary could also charge a fee for treatment.[29] The agents working outside of London were also allowed to charge. The excise fee was 1s per payment, a practice that was allowed, despite raising concerns among the commissioners and at the War Office.[30] The clerks in the Secretary's Office were still levying unofficial charges in the early nineteenth century, as

25 John Woodman, *A Rat-Catcher at Chelsea College; A Tale Alluding to the Manner in which the Out-Pensioners of Chelsea have been a long Time oppress-d by Usurers and Extortioners* (London: printed for the author, 1740), p. 5.

26 Ibid., p. 4.

27 Ibid., p. v.

28 28 Geo. II c.1.

29 TNA, WO245/1.

30 Dean, *Royal Hospital*, p. 217.

evidenced by the several reminders that this practice was banned.[31] Officially, the charge was lowered to 6d in 1815, but isolated cases occurred when men claimed that they were being charged more.[32] Like all other serving officers, the officers of the independent companies of invalids were subject to the credit systems and fees of their regimental agents.[33] The real value of the pensions was far less than the sum originally awarded.[34]

Windham's Act came into force at the end of 1806.[35] It effectively instituted length of service as the main legal qualification for a pension. Several amendments ensured that the level of debility and age of the pensioner were also taken into account when fixing the sum awarded.[36] Furthermore, it was backdated to include all pensioners on the lists. The basic rates remained at 5d, 9d and 1s, but men could legally demand up to 2s depending on their service and disabilities. The original act acknowledged the physiological toll of service in unfamiliar climates.[37] It was calculated that two years' service in the East or West Indies counted for three years in Britain.[38] The act was part of a wider initiative to attract more 'quality' recruits to lives in the army.[39] However, the commissioners continued to recognise the importance of an officer's right to be favourable towards his best and longest-serving old soldiers by providing them with the opportunity to help their men receive higher levels of pension.[40] This was done through their personal

---

31 TNA, WO247/25; WO247/25.

32 Hutt, *Papers Illustrative*, p. 37.

33 TNA, WO245/1.

34 On the real value of the pensions, see: Caroline Nielsen, 'The Chelsea Out-Pensioners: Image and Reality in Eighteenth-Century and Early Nineteenth-Century Social Care' (Newcastle University unpublished PhD thesis, forthcoming).

35 46 Geo. III, c.69.

36 'A Bill as Amended by Committee for the Regulation of Chelsea Hospital, and making better Provision for Soldiers' (London: Stationers Office, 3 June 1806).

37 On medical views of hot climates, see: Mark Harrison, 'Disease and Medicine in the Armies of British India, 1750–1830: The Treatment of Fevers and the Emergence of Tropical Therapeutics', in *British Military and Naval Medicine*, ed. by Geoffrey Hudson (Amsterdam: Rodopi, 2007), pp. 87–120; also Mark Harrison, *Climates & Constitutions: Health, Race, Environment and British Imperialism in India, 1600–1850* (Oxford: Oxford University Press, 2002).

38 Hutt, *Papers Illustrative*, p. 46.

39 On these reforms, see: Patricia Y. C. E. Linn, '"Extending Her Arms?": Military Families and the Transformation of the British State, 1793–1815' (University of California at Berkeley, unpublished PhD thesis, 1997); Linn, 'Citizenship, Military Families and the Creation of a New Definition of "Deserving Poor"', *Social Politics*, 7 (2000), pp. 5–46. For a negative view of the act, see: Richard Blanco, 'Henry Marshall and the Health of the British Army', *Medical History*, 14.3 (1970), pp. 263–8.

40 Examples survive in TNA, WO180/16.

recommendations to the commissioners. The act rapidly attracted criticism. The estimated cost of all out-pensions in 1807 was £357,222 7s 3½d (approximately 11¼d per man). In 1806 it had been 5½ per man.[41]

The main criticism of the act was that it was ruining the morality of the army, instead of improving it. The surgeon Henry Marshall argued that 'the regulations have a tendency to encourage moral depravity' by inducing men to feign injury or chronic illness or to self-harm.[42] He authored some of the first detailed guides on the detection of such injuries and other fraudulent disabilities to aid those discharging men.[43] Marshall went on to lead Sir Henry Hardinge's investigation into fraud among the Chelsea out-pensioners. He did not advocate the removal of the pension from those genuinely debilitated by their service (his texts described the bleak prognosis of many chronic complaints). Instead, he favoured more routine medical examinations for those in service.[44] The act was repealed in 1826, and once again the out-pension became a gift of the state and not a legal entitlement.

Officially, out-pensioners and lettermen could live in any land owned by Britain as long as they kept in regular contact with the hospital through annual affidavits confirming their identity and their continued debility. After both the Seven Years War and the American War of Independence, former commanders and civilians highlighted the benefits of encouraging old soldiers to settle as colonists in North America and Canada.[45] Major Henry Fletcher noted that men often opted to stay in North America as 'they think they have a better prospect of a Livelihood'.[46] Many soldiers did not have a choice. At the end of the Seven Years War, passage was provided only for the limited number of men 'recommended' for the pensions of Chelsea, as Stephen Brumwell has noted.[47] In reality though, settlement beyond Scotland or Ireland caused major problems for any out-pensioner. The commissioners regularly refused to authorise payments for 'American settlers' whom they had not physically examined in years (despite doing so for men in Scotland

---

41 Hutt, *Papers Illustrative*, p. 86.

42 Henry Marshall, *United Service Journal and Naval and Military Magazine*, ii (1829), p. 330 cited in Blanco, 'Henry Marshall', p. 265.

43 Henry Marshall, *Hints to Young Medical Officers of the Army on the Examination of Recruits, and Respecting the Feigned Disabilities of Soldiers: with Official Documents, and the Regulations for the Inspection of Conscripts for the French and Prussian Armies* (London: Burgess & Hill, 1828).

44 Blanco, 'Henry Marshall', p. 265. On the nineteenth-century fraud investigations at Chelsea, see: Cookson, 'Alexander Tulloch', pp. 60–82.

45 Stephen Brumwell, *Redcoats: The British Soldier and War in the Americas, 1755–1763* (Cambridge: Cambridge University Press, 2002), p. 297.

46 Ibid., p. 297.

47 Ibid., p. 297.

and Ireland). This was justified, as the commissioners' instructions stated that they had to physically examine all pensioners every couple of years. The commissioners similarly refused to pay for these pensioners' passage to England when they came to claim their pension arrears, despite numerous intercessions by their former officers.[48] It usually required the formal intercession of the monarch or his closest advisors to the Secretary at War for the pension to be restored without making the journey to England. One such victim was Thomas Gordon, a former sergeant in the Third Regiment of Foot Guards. He was admitted to the 5d pension in 1748. In 1753, unable to find work, he left England in hope of finding employment with the army in North America. He was struck off the pension lists, probably due to his lack of personal appearance or regular affidavits from persons of 'quality'. He did not receive any pension until his personal appearance at Horse Guards in June 1760. The commissioners reluctantly reinstated him but refused him his arrears. Adam Schomberg of the First Troop of Horse Guards was more fortunate. He similarly received no pension during his residence in New York, but was granted his arrears.[49] It is not clear why Schomberg received more, but it was possibly in lieu of loss of property in North America during the War of Independence.

The Invaliding Process

THE APPLICATIONS PROCEDURE changed little over the course of the eighteenth century despite the increase in applications.[50] Sergeant James Hale of the Ninth Regiment of Foot described the process in 1826, approximately twelve years after his admission to the pension lists.[51] His arm was shattered on 13 October 1813, and twelve bones had to be removed from the wound during his five-month convalescence in Bilbao. By March 1814 he was reviewed by the hospital staff and declared fit enough to travel as his arm was 'in a fair way of getting well', a decision he thought was also made because 'sergeants were wanting'.[52] It was standard practice to assign a recovering sergeant or ensign to escort travelling wounded men to help care for them, prevent desertion and maintain military discipline. He helped marshal 100 invalids to their embarkation point. The passage took eight days, and many

48 TNA, WO250/459, 29 June 1742.
49 TNA, WO250/461, 20 November 1783.
50 Hutt, *Papers Illustrative*, pp. 84–6.
51 James Hale, *Journal of James Hale, Late Sergeant in the Ninth Regiment of Foot* (Cirencester: Philip Watkins, 1826), pp. 128–30.
52 Ibid., p. 128.

soldiers' wounds re-opened and turned septic, which he blamed on 'the unfeeling fellow that was put in place of a surgeon'.[53] These men were sent to Plymouth Dock barracks to recover from this experience. In June, Hale and the other wounded were reviewed, presumably by the regimental or garrison surgeon. Hale was declared unfit, discharged, and sent to London to await his turn before the commissioners. Applicants like Hale waited for the day assigned for their regiment to attend one of the commissioners' examination days. These days were advertised, which also allowed pensioners' creditors and potential informers to attend. In the intervening time, the clerical staff of the Secretary's Office collated the information on the applicants sent by regimental surgeons, officers, and persons of 'quality'. Brief descriptions of the applicants were transcribed into the 'Examination Books'. On 24 August, Hale attended the board. Like most other Revolutionary and Napoleonic memoirs, Hale's is frustratingly quiet about the actual process of facing the commissioners and their staff.

Examination days would have been crowded and busy. First, the man would be examined by the hospital surgeon(s) and/or his mates, who would then pass their findings to the commissioners by note. Sir William Sands' defence of the hospital examination provides insight into the experience: 'We have made them strip to the Skin, the better to judge their Inability; after such a strict Enquiry, we could not in Humanity refuse to admit them.'[54] Second (and probably in a different place), he would be publically questioned by the commissioners as to the particulars of his service, age, settlement and disability. Between 1715 and the later 1740s, the man's appearance would be carefully noted, especially if the man did not have a visible injury, disability or scar. This practice was subsequently abandoned, most likely for reasons for brevity. Any discrepancies between their appearance or account and that of their officers were noted down. All successful pensioners were then sworn before a presiding Justice of the Peace, and his documents would be filed in the Secretary's Office. If a man was found 'fit for further service' or 'unqualified under the Regulations', he would be sent to an invalid garrison or returned to his regiment. His discharge papers would be sent back to the commanding officers of his regiment and a note of his unsuccessful application made in the Secretary's Office. This reprimanded the regiment for authorising the discharges of men that the high-ranking commissioners felt were still fit for some form of duty. It also prevented the discharge papers being used fraudulently at a later date. A man had to be able to walk

---

53 Ibid.
54 'Debates in last Session of Parliament', *Gentleman's Magazine*, 2.22 (October 1732), p. 987.

without the aid of another person (crutches were acceptable), and fire a gun over a wall to be considered fit for garrison duty with an invalid company.[55] Madness, incontinence of urine and hectic fevers were the only conditions that consistently excluded a man from any further service.

CHRONIC ILL HEALTH AND DISABILITY
AMONG THE OUT-PENSIONERS

THE COMMISSIONERS' INSTRUCTIONS were enshrined in the Hospital Warrants.[56] They gave the commissioners the power to question the discharge of the men sent to them. If a man was sent to Chelsea because of a prolonged disability, it had to be proven that it had been the result of their *service alone*, with the assurances of medics and officers that they were unlikely to ever recover enough to return to their normal regimental duties. Out-pensioners had to attend the commissioners or their travelling representatives at least once a year to demonstrate their continued decrepitude. Mass re-examinations were held during periods of heightened concern about the financial cost of the invalid establishment. Chelsea commissioned 'inspectors' to attend the Excise Collectors at some of the regional payment dates to assess the attendees from the 1760s. Those who could not attend had to get affidavits from their local churchwardens and, again, from 'persons of Quality'. There are a few instances of men being admitted onto the 5d pension for a six-month period in order to recover, but it was always on the assumption that they would go into an invalid garrison company upon their recovery.[57]

The early detailed descriptions of the disabilities of the successful applicants in the Examination and Admission Books have to be contextualised with the medical history of the military and of working-class men in this period. The applicants to Chelsea were chronic convalescents, and usually had suffered repeated infections and multiple serious injuries. Any recommendation to Chelsea on health grounds was not made because an individual was suffering from one of the many chronic complaints common to serving soldiers. It was because this condition had become incurable or had weakened the man's body to such an extent that he was no longer fit for his normal duties. Simply having a rupture, skin ulcer, damaged arm or rheumatism on its own did not constitute a reason for discharge or a recommendation to Chelsea. The surgeon Everard Home was echoing the views of the commissioners when

---

55 TNA, WO250/459, 9 January 1727.
56 Hutt, *Papers illustrative*, appendix.
57 E.g. TNA, WO250/460, 18 November 1783.

he stated 'ulcers are not a disease nor a reason for discharge […] continuance of a condition is not a reason for discharge'.[58] This was not unduly harsh. It mirrored the experiences of those with chronic sores and skin ulcers in the London hospitals.[59] Having such a condition was normalised. The problem occurred when an individual was no longer physiologically capable of coping with such a condition. This is one of the reasons that we cannot simply assume that the wound or infection listed in a man's examination was the sole or even immediate cause of his discharge.

A large proportion of the out-pensioners were given the ambiguous diagnostic category 'worn out'. This referred to the toll that repeated exposure to different illness, climates and labours had had on the bodies of these men. The hardships of military service (and chronic illness) had literally prematurely aged their bodies, and age affected the body's ability to heal.[60] Older bodies did not generate enough heat to stimulate the blood, humours and nerves effectively.[61] Heavy loss of blood had a similar long-term effect.[62] Military convalescents had also had the opportunity to taste life away from the usual harsh military discipline of their regiments or barracks. This made them particularly troublesome. The surgeon Donald Munro advised his readers to 'send them either to Billet, or to a convalescent Hospital; because recovered Men are always the most riotous besides they crowd the Hospital, and were in Danger of catching fresh Disorders from those who were sick'.[63] Monro's comment highlights that convalescents was in more danger from those around them than vice versa. They were not able to fight off any subsequent infections or adapt to any sudden climatic change.[64] This

---

58 Everard Home, *Practical Observations on the Treatment of Ulcers on the Legs, Considered as a Branch of Military Surgery* (London: printed for G. Nicol and J. Johnson, 1797), p. 46.

59 Ibid., p. 47.

60 Hudson, 'Arguing Disability', p. 109.

61 Ottaway, *The Decline of Life*, pp. 27–9.

62 Hudson, 'Arguing Disability', p. 109.

63 Donald Monro, *An Account of the Diseases Which were most frequent in the British Military Hospitals in Germany, from January 1761 to the Return of the Troops in England in March 1763, to which is added An Essay on the Means of Preserving the Health and Soldiers and conducting Military Hospitals* (London: A. Millar, D. Wilson and T. Durham, 1764), p. 389; Monro, *Observations on the Means of Preserving the Health of Soldiers; and of Conducting Military Hospitals. And on the Diseases Incident to Soldiers in the Time of Service and on the Same Diseases as they have Appeared in London* (London: J. Murray and G. Robinson, 1780), pp. 150–89.

64 See J. D. Alsop, 'Warfare and the Creation of British Imperial Medicine, 1600–1800', in *British Military and Naval Medicine, 1600–1830*, pp. 23–50; also Harrison, *Climates and Constitutions*.

is further supported by the fact that the out-pensioners and their counterparts in invalid companies do not appear to have been seen as harbingers of infectious disease.

NEGOTIATING AND APPEALING THE PENSION SYSTEM

APPLICATIONS to Chelsea relied on the idea that the applicant had undergone numerous hardships during, and because of, their service. As meagre as the pensions were in real terms, they were envisaged as definite markers of the deserving nature of these men and their families. However, changing attitudes towards the poor and their charitable relief in the later eighteenth century meant that many feared that the solid equation of 'deserving' and 'Chelsea out-pensioner' was being fraudulently capitalised upon. The Report on Urban Mendicity in 1798 found that out-pensioners frequently begged using their war stories, elderly uniforms, frail bodies and pension certificates to legitimise their claim to informal alms.[65] Furthermore, a wide spectrum of the population was very willing to give to Britain's former soldiers (or those pretending to be). Most formal charitable endeavour focused on *serving* soldiers and sailors or their bereaved families, usually in the form of charitable subscriptions, often contemporaneous with an expectation of war or during it.[66] Prominent victories often caused wealthy elites to give generous one-off payments to the regiments involved.[67] George Rose noted that soldiers and sailors were also particularly willing to donate to their former comrades if they saw them.[68] Officers' benevolence towards their former men was enshrined by the military establishment in Chelsea's application procedure, which hinged on the all-important character recommendation. While the recommendation was officially an officers' obligation, it allowed both senior and junior officers the chance to show gentlemanly benevolence

---

65 George Ross, *Report from the Committee on the State of Mendicity in the Metropolis Minutes* (London: 1814–15), pp. 46, 67–8; *Report from the Select Committee on the State of Mendicity in the Metropolis* (London: 1816), pp. 7–8.

66 For example, a subscription was raised to be used for 'occasional acts of benevolence as may be useful to the Soldiers who are, or may be employed in his Majesty's Service in America, and for succouring the distressed Widows and Orphans'. See: *St. James's Chronicle or the British Evening Post*, 23–25 November 1775, p. 2. The Marine Society's subscription increased in wartime: Donna Andrew, *Philanthropy and Police*, pp. 54–7, 98–9, 129.

67 John Manners, Marquis of Granby paid for his entire regiment to have a meal, costing £105 5s 6d. See: Richard Holmes, *Redcoats: The British Soldier in the Age of Horse and Musket* (London: Harper Collins, 2001), p. 110.

68 Rose, *Report Minutes*, pp. 7–8.

towards their former men. This factor further complicates the reasons for an admission beyond simply the medical complaint listed.

Some of this concern about fraudulent begging derived from the fact that many pensioners were still seen as *potential* soldiers. The annual reviews of the pensioners demonstrated the hope that some of the younger men's weakened health could be improved with 'gentle' service in the invalid companies or after a period at home with their families caring for them. This coincided with wider concerns about the mass economic migration of the poor and the increases in the south-east poor rates that accompanied it. Furthermore, these parishes were the main thoroughfares for both travelling military families and discharged men, and other types of mobile poor on their way to and from London and the military centres.[69] Large numbers of pensioners settled around London too, and the fact that some of these men worked called the award of disability pension into question.

Both middling and elite members of eighteenth-century British society recognised former soldiers as a deserving group for charitable assistance, but this sat uneasily with concerns about maintaining or encouraging fraudulent applications. Some were clearly prepared to question those claiming to be former soldiers, an event noted by John Douglas in his Napoleonic-era memoirs.[70] The award of a Chelsea pension ensured a level of accountability for those who felt they should check on suspicious beggars or itinerant poor. The production of the Chelsea pension certificates given to pensioners by the hospital would have assuaged most offering one-off informal relief, but it also offered a further opportunity for verification from the commissioners should a man arrive in their local area. Some caution must be exercised here. While the recording of such enquiries is much higher in the later eighteenth-century board papers, it is not clear if this was more to do with a change in the reportage of enquiries, the letters being dealt with by the commissioners instead of solely by the Secretary's Office. Their inclusion in the board minutes has ensured a greater survival of these petitions from this later period. However, Douglas' comment suggests that a level of probity was exercised by some well-off members of society.

Although the position of the applicant or pensioner was weak, they were not passive agents in the pensioning process. The petitions for Chelsea show that they actively solicited the help of both the officers and the gentry

69 See: Steven King, *Poverty and Welfare in England, 1700–1850: A Regional Perspective* (Manchester: Manchester University Press, 2000); Brumwell, *Redcoats*, pp. 290–1. Some surviving travel passes with parish markers survive in TNA, WO180/1.

70 John Douglas, *Douglas' Tale of the Peninsula and Waterloo by John Douglas (former Sergeant, 1st Royal Scots)*, ed. Stanley Monick (Barnsley: Leo Cooper, 1997), pp. 90–1.

mentioned above. Some personally approached members of hospital staff on their behalf, not always legally. The frequency with which Sir Robert Rich brought such applications to the attention of the other commissioners was a notable feature of his time as governor (1740–68).[71] Others appealed to the Secretary at War or the king if they felt that their officers or the commissioners had ruled against them unfairly.[72] Others tried to strengthen their applications through bribery or deliberately worsening their injuries.[73] Clerical staff were reminded to check all handwritten documents and signatures to prevent fraud in the face of an active trade in illicit certificates.[74] The number of proven (or reported) fraud cases was actually quite small. A large amount clearly went undetected due to the profitable nature of fraudulent claims for all involved, including the clerical staff who passed these certificates. Long-distance frauds were also facilitated by the inadequacy of Chelsea's own administrative system.[75] Nevertheless, however small the numbers actually involved, these cases clearly had a resonance in a society increasingly critical of outdoor relief systems.

CONCLUSION

VETERAN SOLDIERS, such as the Chelsea pensioners of this chapter, demonstrate the ambiguity and the fluidity of the historiographical construction of the boundaries of 'military' and 'civilian' in the long eighteenth century. One of the overall themes of this book is the experience of being identified as 'a soldier' during this formative period. Soldiering was a temporary life event for some, but a career and way of life for others. This was also true of the pensioners, some of whom only served a matter of months before being wounded, while others re-enlisted multiple times and served for decades. Military service is looked upon as having a distinct end, a moment when a man is no longer a soldier. It is important to consider exactly where we should draw a line for an old eighteenth-century soldier. Was it at the point of discharge, demobilisation or at death? For the men discussed here, their discharge did not mean their return to being a civilian. For the small number of NCOs and privates recommended to Chelsea, becoming a

---

71 For example, TNA, WO250/460, 7 March 1763.
72 For example, TNA, WO250/460, Alex McCleave of Colonel Holman's Marines, 4 April 1750; TNA, WO250/459, William Brookes and George McDonald, 9 May 1722.
73 For example, TNA, WO116/2, Thomas Stanbridge of Thirty-Ninth Regiment of Foot, 5 December 1748; James Murray of the Twentieth Regiment of Foot, 1 February 1749.
74 TNA, WO247/25.
75 See Nielsen, 'Chelsea Out-Pensioners', ch. 2.

pensioner meant the end of their career but not the end of their relationship or identification with the military and their former officers. The pensioners had the continual (but not altogether unwelcome) intrusion of military administration into their 'civilian' lives in the form of the Chelsea commissioners and their representatives. These disabled and/or elderly men kept the distinction of 'soldier' on their return to their home countries. The 'old soldiers' Chelsea dealt with were men whose manner, customs and physical bodies had been shaped and eventually destroyed by their military service. Their pensions were a limited recognition of this destruction.

This chapter is taken from my forthcoming AHRC-funded PhD thesis, 'The Chelsea Out-Pensioners: Image and Reality in Eighteenth-Century and Early Nineteenth-Century Social Care' (Newcastle University, unpublished PhD thesis, forthcoming).

10

Making New Soldiers

Legitimacy, Identity and Attitudes,
c. 1740–1815

Kevin Linch

ETWEEN 1740 AND 1815, hundreds of thousands of men in Britain took
part in some form of auxiliary military service for home defence, in the
militia, limited service regiments and part-time formations. The history of
these formations has received increasing scholarly attention in recent years,
focused on the role as patriotic citizens (or not), their particularism and
idiosyncrasies, the extent of mobilisation and the politics of their formation.[1]
There is, however, relatively little about them as soldiers, and in particular
how these forms of soldiering came into being and were understood by
contemporaries. Although there were huge varieties in the terms of service
of these men, there were fundamental similarities between them. They were
all fairly 'regular' in that they adopted the uniform, drill and weaponry of
the regular army and, just as significantly, sought to legitimise their role and
behaviour as soldiers through similar mechanisms. This chapter examines
all the men in auxiliary forces in Britain, both full-time and part-time
soldiers outside of the line regiments of the British Army. In most cases
these were temporary military formations raised in wartime with limited
terms of service (at most the British Isles), and this has resulted in them

---

1 See in particular: Linda Colley, *Britons: Forging the Nation 1707–1837* (New Haven,
CT: Yale University Press, 1992); Stephen Conway, *War, State, and Society in
Mid-Eighteenth-Century Britain and Ireland* (Oxford: Oxford University Press, 2006);
J. E. Cookson, *The British Armed Nation, 1793–1815* (Oxford: Clarendon, 1997); Austin
Gee, *The British Volunteer Movement, 1794–1814* (Oxford: Clarendon Press, 2003); John
Randle Western, *The English Militia in the Eighteenth Century: The Story of a Political
Issue, 1660–1802* (London: Routledge & Keegan Paul, 1965).

often being compartmentalised in existing works on the subject. What follows is an examination of all of them to explore the broader military culture that was created in this period, and also consider why it was so homogenous.

Concomitant with a broad approach to auxiliary soldiers in this chapter is an equally wide chronological framework, which also requires some explanation. The military crisis of the Forty-Five Rebellion prompted debates about arming the people to provide additional military forces in Britain to counter any invasion, with equally strong concerns about order and discipline if this was done. Moreover, it provoked deliberations about the nature of British society, particularly around its lack of martial, and often by extension masculine, spirit. These themes emerged again and again through the conflicts in the period, and the response to Earl Shelburne's plan for encouraging local forces in 1782 exemplifies the debates about mass arming and legitimacy. On the one hand, some viewed any such plan with alarm, whilst Charles James Fox saw this as an opportunity to strengthen Britain's military 'and to do this by the consent, and with the concurrence of the people themselves'.[2] This was the crux of the issue: these soldiers needed to be defined and legitimised, and this was a process in which both society and the soldiers themselves had a role to play.

THE LEGAL FRAMEWORK

ULTIMATELY, the law sanctioned the use of lethal force by military organisations, as it defined when such force could be used and, just as importantly, when a soldier's actions were illegal. As Stephen Conway demonstrated in chapter 1, Britain's armed forces were operating in a wider European military culture, which included a pseudo-legal framework that was intended to regulate war, most famously expressed in Emer de Vattel's *Laws of Nations*. Although not subject to any legal authority or court, the European laws of war at the time did indicate the expected behaviour of warring parties, and, particularly relevant in the case of new forms of soldiering, the work discussed the difference between troops and private citizens. In Vattel's view, private citizens were permitted to take actions in self-defence if attacked by the armed forces of an enemy, but were not allowed to take what can be deemed offensive action without orders from their sovereign or officers commissioned by the sovereign. Furthermore,

2 Parliament, *The Parliamentary Register*, 45 vols (London: printed for J. Almon and J. Debrett, 1781), 7, pp. 146–56.

enemy troops were expected to treat civilians humanely because they were not combatants:

> At present war is carried on by regular troops, the people, the peasants, the inhabitants of towns and villages, do not concern themselves with it. If the inhabitants submit to him who is master of the country, pay contributions imposed, and refrain from hostilities, they live as safe as if they were friends.

Within this statement the proviso on the population refraining from hostilities is crucial, for if this was not adhered to then soldiers were permitted to respond and so a delineation between a soldier and the population was essential to ensure that war remained humane and the actions of armies were justified.[3]

In Britain the legal framework for soldiers was codified in the Mutiny Act that was passed each year by Parliament and incorporated the Articles of War. For instance, section eleven of the articles ordered that soldiers and officers who were accused of crimes punishable by the 'known laws of the land' were to be handed over to civil magistrates.[4] However, the exact legal status was complicated by the constitutional sensitivities around a permanent military establishment, such that Blackstone's *Commentaries on the Laws of England* famously stated that 'The laws and constitution of these kingdoms know no such state as that of a perpetual standing soldier, bred up to no other profession than that of war.'[5] Most gentlemen were steeped in the political culture epitomised in Blackstone's work, and these were often the men who were intimately involved in the raising, organising and running of Britain's auxiliary forces.

It is not surprising, then, that there was a prodigious outpouring of Acts of Parliament relating to auxiliary forces in the period. In broad terms there

---

3 Emer de Vattel, *The Law of Nations; or, Principles of the Law of Nature: Applied to the Conduct and Affairs of Nations and Sovereigns. By M. De Vattel. A Work Tending to Display the True Interest of Powers. Translated from the French*, 2 vols (London: printed for J. Newbery, J. Richardson, S. Crowder, T. Caslon, T. Longman, B. Law, J. Fuller, J. Coote, and G. Kearsly, 1759), 2, pp. 52, 89–92. See also: Michael Howard, George J. Andreopoulos, and Mark R. Schulman (eds), *The Laws of War: Constraints on Warfare in the Western World* (New Haven, CT and London: Yale University Press, 1994).

4 11 Geo. 3, c. 6, 'An Act for punishing mutiny and desertion; and for the better payment of the army and their quarters' (1771), Section 11 of the Articles of War. For further details, see: Charles M. Clode, *The Military Forces of the Crown; Their Administration and Government*, 2 vols (London: J. Murray, 1869), 1, pp. 142–51.

5 Sir William Blackstone, *Commentaries on the Laws of England*, 4 vols (Oxford: The Clarendon Press, 1765), 1, p. 395.

were approximately 400 individual acts that related to the military in this period for Great Britain and Ireland, excluding the annual Mutiny Act. It is impossible to give an exact figure because some acts incorporated clauses about auxiliary forces into a larger piece of legislation, such as 3 Geo. 3, c. 17, 'An act for raising a certain sum of money by loans or bills for the service defraying costs' that included clauses on paying the militia, whilst others were routine annual legislation. The rhythm of this legislation was not constant across the period and there was a marked increase in quantity during the 1790s and early 1800s, with peaks in 1796, when twelve acts were passed, and in 1803, when a staggering twenty-nine laws were enacted, compared to the two or three acts passed each year during the Seven Years War.[6] These figures serve as a proxy for the amount of parliamentary time devoted to the subject, and echo the legal and constitutional debates about soldiering.

Much of this regulation concerned technical matters, in particular military finance, the authority of those involved in enacting the legislation, or detailing how the force was to be raised. The militia laws were the most comprehensive. For example, the 1761 Militia Act (2 Geo. 3, c. 20, or 'An Act to explain, amend, and reduce into One Act of Parliament, the several Laws now in being, relating to Raising and Training the Militia within that Part of Great Britain called England') ran to 148 clauses, and although it was unusual in its length it still focused primarily on the process of raising and maintaining the militia, and the property qualifications necessary for those involved.[7] At the other extreme was the 1782 Volunteer Act (22 Geo. 3, c. 79), which had only three clauses and barely made it to 300 words.

Except for the militia laws, government legislation on auxiliary forces often came after local communities expressed a desire to arm and defend themselves, and in some cases after they had began to train. Such wishes were frequently linked to fears of invasion or regional perceptions of military weakness during war.[8] The ability of local government to respond to these requests was curtailed by the comprehensiveness of the militia laws of the 1750s and 60s, which repealed earlier legislation for raising troops locally.

---

6 Danby Pickering, *The Statutes at Large from the Magna Charta to the End of the Eleventh Parliament of Great Britain*, 46 vols (Cambridge: Printed by J. Bentham, 1762–1807); *The Statutes at Large*, 7 vols (London: Printed by George Eyre and Andrew Strahan, 1819).

7 Pickering, *The Statutes at Large*, 25, pp. 101–50. See also: Western, *English Militia*.

8 Stephen Conway, '"Like the Irish"?: Volunteer Corps and Volunteering in Britain during the American War', in *Britain and America Go to War: The Impact of War and Warfare, 1754–1815*, ed. by Julie Flavell and Stephen Conway (Gainesville, FL: University Press of Florida, 2004), p. 144.

For example, during the War of Austrian Succession the county authorities in Sussex were able to raise a military association and organise a watch over the coast,[9] but a plan for arming the population during 1779, suggested by the Duke of Richmond whilst the area was under the threat of invasion from a combined Franco-Spanish fleet, apparently met with concerns of legal propriety. John Robinson expressed his trepidation about the duke's plans for arming the population:

> Should his Grace propose to raise a number of man to be armed, trained, and exercised, under the power of the Lord Lieutenant and magistrates with Commissions from the Lord Lieutenant that measure is not I apprehend legal (the old Militia Laws being repealed when the new Militia was established) unless the men to be raised are to be considered as Volunteer Companies to be added to the Militia of the County under the power of the Act of Parliament of last session.[10]

Nor was John Robinson's view unusual. Lord Amherst, then Commander-in-Chief, was similarly concerned when he first heard about a military association in Devon that had not been approved by himself or the king. Furthermore, the Secretary at War thought that each association should have a letter of service issued to them, a formal, and legal, document setting out their specific terms and conditions to 'bind the Men to some specific engagement'. In the absence of any additional legal framework, the only way Amherst and the Secretary of State felt they could proceed was to utilise a plan already approved for the Westminster Association,[11] and this proved sufficient until the 1782 Volunteer Act.

As Stephen Conway has shown, the politics of the years 1779 to 1782 played their part in this mobilisation, both at a national and local level, as the debate about arming the people became a political battleground for the wider argument about power and patronage relationships between the state, local authorities and the public. It was quite possible for local communities to take matters into their own hands, arm themselves and organise an auxiliary military force without any reference to the government.[12] This was particularly the case in Ireland, where the volunteers had emerged without any legal framework from the Irish Parliament. In correspondence about the

---

9 East Sussex Record Office, Lewes (ESRO), Lieutenancy, L/C/V/1/1, Association Book, 1745–1749.

10 ESRO, Archive of the Pelham Family of Stanmer, Earls of Chichester, SAS/A741/12, John Robinson to Lord Montague (Copy), 24 August 1779.

11 TNA, War Office In-Letters: Government Departments: b. Commander-in-Chief, WO 1/616, Leo Morre to Matthew Lewis, fols 585–92, 17 November 1779.

12 Conway, '"Like the Irish"?'

practicalities of mobilising the Irish volunteers for service in 1782, the then Commander-in-Chief, Henry Seymour Conway, thought that

> If an invasion happens they will be called upon to assist in repelling it. But I don't see how without an Act of Parliament they can be put under Military Law except by the General Principle of Proclaiming Martial Law and even that should be cautiously attempted for fear of disgusting them.[13]

The complexity of the legal situation was made most apparent in the response to a query made by Lord Barrington in 1779, when he was involved in plans for a military association in Berkshire. Even though had been Secretary at War, he felt the need to refer the question about training and arming men to the government, and the reply from Charles Jenkinson, the incumbent Secretary at War, was clear that the people had a right to arm themselves but made a critical distinction that no one could 'exercise any Command or Authority over another, unless what He derives from Government'. Jenkinson's opinion made a clear division between voluntary training with arms for 'play and amusement' and arming and disciplining men under the command of the Crown.[14]

The situation by 1803, when there was a massive mobilisation of part-time soldiers, was significantly different as the government had much greater control over the volunteers and their legal status. First, the government encouraged volunteering through the terms of the Levee en Masse Act, which stipulated that if a sufficient number of volunteers equal to six times a county's militia quota were not forthcoming then counties would be forced to train men.[15] Second, the subsequent huge expansion of these part-time forces meant that arms were not as easily available to the public as they had been in American War of Independence and the early stages of the French Revolutionary War and so the government, through the Board of Ordnance, had an unintended measure of control. If these part-time soldiers did not have weapons, then they were not considered to be volunteer soldiers and therefore did not count towards the counties' total auxiliary force. Furthermore, precedents had been set in 1798 legislation for mass arming, which asserted the authority of government to know about every part-time

---

13 TNA, Home Office: Military Correspondence, HO 50/1, Henry Seymour Conway to Thomas Townshend, 31 July 1782.

14 Charles Jenkinson to Barrington, 9 October 1779, in *An Eighteenth-Century Secretary at War: The Papers of William, Viscount Barrington*, ed. by Tony Hayter (London: Bodley Head for the Army Records Society, 1988), pp. 268–9.

15 J. W. Fortescue, *County Lieutenancies and the Army 1803–1814* (Eastbourne: Naval & Military Press Ltd, 2002), pp. 34, 61–9.

force. Alongside requiring a complete survey of Britain's military manpower from county authorities, this also empowered the king to appoint officers to train men if the Lords Lieutenant did not recommend suitable persons themselves.[16]

The legal situation only went so far though in providing a universal framework for soldiering. The militia acts were clear that once called out into service, either for training or during war, the men were subject to the annual Mutiny Act. The various other full-time home defence forces that were added to the establishment of the British Army were similarly subject to the provisions of the Mutiny Act. However, the position of the part-time forces was more ambiguous. The terms offered to the Westminster Association in 1779, which were copied by other part-time forces in Britain at the time, made no mention of the Mutiny Act but offered a fairly loose contractual assertion that the commissioned officers were 'empowered immediately to train and discipline such Men as shall voluntarily offer themselves for that purpose'.[17] The 1782 and 1794 Volunteer Acts included a provision that men enrolled in these part-time forces could only be tried in a court martial composed of volunteer officers, but no mention was made of the exact legal situation. As a result, many units established their own regulations. For example, in the regulations of the Manchester Military Association (approved by its committee, of course) officers and men who disobeyed orders were to be tried by a court martial of the men in their company.[18] The London Military Association set out fines for inappropriate conduct.[19] The terms of the Sussex Yeomanry Cavalry, detailed in 1794, whilst they appeared more robust in declaring that when they were called out men were 'subject to Military Discipline as the rest of His Majesty's Regular and Militia Troops', still reverted to a contractual arrangement with the caveat of 'every Yeoman then having the option to march or not'.[20]

16 38 Geo. III, c. 27, 'An Act to Enable His Majesty More Effectively to Provide for the Defence and Security of the Realm During the Present War, and for Indemnifying Persons Who May Suffer in Their Property by Such Measures as May Be Necessary for That Purpose' (1798).

17 TNA, War Office: Secretary-at-War, Out-letters, WO4/106, Charles Jenkinson to the Duke of Northumberland, fols 433–5, 22 July 1779.

18 Lancashire Record Office, Preston (LRO), DP/288, Manchester Military Association, Minutes, Accounts, etc.

19 'London Military Association', *London Courant and Westminster Chronicle*, 1 May 1780.

20 ESRO, Archive of the Gage family of Firle, East Sussex: additional, SAS/GM/2/1a, Copy of the Resolutions of the Sussex Yeomanry Cavalry and Infantry, 1794.

INVENTING A TYPOLOGY OF SOLDIERING

THE CONTRACTUAL NATURE of auxiliary military service that appeared between 1740 and 1815 was a product of the fact that these new military forces were not solely directed by the government or parliament. In fact, there was a three-way dialogue between the government, those involved in raising auxiliary forces, and those who joined these forces. The legal situation outlined above was paralleled in the etymology of these soldiers, a heuristic process in which these forms of service were created, and subsequently refined, at the same time as they brought themselves into being. By the mid-1790s this had created a linguistically fairly stable hierarchy of auxiliary soldiering in Britain, comprised of fencibles, militia, volunteers and yeomanry, with a later introduction of local militia in 1808. This development can be traced through the titles of auxiliary military forces, and the myriad of different names of auxiliary units in this period are significant, as they were an outward expression of their identity as soldiers, both real and imagined. Titles, and types, of units, alongside the four mentioned earlier, include associations, provisional cavalry and rangers. These were not necessarily mutually exclusive terms, and some may be considered as subsets of others, for example many volunteer units included the term ranger in their title, albeit with notable exceptions such as the 88th Foot or Connaught Rangers (a regular unit of the British Army). The language of soldiering is a way of exploring the wish of those concerned to be soldierlike but also to distinguish themselves from a regular soldier.

In creating a new lexicon to describe different types of soldiers, those involved drew upon their own experiences and cultural background, which could be both from within the British Isles and wherever else the British Army had served. There was an influx of new terminology during the period 1740–60 because of British military commitment in Europe and North America. This was particularly the case with light troops, who engaged in small-scale warfare. In 1779, John Money proposed raising a corps of light cavalry in Norfolk, and felt he was particularly suited to command such a force as he had served with Prussian Hussars in the Seven Years War; in the same year the government received an offer of 'Chasseurs' to be raised in Germany.[21]

New words were necessary because of the variety of new types of units that appeared from the 1740s. The militia as a home defence force was fairly well

---

21 TNA, War Office: Baron Jeffrey Amherst, Commander in Chief: Papers, WO34/153, John Money to Lord Amherst, fols 453–4, 20 July 1779 and Jonathan Williams to Viscount Weymouth, fols 11–12, 1 July 1779.

established and it solely applied to units raised under the terms of the Militia Acts, yet additional full-time auxiliary forces with limited terms of service were established during the Austrian War of Succession and in each conflict thereafter. These units are often anachronistically described as fencibles,[22] but contemporaries would not have recognised this as a universal term to describe a particular type of military force until the French Revolutionary Wars.[23] By then, such was the pervasiveness of the term that offers came in to the government specifically stating the wish to raise a fencible regiment, and in 1802 the expression was defined in James's *A New and Enlarged Military Dictionary*.[24] There was, therefore, a linguistic journey by which this rather specific term became common across Britain, and indeed the United Kingdom.

In the 1740s and 50s there was no such clarity. In response to the Jacobite invasion a number of 'volunteer' regiments were raised through country subscriptions for service in Britain, such as the Hampshire Regiment of Foot,[25] but this use of the term subsided thereafter, making spasmodic reappearance in later wars to describe individual full-time units for the raising of which the government did not pay.[26] It was in the Seven Years War that the first officially titled fencible regiment – the Battalion of Fencible Men of Argyllshire – appeared.[27] The initial background to this term was peculiar to Scotland. By 1759, Pitt the Elder was conscious of the need for some kind of home-defence force for Scotland in the absence of a militia there, yet was not prepared to sanction a Scotland-wide force. Discussions ensued between Pitt, the Duke of Newcastle and Archibald Campbell, 3rd Duke of Argyll (the latter was probably the most powerful political figure in Scotland) about a selective arming in Scotland. Argyll, keen to further his patronage of the

---

22 See for example Conway, *War, State, and Society*, pp. 62–3, J. A. Houlding, *Fit for Service: The Training of the British Army, 1715–1795* (Oxford: Clarendon, 1981), p. 10.

23 Ron McGuigan, *The Forgotten Army: Fencible Regiments of Great Britain 1793–1816*, The Napoleon Series <http://www.napoleon-series.org/military/organization/fencibles/c_fencibles.html> [accessed 3 July 2011].

24 Charles James, 'Fencible', in *A new and enlarged military dictionary, or, Alphabetical explanation of technical terms: containing, among other matter, a succinct account of the different systems of fortification, tactics, &c. also the various French phrases and words* (London: printed for T. Egerton at the Military Library, 1802), p. xxxv.

25 Hampshire Record Office, Winchester (HRO), Jervoise family of Herriard, Militia papers 44M69/G6/3/1/2, Printed Notice of Subscriptions for the Raising of Two Volunteer Regiments in the County of Southampton, 12 Oct 1745.

26 See for example TNA, WO34/153, Proposal for Raising a Corps of Volunteers in the Cinque Ports, 19 July 1779.

27 TNA, War Office and predecessors: Indexes to Out-letters, WO 2/32, Entry for Battalion of Fencible Men of Argyllshire, fol. 206, 1759–1760.

Campbell family through the armed forces, utilised existing Scottish laws and raised a fencible regiment.[28] The actual term was chiefly of Scottish origin, a shortening of the middle English term defensible, and actually refers to men 'fit and liable' to be called out for defence.[29] Officially, the term only applied to Argyllshire's corps, and the other unit raised in Scotland for limited service was titled Earl of Sutherland's Battalion of Highlanders.[30] The diffusion of fencibles as a certain type of military formation gathered pace during the American War of Independence. The government described offers of units for limited service from Scotland as fencibles, broadening its usage to the country as a whole. Mr Wemyss' offer from Sutherland was approved on 'the same terms on which the late Fencible Regiments in North Britain were raised',[31] and four fencible regiments were formally established in 1779.[32]

Just because the phrase came into official military parlance did not mean that it was fully understood by the men joining them. The terms for the Argyllshire fenciblemen in 1759 had to be made explicit to potential recruits, noting that they were 'unlike any other regiment in the service'.[33] In response to a rejected offer on a fencible regiment in 1779, Lord Newhaven was careful to stipulate that the title of fencible only applied to the 'mode of recruiting' not the geographical extent of its service.[34] A recruiting poster from 1779 for the Southern Regiment of Fencibles went further and sought to distinguish fencibles from other soldiers, for although they acquired the privileges of soldiers,

> every possible indulgence, consistent with their duty, will be given to the private men; they will be allowed to work for themselves during hay-time and harvest, (and at all other times, when they are quartered in places where work is to be had, to as great degree as circumstances will permit), so that the men

28 John Robertson, *The Scottish Enlightenment and the Militia Issue* (Edinburgh: John Donald, 1985), p. 106.

29 'Fencible, Adj. And N.', in *Oxford English Dictionary* (Oxford: Oxford University Press, 2011); Bruce P. Lenman, 'Militia, Fencible Men, and Home Defence, 1660–1797', in *Scotland and War: AD 79–1918*, ed. by Norman Macdougall (Edinburgh: John Donald, 1991), pp. 170–92; Western, *English Militia*, p. 165.

30 TNA, WO 2/32, Entry for Earl of Sutherland's Battalion of Highlanders, fol. 210, 1759–1760.

31 TNA, WO 1/616, Lord Amherst to Charles Jenkinson, fol. 161, 5 February 1779.

32 Officially titled the West Fencible Men of Argyllshire, North Fencible men, South Fencible men, and Colonel Wemyss' Fencible men: TNA, WO 2/34, fols 243–7, 269, 1779–1783.

33 National Archives of Scotland, Edinburgh (NAS), Inveraray Sheriff Court, SC54/24/4, Draft Advertisement [1759?].

34 TNA, WO34/153, Lord Newhaven to [Weymouth?], fols 211–12, 12 July 1779.

who enlist in these regiments do not become soldiers in the common sense of the word.

As a finale, the poster epitomised this new form of soldiering by stating that 'Regulars, militia, and fencible men, are equally the defenders of their country.'[35]

In the 1770s fencibles were still limited to Scotland. Other units created for limited service in Britain, such as Sir Thomas Egerton's Regiment of Foot (Royal Lancashire Volunteers) or Thomas Lister's Corps of Light Dragoons, made no use of the term. Only one unit within Britain broke the Scottish monopoly of the expression, and this was the Isle of Man battalion, which by 1781 was being described by War Office officials as a fencible battalion. This exception can largely be attributed to the considerable Scottish influence on the island, as the Dukes of Atholl still retained several rights there and the British government had only gained suzerainty over the island in 1765.[36] A second exception was the Royal Fencible American Regiment raised in North America by Joseph Goreham – an army officer from Nova Scotia with good relations with Lord Amherst and a frequent visitor to Britain in the 1760s and 70s.[37]

Although fencible soldiers became a much more universal term during the Revolutionary Wars, Scotland still led the way in raising troops of this type in the early 1790s.[38] Crucial to the diffusion of the fencible soldier across Britain, both the term and the understanding of its meaning, was the government's March 1794 'Plan of augmentation of the forces for internal defence', which encouraged counties 'to raise volunteer troops of Fencible cavalry'.[39] The influence of Scottish officers familiar with the term was still important though, and can be seen in the 1799 offer to raise a regiment in Jersey, to be commanded, of course, by Lieutenant-Colonel Campbell.[40] There was an abrupt end to the history of fencibles in Britain, as all the units were disbanded

35 NAS, Papers of Clerk family of Penicuik, Midlothian, GD18/4210, Copies Advertisement 'to the Brave Lowlanders' Urging Them to Join the South Fencible Regiment Commanded by Henry, Duke of Buccleugh. (Printed), c. 1778.

36 TNA, WO 1/682, G. Aust to Secretary at War, fols 329–31, 2 January 1781.

37 David A. Charters and Stuart R. J. Sutherland, Goreham (Gorham), Joseph, ed. by John English, Dictionary of Canadian Biography Online (University of Toronto and the Université Laval, 2000) <http://www.biographi.ca/009004-119.01-e.php?&id_nbr=1918> [accessed 31 January 2012].

38 J. R. Western, 'The County Fencibles and Militia Augmentation of 1794', Journal of the Society for Army Historical Research, 34.137 (1956), pp. 3–11.

39 British government, 'Plan of Augmentation of the Forces for Internal Defence' (London, 1794).

40 NAS, Maclaine of Lochbuie Papers, GD174/2296, Printed Notice of the Recommen-

between 1801 and 1802, and they were not re-raised during the Napoleonic Wars, partly due to the fact that both Scotland and Ireland then had militias, and also because of the competition it caused with regular recruiting. This particular type of service was exported to forces outside Europe.

The government's 1794 plan caused some confusion as alongside fencible cavalry it also encouraged 'gentlemen and yeomanry' cavalry and the difference was not clear to many contemporaries. However, if the linguistic journey of the fencibles was a story of steady exportation across the United Kingdom, the articulation of the yeomanry was rapid. The government was an essential agent in the swift rise of the yeomanry as it took resolutions from county meetings, notably Rutland and Northampton, and circulated them to other counties to help define the yeomanry.[41] Other units soon copied these resolutions and forms of enrolment.[42] Once the yeomanry was established there were still debates about its military nature. Although they have often been portrayed as the militant wing of the propertied forces of repression, this identity was far from universal. The end of the war in 1801 in particular demonstrated this. The 3rd Earl of Egremont, writing about the Sussex Yeomanry, was prepared to withdraw from the service and also oppose it if it were to be 'merely as a measure of internal Police'.[43] In coastal counties, the yeomanry also became intimately involved in plans to evacuate the coast during an invasion. The yeomanry units in Hampshire can be considered a form of military police or mounted *gendarmerie* as they were expected to patrol roads and direct the evacuation.[44]

There were also other less pronounced expansions in the military lexicon, such as the ranger units that emerged in Britain after the Seven Years War. In part a corruption of the German *jäger*, an adaptation of the existing definition of 'an officer that tends a game forest',[45] and borrowing from its use in North

dation by the States of the Island of Jersey to the Duke of York That Lt. Col. Campbell Be Permitted to Raise a Regiment Called the Loyal Jersey Fencibles, 31 Aug 1799.

41 TNA, William Pitt, 1st Earl of Chatham: Papers, PRO30/8/244, General Meeting of the County of Rutland, fols 188–9, 22 March 1794.

42 See for example: East Riding of Yorkshire Archives and Local Studies, Beverley, County Library Collection, DDX17/57, Thomas Grimston to Duke of Leeds, 8 July [1794].

43 ESRO, The Shiffner Archives, SHR/3327/34, Extract of a Letter from Earl of Egremont to Duke of Richmond, 9 January 1802.

44 HRO, Papers of Thomas Orde, 1st Baron Bolton – Lord Lieutenant: letter book: '1801, 1802, 1803, 1804 and Defence of the Realm', 11M49/231, G. H. Rose to Lord Bolton, fols 25–7, 19 August 1801, and George Rose to Lord Bolton, fols 14–16, 29 July 1801.

45 J. Johnson, D.D., F.R.S., 'Ranger', in *The new royal and universal English dictionary. In which The terms made use of in Arts and Sciences are defin'd [...]* (London: printed for A. Millard in the Strand, and R. Dorsley in Pall-Mall, 1763).

America to describe frontier woodsmen, the term was especially popular in Ireland in the 1770s, perhaps in part due to the re-publication of the *Journals of Major Robert Rogers*, commander of Rogers' Rangers in the Seven Years War, in Dublin in 1769.[46] Also, there was a strong correlation of the use of the term with mountainous and forested areas of the kingdom during the French Revolutionary and Napoleonic Wars.[47] The government also attempted to force the link too between social and geographical groups and forms of military service, and in 1798 attempted to enlist gamekeepers and foresters into part-time military service.[48] It is clear that in choosing such titles there was as much of an element of cultural distinction as there was military demand. This is particularly the case at the opposite end of the military social hierarchy: the artillery. Perhaps the most militarily useful form of part-time soldier along coastal areas of Britain, it was only really in Cornwall and Devon that this form of military service really took hold, a result not of military need but because of its links to the Stanneries, the ancient political and social mining enclave in these counties.[49] Attempts to form artillery elsewhere were not so successful. Despite the Lieutenancy meetings in Sussex advocating volunteer artillery companies in 1794, recruitment for these forces did not go well and many preferred to join infantry units rather than use 'the Great guns'.[50]

Yeomanry and rangers were just part of the wider language of the biggest group of soldiers in Britain: the part-time forces. Until the late 1770s many of these units styled themselves 'associations', such as the Manchester Military Association of 1779–82. This term was borrowed from the existing language of extra-parliamentary organisations, a specific and contractual agreement to

---

46 Robert Rogers, *Journals of Major Robert Rogers: Containing an Account of the Several Excursions He Made under the Generals Who Commanded Upon the Continent of North America, During the Late War [...]* (Dublin: printed by R. Acheson, for J. Milliken, No. 10. in Skinner-Row, 1769), p. 353. See, for example, the offer in 1779 for a unit to be called the Royal Irish Rangers: TNA, WO34/153, Mr Fitzwilliam to [Lord North?], 20 July 1779. Interestingly, three Irish regiments of the British Army that were amalgamated in 1968 now use this title.

47 'Volunteers of the United Kingdom, 1803', in *House of Commons Papers*, Vol. IX, p. 9, < http://o-gateway.proquest.com.wam.leeds.ac.uk/openurl?url_ver=Z39.88-2004&res_dat=xri:hcpp&rft_dat=xri:hcpp:rec:1803-000613> [accessed 2 February 2012].

48 HRO, 11M49/231, Charles Hodges Junior to Lord Bolton, fol. 41, 29 August 1801.

49 The Royal Stannary Artillery accounted for one-eighth of the volunteer artillery in Britain: 'Abstract of the return of all the volunteer and yeomanry corps, accepted by His Majesty; describing each corps', in *House of Commons Papers*, Vol. IX, p. 1, < http://gateway.proquest.com/openurl?url_ver=Z39.88-2004&res_dat=xri:hcpp&rft_dat=xri:hcpp:rec:1803-000611> [accessed 2 February 2012]; George Randall Lewis, *The Stannaries a Study of the English Tin Miner* (Boston, MA; New York: Houghton, Mifflin, 1908).

50 ESRO, Lieutenancy, L/C/V/1/2, 'On Lieutenancy. General Defence', 1794–1797.

come together for an explicit purpose.[51] Often linked to radical or reforming activity, the term 'association' had a much wider use in part-time military formations, particularly regarding the creation of a new unit. 'Association' appeared less and less in the titles of units after the 1780s. It was during the 1780s that the term 'volunteer' began to be more closely connected to part-time soldiering, in both official discourse (such as in the 1782 Volunteer Act), in the terms of enrolment itself, and in unit titles. In the 1790s associations were degraded to the most local of military forces, in effect an armed constabulary, with the armed associations of 1798. This change was brought about by the clearer delineation in the auxiliary forces with the emergence of 'fencibles', which was utilised for the full-time home defence forces that had sometimes utilised 'volunteer' in their titles. Furthermore, this change was about identities: men could describe themselves as volunteers whilst they could only belong to military associations. Yet the idea and process of coming together for mutual defence did not disappear and many offers of service for part-time units continued to utilise 'associating' in the proposals.[52]

AUXILIARY SOLDIERS AND THE PUBLIC

THE TYPOLOGY of auxiliary soldiering was one just form of their culture and these men demonstrated their qualities and attitudes through their engagement with the wider public in a variety of forms and media. Like the emergence of reasonably well established types of soldier, the legitimisation of these auxiliary soldiers in the public sphere was a process of negotiation, which in this case relied on interaction between the public and new soldiers. With the constitutional and legalistic concerns mentioned earlier, it is not surprising that there was a general anxiety amongst those involved in raising auxiliary forces about official sanction for their actions. First, this took the form of seeking approval from secretaries of state and the monarch. This was not sufficient and in many cases before anything more could be done to

---

51 Eugene Charlton Black, *The Association: British Extraparliamentary Political Organization, 1769–1793* (Cambridge, MA: Harvard University Press, 1963); T. M. Parssinen, 'Association, Convention and Anti-Parliament in British Radical Politics, 1771–1848', *English Historical Review*, 88.348 (1973), pp. 504–33.

52 See for example: TNA, War Office: Secretary-at-War, Out-letters, WO4/106, Charles Jenkinson to Thomas Pryce, Sheriff of Cardiganshire, fol. 490, 31 July 1779; HRO, Miscellanea W/K5/7, Jacob's Scrapbook Number Six; HRO, Papers of Thomas Orde, 1st Baron Bolton – Lord Lieutenant: letter book: 'Volunteer Correspondence. Volunters – Offers of Service – Establishment – Staff – Allowance: 1: 1801, 1802, 1803', 11M49/234, Richard P. Baker to Lord Bolton, 7 August 1803.

progress the establishment of a unit there needed to be a public declaration about it. This was provided by the *London Gazette*, the official newspaper of the British state.

As well as delivering an official public sanction for new units, the *Gazette* also provided a national record of the rank and precedence of officers and units. As such, it was a frequent source of disputes about these issues. In 1803 George Rose noticed that a lord had been given the rank of colonel in the South Devon Yeomanry, and so argued that 'If the appointment has really taken place, I cannot conceive that an objection can now be stated to the same rank being given to me.' This is despite the August before stating to the Lord Lieutenant, Lord Bolton, that rank was of no consequence to him.[53] In December 1803 John Goodeve pointed out that others had been appointed to the rank of captain-lieutenant, and so there could be no impediment to him having that rank. The South Hampshire Yeomanry was somewhat of a headache for Bolton, and in the same month as dealing with John Goodeve, he received a curt letter about the social status of the officers in that corps from William Sloane, who in consequence was tendering his resignation, but held back his expressions of unhappiness at the situation until he had read the *Gazette* that morning.[54] It is little wonder that the Lieutenancy records for Lancashire include a vast bundle of copies of the *London Gazette*.[55]

Would-be soldiers could be punctilious about the *Gazette*, and it went much further than a concern with precedence and rank. In July 1803 the former commander of the Christchurch Volunteers in Hampshire pressed Bolton for this unit and its officers to be named in the *Gazette* so that he could enrol and exercise men.[56] In the same year, John Medley would not act as an officer in the Loyal Volunteer Artillery in Portsmouth until his name appeared in the *Gazette*.[57] Concern about official status was not limited to officers. In the same year, John Whitelocke, commander of the Portsmouth garrison, thought the volunteers there would recruit much better if the unit and officers appeared in the *Gazette*. Once they had been announced, Whitelocke was happy to report that the men had returned to their former good humour.[58] During the Amiens peace, one

53 HRO, 11M49/234, G. H. Rose to Lord Bolton, 24 August 1802.
54 Ibid.
55 LRO, Lieutenancy, LV/1, Copies of the *London Gazette*, 1797–1852.
56 HRO, 11M49/234, Edmund Walcott to Lord Bolton, 12 July 1803.
57 HRO, Papers of Thomas Orde, 1st Baron Bolton – letter books and papers of Lord Bolton, Lord Lieutenant: letter book: 'Isle of Wight Volunteers 1801 to July 1807', 11M49/241, R. B. Watkins to Lord Bolton, 12 September 1803.
58 Ibid., letter book: 'Portsmouth etc Volunteer Correspondence, 1803–1804: 1', 11M49/239, John Whitelocke to Lord Bolton, 6 October 1803.

officer felt that the recruitment into the South Hampshire Yeomanry, which was in the process of being created from disparate squadrons across the county, would go much better once the regiment had been officially announced.[59]

Alongside propagation through the *London Gazette*, auxiliary soldiers also made themselves through their behaviour. A prominent feature of making themselves into soldiers was massed, collective activity of the men. The terms of the Sussex Association of 1779 made this quite clear, as the first thing the subscribers thought the men who joined up should learn was to be quiet whilst in the ranks so that they could hear commands.[60] The silence of a large group of people, in some cases it could be up to several hundred, in a single place and time was unusual and quite distinct from the bustle of other communal activity, such as election hustings, collective bargaining or public celebrations. In fact, the only other time most of the population would have experienced such quietude was in church. The visual impact of collective activity was significant too. Emma Smith, writing to her sister, was initially quite dismissive of the military prowess and behaviour of the Devizes Yeomanry, relating some personal disputes between members of the corps and the town. But her attitude and language changed once she saw them riding and drilling together. When thirty-five of them were together they 'made a very handsome appearance, turned and wheeled, mounted and dismounted capitally'.[61] The visual ephemera of the militia and volunteers provide another means of exploring attitudes towards them. Rowlandson's 'The Light Horse Volunteers of London & Westminster' is good example of the concern for order in the military, as the volunteer cavalry are all identical in their ranks, even to the point that the horses are in step together, in contrast to the spectators watching them. Many of these viewers are in uniform themselves, suggesting that it was only in acting together that men became soldiers.[62] Equally, disorder whilst acting collectively was unsoldierlike, and a particularly common theme of satires of auxiliary soldiers. Amongst the numerous examples is the 'Advance three steps backwards, or the Militia Heroes', in which not only are all the men

59 HRO, 11M49/234, William Smith to Lord Bolton, 28 November 1802.
60 ESRO, Archive of the Pelham Family of Stanmer, Earls of Chichester, SAS/A741/15, Minutes of Meetings of Committee of Subscribers, 19 November 1779.
61 HRO, Austen-Leigh family papers, 23M93/70/3/32, Emma Smith to Eliza Chute, 16 Nov 1794.
62 Thomas Rowlandson, 'The Light Horse Volunteers of London & Westminster, Commanded by Coll Herries, Reviewed by His Majesty on Wimbledon Common 5th July, 1798' (London: Mr. H. Angelo, 1798), British Museum (BM), London, BM Satires 9238, 1917,1208.2827.

visually different in size and shape but also in their dress, besides their obvious military deficiencies.[63]

These views about soldiers acting together in unison being beneficial, and about a concern for public appearance, were also shared by the military. The Inspecting Field Officer in Hampshire during the early part of the Napoleonic Wars (a role created in 1804 to improve the volunteers across the kingdom) felt that many of the disputes in the volunteers over precedence would be helped if they could be amassed and act in one formation. As an example of what he had to deal with, only three volunteer companies at Gosport would meet together because they could not agree which company should take the place of honour at the right of the line.[64] This belief in the efficacy of acting in unison lay behind his careful attempts at encouraging units to join and act together:

> but as volunteers must be treated like Children, this junction can only be formed by degrees, by getting them to act together occasionally, and getting acquainted together in the Field, so as to imperceptibly to destroy all former jealousies and animosities, this must be my province and arduous as the task seems, I hope to satisfactorily accomplish it.[65]

In the importance of public display in legitimising soldiers, the flurry of activity that surrounded the auxiliary forces in the eighteenth century is explained. The eager adoption of all aspects of public military ceremony by volunteers and militia, and so avidly reported in the local press, signalled the way in which military units became accepted as soldiers by their communities. The Cumberland Rangers are a case in point, and their activities were well reported in the *The Lancaster Gazette and General Advertiser, for Lancashire, Westmorland*. Here we find not only details of appointments (echoing the *London Gazette*'s role in a local context), parades and inspections, but also ways in which belonging to this unit came to be part of the men's lives, and indeed their deaths. Members who died during the Napoleonic Wars were buried with military honours, and at the marriage of one of the men the unit paraded and fired three volleys in the couple's honour. The Cumberland Rangers engaged with the honorific aspects of military culture in other ways too. In 1808, the members of the corps presented a 'beautiful silver embossed cup' to Henry Howard, their commander, and similar examples of trophies and objects signifying gratitude and esteem for volunteer commanders abound

---

63 'Advance Three Steps Backwards, or the Militia Heroes', (London: Matthew Darly, 1778–1780), BM, BM Satires undescribed, 1948,0214.585.

64 HRO, 11M49/239, Bgd. Gen. George Porter to Lord Bolton, 14 September 1804.

65 HRO, 11M49/240, Bgd. Gen. George Porter to Lord Bolton, 7 January 1805.

in the period. Much of this activity was internal to the corps and reinforced the corporate identity, albeit that the public were able to read about it, via newspapers, or attend events when they happened. The presentation of the cup to Henry Howard noted the attendance of 'ladies and gentlemen of the neighbourhood'.[66]

Despite the focus on the motives for enlisting and their intense localism, Britain's auxiliary forces had many things in common in this period. The legal situation only went so far, and so the invented typology and their behaviour, widely defined, was an attempt to describe and delineate the attributes of these military forces or, more accurately, the attributes that those involved hoped the force would embody. Often the language of auxiliary soldiering indicated a desire to match military functions with social and cultural status, which drew upon and adapted existing terminology. In many cases the durability and popularity of these terms throughout the period and beyond were predicated on the success of matching this language to the wider social context. When looking at the process of making new soldiers we can see that the men and organisations helped shape it with important input from the government and the public. It was contested and negotiated and also had different legacies, such that some aspects survived, flourished and became an established part of British military culture in the period and well beyond, whilst other features became obscure and forgotten. Gillian Russell has highlighted how Georgians experienced war as theatre, and has argued that public martial displays were a demonstration of loyalty to the king and constitution and preparedness to act,[67] but such displays had a more important and fundamental function in legitimising the men's role as soldiers within their communities. To do this, these men in their units adopted much of the practice and behaviour of the regulars, and this was driven by a quest for legitimacy in the absence of activity that related to combat, which rationalises their focus on militaria. They may have been an untested military force, and it is sometimes easy to disparage their exaggerated uniforms and sense of pride, but this was a manifestation of their quest to define and legitimise themselves as a new form of soldier.

---

66 *The Lancaster Gazette and General Advertiser, for Lancashire, Westmorland, &c.* (Lancaster, England), 28 April 1804, Issue 150; 2 March 1805, Issue 194; 28 December 1805, Issue 237; 10 May 1806, Issue 256; 2 July 1808, Issue 368; 9 July 1808, Issue 369; *The York Herald* (York, England), 10 December 1808.

67 Gillian Russell, *The Theatres of War: Performance, Politics, and Society, 1793–1815* (Oxford: Clarendon Press, 1995), pp. 17–19.

Index